Analysis of the Literary Works of Rabindranath Tagore in the context of Indian Education System

Dr Jumisree Sarmah Pathak
Centre of Education
Indian Institute of Teacher Education
Gandhinagar, Gujarat

TABLE OF CONTENT

Chapter No.	Title	Page No.
1	**Introduction**	4 - 48
	Introduction	5
	Key Words	36
	Objectives of the study	38
	Rationale of the Study	42
	Significance of the Study	45
	Delimitations of the Study	47
2	**Review of Related Literature**	49 -51
	Introduction	50
	Importance of Review of Related Literature	51
	Review of related studies	51
	Research Gap	100
	Implication of the present study	101
3	**Fundamentals of Research and Research Design**	102 - 112
	Introduction	103

		Origin of the Study	103
		Research Methodology	104
		Population of Research and sampling	105
		Tools and Techniques of Data Collection	107
		Data collection	108
		Data Analysis Technique	109
		Researcher's Experience during Research	110
4	**Data Analysis and Interpretation**	113-174	
		Introduction	114
		Nature of Data	115
		Classification and Presentation of Data	116
		Data Analysis and Interpretation	117
5	**Summary, Findings and Implications**	197 - 122	

	Introduction	198
	Summary of Research	199
	Findings of Research	232
	Discussion on Findings	243
	Implications of the Study	246
	Recommendations for Further Research	248
	Conclusion	249
	Bibliography	252-259

CHAPTER 1
INTRODUCTION

Introduction

Concept of Education

The word Education is originally derived from the Latin words *Educare, Educere* and *Educatum,* which mean to nourish or to bring up, to   lead forth and to draw out respectively. Considering these root words, it can be said that education is a broad appellation, which cannot be defined easily as it covers all the aspects of life. It is often said that Education is a lifelong process, whichcontinues from womb to tomb. As life involves many different aspects,   i.e.   biological,   physiological,   physical, sociological, philosophical, psychological, etc.; no single definition can be enough to give the proper idea of the term education. Different people have got different perspectives about life, different goals of life and different expectations from the life. As education serves towards the betterment of life, it becomes very complicated to decide the objectives of education.

Meaning of education keeps changing from time to time, place-to-place and person to person. So many different philosophers and thinkers from around the worlds have tried to define education as per their own understanding and the need of the society. There are many reasons behind different meanings and definitions given for education. Human personalities are very complex in nature, which consist of different areas like physical, social, intellectual, spiritual, moral, aesthetic, etc. Meaning of education given by any person depends on which area is more important to him/her. Another reason is that human environment is different for different people, which comes with different needs. Environment also has different aspects like social, physical, cultural, economic, etc. Education leads an individual to adjust in the environment. Difference in all such aspects of environment demand different inputs from education. Philosophies of life are also different for different societies and times, which define the goal of life as well education. Different psychologists have given different theories about mental processes of human that also make it complex to define education.

Some of the educationists have given more importance to internal aspects of human life while talking about the aims of education. They focus on the development of the aspects which are not physical in nature but take into account the inner potentialities of an individual; like mind, soul, self-realisation, etc. For example, Gandhiji defines education as all-round drawing out of the best in man-body, mind and spirit. Aurobindo calls it as a process of helping an individual to draw out which is already present internally in one's self. Swami Vivekananda defines education as the manifestation of divine perfection existing in man. Aristotle calls it a process of creating sound mind in a sound body. Pestalozzi considers education as the natural, harmonious and progressive development of Man's innate powers. Plato considers education capable of developing all the beauty and all the perfection in the body and the soul of a pupil, which he is capable of. On the contrary, many educationists and philosophers have given more importance to external aspects of human life, i.e. Social, Environmental, etc. According to Thomson (as cited in Theory and Principles of Education),

> *"By education I mean the influence of the environment upon the individual to produce a permanent change in his habits of behaviour, of thought and of his attitude. Environment has many aspects- physical, social and cultural. Education should facilitate the task of adaptation of the child to his environment." (p.6)*

Gandhiji also considered the practical aspect of education as very important and he gave the concept of craft in education in order to nurture the students in a way that they can earn their living in future. Apart from this, education is viewed from many different angles. It is regarded as a bipolar process where educand and educator are two poles that influence each other and the behavioural changes happening in the educand are shaped by the educator and the personality of the educator is also affected by the educand. It is deemed as a tri-polar process by some people where social setting is the third pole. Educand, Educator and the social setting; all three affect each other. The behaviour of the educated is modified by the educator in the social setting which actually plays important role in settingthe goals of education and also puts some limitations on the educand and the educator. Education is accounted as a lifelong process that involves the development of an individual from infancy to maturation and all the physical, social and psychological aspects of the life influence such a development. Education is a deliberate process where the process of educating and being educated is done consciously towards predefinedaims and objectives.

In order to define the goals and objectives of education, it is important to understand the roles and functions which education has to play in the society. Such functions are influenced by many factors. These factors include Geographical factors, Economic factors, Religious factors, Political factors, Social factors, Linguistic factors, etc. Depending uponthese factors, educational processes taking place in the society will change from time to time. In the context of Indian society, main features of Indian society need to be considered.Indian society is democratic, socialist and secular in nature and India is developing country. Therefore, the functions of education will be determined accordingly. Factors influencing the functions are Social Development, Human Resources Development, Development of physical resources in the country, Skill development, creating equal opportunities for all, democratization of education, Fulfilment of needs of the society with diversity, involvement of people, secular values, etc. Once the functions of education are defined, it becomes easy to develop the educational policies based on it by seeking the answers of the questions like Why to educate, Whom to educate, Who is to educate, Where to educate, What to educate, How to educate and When to educate.

The process of education involves many terms, which seek to be defined clearly to explainthe process of education clearly. Teaching, Training, Instruction, Literacy, Learning, Schooling, Indoctrination, etc. are some of the terms, which are parts of educational process.Teaching is the important instrument of education that imparts knowledge, understanding and skills. According to H.C. Morrison (as cited in Theory and Principles of Education),

"Teaching is an important contact between a more mature and a less mature personality which is designed to further the education of the latter." (p.20)

Teaching can be formal as well as informal which causes an individual to learn, to adjust in the environment and to respond to the environment effectively. The process of teaching is art as well as science, which involves interaction, training of emotions and imparting information. Effective teaching depends of many factors like knowledge and skills of a teacher, the level of relations between the teacher and the learner, planning, availability of resources, classroom environment, etc. Training is another term which is often used in theeducational scenario which is little different from teaching. Training is focused on the development of particular skills and is limited in scope, which is imparted during the limited period. Another term is instruction which mainly deals with the intellectual development and is limited to a particular subject and is also provided in the particular time period. Schooling is also a part of education, which is concerned with mental development.Curriculum is fixed for schooling, which is transacted in the school for several years. Literacy being a part of education is concerned with three basic aspects, i.e. Reading, Writing and Arithmetic that are considered very basic skills in the process of education.

Education is often classified in three types, i.e. Formal, Informal and Non-formal. Formal education takes place in the formal educational institutions, i.e. school or college. Formal education is a planned process, which works towards definite set of goals, is well planned in terms of objectives, curriculum and time, and is related to some degree or certificate, which often starts and ends at particular age. It is organized by government or private agencies. Informal education is something that takes naturally under the influence of family, society and environment. There is no fixed aim, curriculum or teaching methods in informal education as it happens in natural setting throughout life and involves learningthat takes place unconsciously and is affected by the press, films, libraries, etc. Non-formal education revolves around flexibility in education in different aspects like curriculum, age, admission process, evaluation, modes of teaching, extra-curricular activities, etc. It works on the principle of education without barriers. One can continue education at any age, anytime and anywhere if he/she wishes for the advancement of knowledge in any area.Open Universities, distance learning courses, etc. are the examples of Non-formal education, which enable the learners to continue learning as per their own convenience. It is learner-centered, multi-dimensional, does not demand any formal qualifications, and is regarded as supplementary to the formal education.

While a lot has been developed in the field of education with time, Aims of education has always been a debatable matter. As aims of education are related to real situations of societyand community, they can never be free from the influence of time and place. Aims of education can be classified in various categories like Individual aims, Social aims, Knowledge aim, Moral aim, Religious aim, Vocational aims, etc. Individual aims are derived from the idea that every individual is different and unique. Education must help anindividual to develop and maintain this distinct identity of each individual. Some thinkers have also criticized this idea of individual aims saying that an individual can never be considered in isolation from the society. This thought give the emergence to the social aims of education. Social aims of education include the development of an individual to fit in the society. In a broader context, social aims also include education for social efficiency, citizenship and social service. Education should work towards nurturing an individual as a responsible citizen who can contribute towards the betterment of the society. One of the important aims of education is knowledge aim. Indian philosophies put emphasis on true knowledge, which is free from errors as an ultimate goal of life. Socrates considers knowledge as power. Knowledge is not just knowing many things or gathering information, but true knowledge is something that can make one realise the true essence of life. Moral aims of education are related to the character building of an individual. Many philosophers like Gandhiji, Aurobindo, etc. have given importance to the character building of a person. This aim focuses on developing good habits and qualities like forgiveness, kindness, sympathy, truth, charities, selflessness, etc. Religious aims of education are more or less related to moral aims as every religion also talks about making a man with good character. Some religious goals also include learning of specific religious practices. Vocational aims of education focus towards making an individual capable of earning the livelihood. Some educationists like Gandhiji and Rabindranath Tagore gave importance to this aspect and included craft and skill based activities in education. After the independence, India has worked towards the democratic and totalitarian aims of education, which include economic development of the society and transforming the society into a developed society. Totalitarian aims are concerned with training of each individual in the interest of the state. Democratic aims encourage independent and constructive thinking and take into account originality and inventiveness. They are in favor of broad choices to be provided to each individual.

Education and Philosophy

As the present study deals with educational philosophy of Rabindranath Tagore, it becomesimportant to understand the meaning of philosophy and establish a meaningful relation between the two terms.

The word Philosophy is originated from Greek word 'Philosophia', which is a combination of two words 'phileo' and 'sophia'; meaning love and wisdom respectively. Thus, the literal meaning of philosophy is 'Love for wisdom'. Philosophy leads an individual towards finding the truth of life. Every philosophical investigation follows the path of wisdom. Like every social construct, philosophy is also defined with different angles by different people. Alexander considered philosophy as similar to metaphysics. Some thinkers consider philosophy as a science while others reject that idea, as it cannot be proved experimentally. Philosophy is more of interpreting and giving meaning to something after enough of intellectual processes taking place in mind rather than providing mere factual information. It aims at searching the reality based on inquiry. No philosophy is universal, but rather it is individual or is dependent on the group of people who believe in the same thing or keep similar thoughts. It is a driving force of life, which is zestful and provides guide to live a life in a purposeful manner. As Carlis Lamont defines (cited in Theory and Principles of Education) *"Philosophy is the tenacious attempt of reasoning men to think through the most fundamental issues of life, to reach reasonable conclusions on first and last things, to suggest worthwhile goals that can command the loyalty of individuals and groups."* *(p.53)*

Life is full of contradictions and extremes like right and wrong, good and bad, beauty andugliness, truth and falsehood, etc. There are times when an individual is confronted with some situations, which make it difficult for him/her to decide which way to go or which isthe right move and which is wrong. Philosophy helps that individual to be free from the confusion and take the decision wisely. Thus, philosophy equips us with the grounds of conducts both on personal and social level. Philosophy covers very vast scope in different branches under study, i.e. Metaphysics, Theology, Ontology, Cosmology, Epistemology, Aesthetics, Ethics, Logic, Cosmogony, Axiology, etc. Metaphysics deals with the concepts which are beyond our cognition, i.e. soul and seeks to answer the questions like why do we exist? , what is being? , etc. Theology is concerned about the existence of God and discusses about the nature of God and if it can be proved somehow. Ontology is the study directed towards finding out the eternal constituents of the universe and their relations with the mortal ones. It is further classified into Monism, Dualism and Pluralism. Epistemology is the branch of philosophy, which deals with knowledge and seeks the answers of the question about truth, doubt, true knowledge, etc. Aesthetics is centered on distinguishing beauty and ugliness. Cosmology talks about the unity of the universe as well as origin and development of the universe. Ethics revolves around the moral conduct and differentiates good act from the evil act. Logic is the branch that promotes logical thinking and gives the ways of inductive and deductive reasoning. Cosmogony tries to find the answer if the universe is created by someone called God. Axiology studies values, both moral and aesthetic.

Education and philosophy are interdependent on each other as they serve towards the common goal of life. It is already discussed earlier how education shapes an individual's behaviour to live the life and deals with physical, social, academic, moral and spiritual aspects of life. Philosophy also guides an individual to live a meaningful life and the goalsand needs of philosophy as discussed above also deal with similar aspects, it is obvious that philosophy and education are inseparable parts of each other. Philosophy helps define the goals of education. Education without Philosophy and Philosophy without Education can never be enough to lead someone towards the achievement of life goals. In the words of Fichte (cited in Theory and Principles of Education),

"The art of education will never attain complete clearness without philosophy."(p.58)

Role of Philosophy in education starts from the individual and extends to educator, societyand education system. Philosophy serves education to find the reasons and understand human virtues, beliefs, life, actions and ideals. It assists the policy makers and educators to construct beliefs, suppositions and judgments related to teaching-learning process. It helps to emerge devotion and a sense of responsibility, which enables the educand and educator both to put in positive efforts towards teaching learning goals. A guiding philosophy is always required to set the objectives of education. Philosophy gives a holisticview to education prevents it from compromising even with a single aspect. Philosophy in present scenario provides with rational approach towards solving a problem and enables one to look at the problem with every possible angle before deriving any conclusion. Philosophy assists in curriculum planning as well. For example, various co-curricular activities included in education are the result of the philosophy of all round development of the educand. Emphasis given on art in education is because of the philosophical valueslike aesthetics, manifestation of self, etc. Philosophy helps teachers to handle tough situations coming in during the process of teaching and paves the way to take difficult decisions. Philosophy enables us to understand the importance of discipline in education and defines the extent to which one should be strict. Democratic philosophy believes in giving maximum freedom to the individual while orthodox philosophies are focused more on strict rules.

Philosophies of education can broadly be defined as Western philosophies and Indian Philosophies.

Philosophers in the east as well as in the west have come up with changing views in the thought process over time. Western philosophies are usually named according to the cardinal thoughts behind any philosophy. Indian philosophies are mainly grounded to ancient times where the focal point is mainly self-realization or achievement of the ultimate goal of life. India is known as the land of knowledge. This knowledge is collected in the scriptures, which are created as the result of worshipping knowledge for years by the great sages. Indian ancient philosophies are present in the form of literature which comprises of four Vedas, six Vedangas, Brahmanical scripts, Upvedas, Upanishadas, six systems of philosophy, Smritis, Bhagavad Gita, Buddhism, Jainism and Islamic studies. Most of the Vedic scriptures are written in Sanskrit language which is the oldest Indian classical language.

Indian Thinkers and their Educational Philosophies

Maharshi Aurobindo, Swami Vivekanda, S. Radhakrishnan, Mahatma Gandhi, Rabindranath Tagore, J. Krishnamurti etc. are some thinkers of India who have given theirideas on education and have also contributed in the field of education by establishing educational institutions and improving educational opportunities.

Sri Aurbindo and his Philosophy

Aurobindo was born in Calcutta and acquired his primary education in England. He returned to India after that and joined further studies. He contributed in India's anti-British movement and later on left these political activities to walk on the path of spirituality. He established Sri Aurobindo Ashram in Pondicherry to continue and spread the spiritual activities. He propagated Internal Yoga through which one can realise the true self within.He was no extremist but gave equal importance to science and spirituality, matter and souland the East and the West. True education according to Aurobindo was the one which was for the good of people, nation and the whole universe. Discovering our own soul was the main purpose of education according to Aurobindo. He considered teacher as a guide and not a taskmaster as he believed that nothing can be taught to anybody but he/she learns onhis own; one can just provide the direction. Aurobindo suggested providing liberty to the child rather than imposing harsh rules.

Aurobindo proposed integral education, which involves vital, physical, mental, psychic and spiritual development of the person. The integrated education proposed by Aurobindo stressed on treating the individuality and the humanity as whole and one. Fundamental principles of integrated education are harmonious development of individuality, integrating various dimensions of self as 'one' and whole, integrating mental training with academic perfection and integration of socio-economic and political training. Aurobindo believed that the entire universe is nothing but multiple cells of a single consciousness. Inner and outer realization is necessary to unite with this consciousness.

Mahatma Gandhi and his Philosophy

Mohandas Karamchand Gandhi, The Father of the Nation, was inspired by Tolstoy. His philosophy of life and education was actually inspired from Toltstoy, his visit to Durban, South Africa and his experiences in England. Gandhiji strictly followed and believed in Self-discipline and Self-purification. His core philosophy of life was service of humanity. Aims of Education as suggested by Gandhiji include education for a harmonious and well balanced society and all round development of an individual, i.e. body, mind and soul. Village crafts should be the part of education which can train the individuals to be self- dependent. He proposed 'Dignity of Labour' to make children understand the importance of labour in life. Truth and Ahimsa should be at the centre no matter which religion is followed by an individual. He promoted the use of mother tongue for education as it can help to learn in a natural manner. Women's education should not be any different from Men's education as they are equal, Gandhiji said. He also put stress on importance of good handwriting.

Gandhiji's views were very flexible which reflected naturalist, idealist as well pragmatist characteristics. He believed in education taking place in natural surroundings and agreed with the idea of freedom that comes with self-discipline, which supports his naturalist views. Gandhiji was also an idealist as he emphasized character development through following Anuvratas, i.e. Satya (Truth), Ahimsa (Non-violence), Aparigraha (Not to store if not needed), etc. He also kept pragmatist views as he advocated craft education, which follows the principle of learning by doing. Gandhiji gave the concept of basic education. He introduced Wardha scheme of education in Pune based on the principle of basic education. The key characteristics of basic education are as follows:

> Education should be based on craft to increase the productivity

- ➤ Education should be free and compulsory for all at least for seven years where some basic skills should be taught and sense training should be done
- ➤ Self-sufficient education system which can be capable of managing own financialneeds
- ➤ Medium of instruction should be mother tongue to get maximum outcomes ofeducation
- ➤ The spirit of nationalism and a responsible and aware citizenship should beinculcated in children, which will lead towards the development of the society.

Sarvapalli Radhakrishnan and his Philosophy

Radhakrishnan happens to be one of the greatest scholars of time who became well- known for his book 'Philosophy of Tagore's life' and has served as the chairman of University Grant Commission as well as the first leader of UNESCO Indian team. He was also appointed as the Indian ambassador of USSR (Union of Soviet Socialist Republics) and second president of Republic India. He was also awarded with Bharat Ratna in 1967 for his contributions in the field of politics as well as education. Although he supported theimportance of religion in one's life, he was in favor of a secular state with respect for all the religions, faiths and sects and treating all the individuals with equality. He considered Science and Religion as two sides of a coin as both seek truth.

Radhakrishnan proposed some important functions of education. Education should be such that can train individual's intellect, heart and spirit. Like Gandhiji and Aurobindo, Radhakrishnan also believed in education, which can serve towards human welfare and not mere academic advancement. Education should ingrain democratic spirit in the learners and should infuse in the tolerance for all the beliefs. It should forbid the learners from following the path of superstitions and should implant scientific attitude. Values are like soul to the body of any society, which should be instilled through education. Spirituality should not be overlooked for materialistic advancement through education. Education should enable the individual to integrate all the aspects of life, i.e. physical, social, and organic, etc. One of the important function of education is to empower an individual to take own decisions and judgements in life. Inquisitive spirit should also be developed by providing such educational activities. Harmony with the surroundings should be established through self-discipline. Education should make one maintain the young and passionate soul throughout the life no matter what the age is. Women should be encouraged to take education. Radhakrishnan's birthday is celebrated as Teacher's day in India.

J. Krishnamurti and his Philosophy

Jiddu Krishnamurti was born in a Brahmin family in Chennai whose father was an activemember of theosophical society. He was closely associated with Mrs Annie Besant and accompanied her while she travelled to England for the meetings of theosophical society. He delivered his speech in London and was inclined towards the path of spirituality. Lateron, he was recognised as the most mystic member of the theosophical society and was named as 'World Teacher' by Charles Webster. Krishnamurti was a strong opponent of discipline and rejected the authority of mentors. He proposed that an individual shouldbe free from all the burdens of rules and society for the transformation. Every individual must follow the independent path rather than following someone blindly. Krishnamurti spotlighted the training of a strong mind, which can deal with any tough situations in life and can stay calm. He said one must be free from ego, i.e. the self, me and mine; to be freefrom the conflicts of life. One cannot live freely until he/she has become free from his/herself. One has to become conscious of his/her own feelings, thought process, temperament, intellectual characteristics and behaviour in order to get relieved from mental conflicts. Such a training of mind is the most important need of education according to Krishnamurti.

Krishnamurti was not in favor of the education system prevailing at that time as it was oppressing the real nature of individuals. According to him, the present system did not allow the learners to think independently and with spontaneity as it focused on training everyone in the same manner without taking care of their individual differences, which actually would end up creating machines, rather than letting them be human beings. This system was overemphasizing academic aspect while overlooked the training of a healthy mind. It produced employment but ignored the holistic development of the learner who candeal with the environment and maintain the stability. It trained the individuals with some specific skills required for the job but did not prepare them for the unpredictable circumstances of life. The holistic approach of education is to prepare a fearless individual,an integrated man and not just a doctor, a scholar, a technician or a job seeker. It is beyondthe process of acquiring knowledge or to be fit for a specific job.

Krishnamurti proposed integral education, which can build the capabilities to face challenges of life in the learners. Academic knowledge of certain discipline is not enough,　rather it should work towards building self-knowledge and self-awareness. Pre-established ideals should be vanished from the system and one should be made free to develop and follow own ideals. Education should enable the individuals to develop proper understanding of the environment and behave accordingly. Wisdom should be given moreimportance than collection of knowledge. Once a person learns to love the self, he/she can extend the love for the whole humanity, which is the value to be inculcated by education. Freedom opens the path for flourishing goodness and love. Education should create open-minded individuals who can respect and accept internationalism and promote brotherhood among people belonging to different places, having different cultures and followingvarious sects. The child should be taught how to think rather than what to think, thinking individually, independently and for the self is very important. Student is not a subordinatebut rather should be treated as the partner in the process of creating knowledge. Creativityshould be encouraged over monotonous way of teaching learning. A child should be observed properly by the teacher to identify the potentials and nature of the child, which can open so many possibilities rather than pushing towards a specific direction. Wisdom comes with experiences; teacher should work towards providing maximum possible experiences to the learner.

Krishnamurti visualized an ideal school where there is limited number of students as instruction provided in a huge mass is worthless. The school should be free from rigid ideologies and rules. Authoritarian attitude of teachers should not be encouraged. Child should be treated as an important individual should be allowed to discover the own interestsand potentials. Krishnamurti had tried to put in his ideas into practice by founding more than ten co-educational schools with the goal of providing maximum opportunities to the children to grow and flourish as much as they can. Rishi Valley Education centre is one of the prominent educational institution running under Krishnamurti Foundation which runs on the ideas of Krishnamurti. Several other schools are Brockwood Park school, UK; Oak Grove School, US; Rajghat Besant School, Varanasi and The School KFI, Chennai.

Brief Biography of Rabindranath Tagore

When we look back into the great history and development civilization of India, we can see that India has seen today's glory owing to the unforgettable contributions of many a talented and great persons along the ages. One of such gems that history has ever produced is Gurudev Rabindranath Tagore, India's first recipient of the prestigious Nobel Prize.

Rabindranath Tagore, world's famous poet, great philosopher and humanist, novelist, dramatist and a prophet was born in Calcutta, India on 7th May, 1861 to Devendranath Tagore and Sarada Devi. He was his parent's fourteenth child. He was named Rabindranath or Rabi for short, meaning "the sun". It was an unusual coincidence that he was born on the same day that famous Indian diplomat Motilal Nehru was born in Agra. His original family name was Banerji. However, the term Thakur which means literally a lord was used to address the Brahmans. The early British officials anglicized "Thakur" as "Tagore" and it was taken over by this family as their surname. Rabindranath's grandfather Dwarkanath Tagore was a highly respected leader of Calcutta's Hindu community. He was primarily called Prince Dwarkanath Tagore because of his elegant appearance, magnificent way of living and his generous public charities. Many public institutes received his generous help. He helped to establish several institutions in Calcutta. The oldest and finest library in India, the first medical centre of modern education in India and the first medical college and hospital in Calcutta and the Presidency college of Calcutta are a few of the Institutions assisted by his generosity. Rabindranath's father, Devendranath was highly respected among the people of Calcutta as a saintly man. He was popularly known as "Maharshi", an enlightened man of God in the tradition of great sages in India. Devendranath's translation of the Rigveda and Upanishads into the Bengali language proved his profound knowledge of Hinduism and Bengali literature. He also had an excellent command in English, Persian and Sanskrit. Although private tutors were engaged for the children's lessons, Tagore's father took a personal interest in their education. The Maharshi was a gifted linguist and made sure that young Rabindranath was multilingual: Bengali, Sanskrit and English.

For only a short time, Rabindranath received formal schooling from the schooling from the schools. First, he attended the Oriental Seminary and later moved to Bengal Academy. He stayed only a short time at these schools. The atmosphere and daily life at school failed to attract him. Then he was transferred to St Xavier's High School in

Calcutta. There he stayed for a while. Thus, he never completed formal schooling . Rabindranath's elder brother, Satyendranath, who himself was highly educated and cultured, suggested to his father that Rabindranath go to England for an education to prepare him for the civil service or the law which were then very respectable positions in India. Satyendranath was the only Indian among fifty successful candidate at the civil services examination held in London in 1863. With his father's consent, Rabindranath moved to Ahmedabad to stay with Satyendra where he was the District and Sessions Judge. During this period, the reading of books of English history and literature contributed a lot to Rabindrath's intellectual growth. After his further studies of the English language, culture and history, Rabindranath was ready for his venture to England. It was in September 1879, that he sailed to England with his brother Satyendra.

Rabindranath married Mrinalini Devi on Dec 3, 1883 in the family home at Jorasanko. Mrinalini never attended any school, so taking special interest in his wife's education Tagore taught her Sanskrit and Bengali. She also learnt English and the Hindu scripture which made her mature socially and culturally. They had five children: three daughters and two sons. However, as the greatest tragedy of his life, Tagore lost his wife and two children to illness during a span of five years.

One of the supreme lyric poets of the world, Tagore was influenced by two important forces, which helped to mould his thinking; one was his own father, the Maharshi and the other was Vaishnava poetry. In all his poems, we can see the vivid description, clear imagery and true feelings with music. Perhaps the most characteristic trait of Tagore's poetry is the fusion of nature and man. This unity of nature and man is identified in all his poetry.

Tagore wrote extensively to the last days of his life. His published verse and dramas amount to about 150,000 lines. His essays on various topics, non-dramatic prose, short stories, novels, criticism and autobiography are more than twice his poetic works. There is also a mass of unorganized and uncollected works. Tagore wrote his first poem when he was only eight years old and his last verse was completed just a few days before his death. Tagore's dramatic work is the vehicle of ideas rather than the expression of action. Tagore, a great actor appeared in many plays. Tagore's dramas are more suitable to be acted in open courtyard than in a packed theatre. The finest work of Tagore is not found in his plays or his songs but in his short stories. He wrote short stories throughout his life. He wrote his 1st story "Bhikharini" (the Beggar Woman) which was published in 1877 when he was sixteen years old and his last few stories were written a few months before his death in 1941. As a short story writer, Tagore was very particular to construct plots to elaborate human life and to reflect human feelings. He preferred to take simple incidents and in most cases his stories are plain, simple and straight forward. Tagore's great desire to express his profound thinking was not satisfied with his literary works alone. He engaged in many expressive art forms and endeavoured to express himself in arts such as music, drama, opera, ballet and at the end of his life in painting.

About his musical talents, Tagore was influenced by three different types of music, European Music, Hindustani Classical Music and popular Religious Music of Bengal. Tagore composed more than two thousand songs. These songs formed a wide variety of styles and themes. Tagore composed two types of songs: songs which are dominated by melodies and songs that are dominated by words and phrases. The moods of Tagore's songs are multitudinous and the variety is bewildering. As a prolific musician, Rabindranath Tagore influenced the style of such musician such as Amjad Ali Khan and Vilayat Khan. He composed the words and music of the Indian national anthem "Jana Gana Mana", which was accepted as the national anthem in 1950. His song "Amader Shonar Bangla" has been accepted as the national anthem of Bangladesh as well, thus making him the first ever person to have written the national anthems of two countries. For Bengalis, the songs' appeal, stemming from the combination of emotive strength and beauty described as surpassing even Tagore's poetry, was such that the Modern Review observed that "there is in Bengal no cultured home where Rabindranath's songs are not sung or at least attempted to be sung... Even illiterate villagers sing his songs".

It is interesting to note that Tagore began painting at the age of sixty-six and continued to paint with great vigour and charm until his death. He produced about two and a half thousand pictures of which many are ranked among the world's greatest. Since Tagore did not follow any conventional methods and principles in his paintings, his pictures did not conform to any prevailing Indian style. It is simply the creative expression of the individual's mind.

T Surge Moore, a famous English author and member of the Royal Society submitted Tagore's name for the consideration of Nobel Prize in literature. The proposal of Tagore's name was a real surprise for the Swedish Academy. The chairperson of the committee Harold Hjarne had a very difficult time to recognize the originality of Tagore's creative work. However, with the support of the other scholars, Tagore was finally awarded the Noble Prize in Nov 13, 1913 for "Gitanjali". The Noble prize made Rabindranath Tagore not merely aware of his literary excellence but of the West's recognition of Asian excellence by Western standards.In the same year Calcutta University adored him with Doctor of literature. In 1915, the Indian Government endowed him with knighthood, which he returned after the notorious Jallianwalabagh massacre to express his emotions of anger at the episode.

In 1921, Shantiniketan Ashram became a world famous university known as Vishva Bharati Univesity. The aim of the University was to bring about a synthesis of the East and the West. For the development of Vishva Bharati, Tagore toiled carelessly and untiringly for twenty years and was able to gain support from the Government as well as stable foundations. He appointed scholars from many places to share their knowledge with the students. As education reformer, he introduced Upanishad ideals of education and widely contributed towards uplifting the 'untouchables'.

It was Tagore's profound desire to see in his own lifetime the unity and peace among the nations. He was much troubled in his mind and heart when people were destroyed and countries were devastated during both the wars. He also cherished the strong hope to see free India in his own lifetime. He was close to the leaders of India's fight for freedom, Mahatma Gandhi, Jawaharlal Nehru, Subhas Chandra Bose etc. and continuously used to lend support towards India's fight for freedom. However, his dream to see India independent was not fulfilled in his lifetime as he breathed his last on August 7, 1941.

Key words:

Essays:

Essay is an analytic or interpretative literary composition usually dealing with its subject from a limited or personal point of view. The Essays considered for the study are the Essays written by Rabindranath Tagore on Educational Theory and problems in various newspapers, edited books and periodicals. The source of data is Primary Data taken from Vishbharati Archive titled as '*Rabindra Rachanabali*' [Volumes 1 to 16, published by Vishvabharati in Bangla] and the series 'The English Writings of Rabindranath Tagore [Volumes 1 to 8] edited by Mohit

Kumar Ray and published by Atlantic Publishers (2007) and some reliable Internet sources.

Letters:

A letter is a direct or personal written or printed message addressed to a person or an organization. Rabindranath Tagore wrote thousands of letters to his family members, close friends and associates as well as eminent persons from different circles of life in both Bengali and English. Most of the significant Bengali letters have been published in the half-century since his death, but not translated, while few noteworthy English letters are in print. These letters show as many facets of his experience, interests and ideas as possible. Students of history, politics and literature find them an invaluable tool, not only for an understanding of the complexity of Tagore's personality, but also of the times in which he lived.

Lectures:

Lecture is an educational talk to an audience, especially to students in a university. Rabindranath Tagore delivered lectures/ speech in different points of his life in India and abroad in varying aspects of life. These lectures are transcripted and published by Vishva Bharati in different

Volumes of *Rabindra Rachanabali*. For this study only those lectures are considered where education in the central theme.

Education: Indian Context:

Education in Contemporary India is about learning the importance of education in today's Indian context. For prospective as well as practising teachers, it is required to have a sound knowledge of philosophical and sociological bases of education, the relationship of education with culture and its role and understand teaching in the context of modernisation especially in the context of India. An understanding of Tagore's Educational philosophy through the study of his literary work would certainly be of great help in these areas.

Objectives of the Study

Research Objectives:

1. To analyse educational thoughts depicted in the literary works, viz, Essays, Letters and Lectures of Rabindranath Tagore.
2. To evaluate the impact of Rabindranath Tagore's educational philosophy on Education in the Indian context.

Type of Research

The present study is of the nature of qualitative research through content analysis. *"Qualitative research is the collection of extensive narrative data on many variables over an extended period."* (Best and Kahn, 2005, p.255)

The study is conducted based on various primary and secondary sources. The original works of Rabindranath Tagore i.e. Essays, Letters, Lectures and other relevant literature by Tagore is used as a reference. The other similar studies and research works conducted on the philosophy of Tagore are referred. Books of other authors on the educational philosophy of Tagore are reviewed.

Scope of Study

As an educator, it is very important to understand the needs of the children with changingscenario and also what needs to be done to nurture the children to make them survive in the present world and to build good citizens. With the time, the attitude towards the Education should also be updated according to the need of the society and the child. Tagoreargued that, *"Don't limit a child to your own learning, for he was born in another time"*. But apart from all these, it is important to make them good human beings, to drive them towards the nature and make them understand the importance of the nature. Nature is the source of everything that is needed for the living of the human and the true education comesfrom the nature. Tagore's philosophy of education puts emphasis on the 'Naturalism'which can help the teacher to understand how to make children love the nature which is really very important in this technological era where the society is getting disinclined fromthe nature gradually.

Bose (2016) stated in her study on 'Rabindranath Tagore's Philosophy of Education and Development in India' that,

> *"Tagore believes that nature is the best educator and man learns through his own experiences from the nature. For him, nature, man and god can never be visualised in isolation from one another, they exist in harmony. Education develops the faith in the universal soul and leads to the realisation of the universal man."*(p.2)

Rabindranath believed in the holistic development of the child and was against the conventional classroom education done inside four walls. He believed that education system should be able to nurture the child in all the aspects, physical, intellectual and spiritual. Tagore said,

"The object of education is to give man the unity of truth. Formerly when life was simple, all the different elements of man were in complete harmony. But, when there came the separation of the intellect from the spiritual and the physical, the school of education put entire emphasis on the intellect and the physical side of man. We devote our attention to giving children information, not knowing that by this emphasis we are accentuating a breakbetween the intellectual, physical and the spiritual life." (Tagore, 1917, p.153)

Rabindranath believed that education should be joyful. It should be vast and not limited. He also put emphasis on creativity in education. Creativity is important because it is the expression of joy. Explaining a verse of Upanishada, Tagore said that,

"From joy does spring all the creation, by joy is it maintained, towards joy does it progress, and into joy does it enter. It means that God's creation has not its source in any necessity; it comes from his fullness of joy; it is his love that creates, therefore in creation is his own revealment." (Tagore, 1915, p.45)

Research Questions

1. What are the views of Rabindranath Tagore towards aims of Education?

2. What are the views of Rabindranath Tagore towards roles of a teacher?

3. What are the views of Rabindranath Tagore towards qualities of a teacher?

4. What are the views of Rabindranath Tagore towards methods of teaching?

5. What are the views of Rabindranath Tagore towards problems of Education?

Rationale of the Study

Rabindranath Tagore, by his efforts and achievements, is part of a global network of pioneering educators such as Rousseau, Pestalozzi, Frobel, Montessori, Dewey and in the contemporary context, Malcolm Knowles. Although Tagore is a superb representative of his country – the man who wrote its national anthem, he is truly a man of the whole earth, a product of the best of both Indian traditional and modern western cultures. The core of Tagore's educational philosophy was learning from nature, music and life. He created Shantiniketan to realize his educational ideals. This is the reason why his education is easily acceptable by human mind. Tagore extended the meaning and functional importance of certain aspects of personality as nobody else had done before him. The ideal educator must combine in himself the gifts of a philosopher, a poet, a mystic, a social reformer, a scientist and a veritable man of action can he has to take into account all types of men and their aspirations ,all facets of the human personality, all levels man's experience, all fields of endeavour and achievement.

Rabindranath Tagore, in his own person was a living icon of the type of mutuality and creative exchange that he advocated. He deliberated on different problems of Indian society particularly that of the rural people and tried to remove them through education. His educational system was a synthesis of East and West, Ancient and Modern, Science and Vedanta although he protested against the emphasis on foreign language. He was one of the first Indian to argue for a humane educational system that was in touch with the environment and aimed at over-all development of educational system on essential human virtues like freedom, purity, sympathy, perfection and world brotherhood.

Thus, it is always helpful to go through the lectures, essays as well as the letters of Rabindranath Tagore to get a comprehensive understanding of his educational thoughts and ideas, so that they can be implemented in the Indian Education system in one way or the other as it is being done from the last few decades. In a rapidly changing world, relearning is always as important as learning. Deep reading is an important element for wiring our brains that allows us to grasp deeper concepts, ideas and thoughts. As the nation is embracing the New Education Policy in 2020, for its effective implementation, an insight into the thoughts of a genius and gem like Rabindranath Tagore is believed to be of utmost importance. Out of the vast volumes of the writings of Rabindranath Tagore in both English and his mother tongue *Bangla*, which are skilfully and meticulously archived by Vishvabharati and Ministry of Cultural Affairs, Government of India in the original format, only those writings are selected which has direct link or reference to the Education system in India. These writings are in the form of Essays, Lectures and Letters written or delivered by Tagore at different points of his life. The understanding of Bangla on the part of the researcher is found to be an aiding factor in the analysis of the Text in the original format. Another important fact is that the researcher is actively involved in the field of teaching from the last twelve years and is in constant touch with students and academicians in the first hand. Thus, the findings of the study can be directly useful to be applied in the teaching learning process or in active classroom teaching experiences of the researcher as well as the academic fraternity with whom the findings of the study would be shared.

Significance of the study

During the course of study, a review of Tagore's writings on education is presented. The core of Tagore's educational theory puts greater emphasis on the complete development of individual personality. He believed that education should help an individual to attain manhood, so that all his powers may be developed to the fullest extent for his own individual perfection of the human society in which he was born. He believed that education was not merely a means for the growth and fullness of the individual, but it was also concerned with the whole physical and social milieu in which his life was lived. He wanted the boys and girls to be fearless, free and open minded, self-reliant, full of spirit of inquiry and self critical, with their roots deep in the soil of India but reaching out to the world in understanding, neighbourliness, co-operation of material and spiritual progress. Tagore's concept of ideal education covered the description of ideal education covered the description of ideal atmosphere, institution, teacher and method. Actually,

Tagore's success lies in the fact that he did not try to control directly the ideas, feelings and values of his children but imaginatively designed an environment and a program of activities and experiences which evoked the desired responses. He also believed that the education of a country acquires shape and substance only against the entire background and it is important that there is a strong relationship between education and society.

Tagore's educational theory was put into practice in his school in Shantiniketan, which started with only five students on the roll. A history of the origin and development of the institution reveals that from such a small start, the school has grown to a university, Vishva Bharati, with different departments in humanities, science, art, music, education, Chinese studies, advanced studies in philosophy and village welfare. Tagore's practical aspect of education also includes a description of organisation of daily activities in which freedom, games and sports, art and entertainment are emphasized. Tagore's organization of curricula was not narrowed down to only textbook learning, but it provided a fullness of experience for children from multiple sources.

Delimitations of the study

Since the intended research is a qualitative and descriptive one, it has the following delimitaions.

1. In the duration of the Dissertation, only a limited number of literary works of Rabindranath Tagore are studied. Out of a large number of literary works available in the Internet archive generated by Vishva Bharati, selected number of Essays, Letters and Lectures are taken into consideration, which has direct implication to Education in the Indian Context in terms of content

2. The intended research requires gathering a plethora of writings of high quality and standard by a Noble Laureate. It would take lot of time and skill on the part of the researcher to analyse all the qualitative data and co-relating it to the Indian system of Education

3. The content are not analyzed in view of a literature analyst or from linguistic point of view. Here, only the educational thoughts and philosophies of Rabindranath Tagore are studied and analyzed. Therefore, many other literary works of Rabindranath Tagore with Educational context can

be studied further as well as the content can be studied from literature and linguistic point of view of analysis.

4. Here, the literary works that are selected does not have any chronological sequence. Relevant literary works from different era or the progress of the thoughts of Rabindranath Tagore can also be done in the chronological order

5. It is tough to validate an accurate and complete representation of a study.

6. The study cannot test or verify the result statistically.

CHAPTER 2
REVIEW OF RELATED LITERATURE

Introduction

This study typically takes the form of a descriptive study. This is aimed to be done through extensive study of his books, lectures, articles and Interviews both in English and Bengali language. The method used is historic analytic method. Available reports and publication on Tagore's educational theory and his institutes are also carefully examined.

Tagore's educational writings constitute a voluminous literature, mostly scattered in Independent essays, speeches and letters. A majority of Tagore's educational writings are in Bengali and a few of them are in English. Due to the extraordinary efforts of Publication Department of Vishva Bharati, all the writings of Rabindranath Tagore are preserved in online archive in the nature of 'Rabindranath Rachanabali' in a total of 27 volumes. Translated versions of the Bengali works are also available.These literature are mainly taken from the volume 4, 5, 6, 7 and 8 of "English Writings of Rabindranath Tagore" published by Atlantic Publishers Distributors (P) limited and edited by Mohit K Ray (ISBN 81-264-0757-6, 81-264-0757-4, 81-269-0740-1, 81-269-0760-1.

The researcher's knowledge of Bengali is hoped to be useful in obtaining significant understanding of Tagore's writings, as it is always best to try to understand the author's viewpoint by studying his creations in the original language in which it was written. Despite of all the efforts made by the able and expert translators, a look into the original version is always necessary and worth analysing.

Importance of review of related literature

Review of related literature helps to gain insight into the area of study. It provides a direction to the investigator and enriches with the existing knowledge and debates in the area of research. It also guides the researcher about the research methodology to be followed. Researcher also comes to know about various reference material available regarding the study after reviewing the related studies. It also suggests the ways in which research report can be written and presented.

Review of related studies

There are many scholars and well known personalities who have worked on the life and writings of Rabindranath Tagore throughout the years. Among them, one of the earliest workers is Krishna Kripalini, noted freedom fighter, parliamentarian and author. His biography on Tagore Rabindranath Tagore, a Biography inspired many budding researchers and educationists to go deep into the educational thoughts of Tagore. His work is referred exclusively in this study. Another early writers to work in depth on the life and work of Rabindranath Tagore is Edward John Thompson in his book Rabindranath Tagore, His Life and Work and Rabindranath Tagore's Philosophy of Education by Sarvapalli Radhakrishnan. Apart from that, two another classic biographies of the Noble Laureate, namely Rabindranath Tagore: A biographical Study by Ernest Rhys and Rabindranath Tagore: an illustrated life by Uma Dasgupta are also considered for the study. Two PhD thesis Tagore- His Educational Theory and Practice and its impact on Indian Education by Radha Vinod Jalan submitted to University of Florida in 1976 and Rabindranath Tagore's Philosophy of International Education by Asirvatham Periaswami submitted to Loyola University of Chicago in 1976 are also discussed in taking references for the study.

Chakraborty, A. (2018) carried out a research under the title "The Educational philosophy of Ravindranath Tagore and Rishi Aurobindo Ghosh."

The educational aims according to these great men are discussed in the studies. The objectives of the study are,

a) To compare the educational aims, curriculum, teaching methods, the teacher- pupil relationship and school organisation proposed by Tagore and by Aurobindo.

b) To discuss the merits and demerits of the educational philosophies of Tagore and of Aurobindo.

c) To suggest educational implications of the philosophical thoughts of Tagore and of Aurobindo in the present context.

As mentioned in the study, Tagore was a Vedantist, Individualist, Naturalist, Idealist, Humanist, Internationalist and Spiritualist. He believed in giving right type of freedom to individual. He believed that every individual should try to attain spiritual perfection. He preached human brotherhood, having faith in fundamental unity of mankind. He considerednature as a great teacher and God revealed himself through various forms, colours and rhythm of nature. According to Tagore, Education not only promotes the acquiring of some knowledge but develops the curiosity & faculty of learning and knowing so powerfully that no class room teaching can match it. Education should strive for a number of moral and spiritual qualities like self-discipline, tolerance, courtesy and inner freedom. Believing inpurity and in his own experiences, innocence of child, the teacher should behave with himwith great love and affection, sympathy, affection. . Instead of emphasizing on book learning, the teacher should provide conducive environment to the child so that he engages himself in useful and constructive activities and learn by his own experiences. Tagore's educational model has a unique sensitivity and aptness for education within multi-racial, multi-lingual and multi-cultural situations amidst conditions of acknowledged economic discrepancy, political imbalance and social evils.

Chaudhari, B. (2018) conducted a study on "Tagore and Nationalism".

The study was done to cognize the views of Tagore on Nationalism. The study reveals that,according to Tagore, knowledge should not be restricted to particular caste or class, but should be free to all without any bias. People of this nation should strive untiringly towardsexcellence and their mind should be led into widening thought and action forever as appealed by Rabindranath. The poet seeks the awakening of country in the heaven of freedom. Tagore wanted the nation to be classless and casteless. Tagore had deep faith in universal humanity and wished to have freedom of heart, not as nationalist, but as an internationalist. Tagore was one of them who were trying to survive the national unity. He could visualize the integrity in India's glorious civilization of past, its ideals and sacrifices, spiritual and mantra meditation. As a result of Tagore's acquaintance with people, disputes and discussions over a variety of issue, the idea of integrated life-philosophy took place in Tagore's mind. Tagore's philosophy also seems relevant in existing situation as we find the variety of social and political issues unsolved even after achieving the freedom from British hegemony.

Janaiah, C. (2018) conducted a research under the title "S Radhakrishnan and Rabindranath Tagore's Philosophical Perspectives on Education -A Comparative Study"

The research was carried out to throw light on the contributions of S Radhakrishnan and Rabindranath Tagore's philosophical perspectives on modern education. The objectives of the study were,

a) To assess the Educational Philosophy of S. Radhakrishnan with regard to curriculum, teacher's role in teaching.

b) To study the contribution of the Educational Philosophy of Rabindranath Tagore to modern Indian Education.

c) To compare the philosophical thoughts of Sarvepally Radhakrishnan and Rabindranath Tagore.

The study is philosophical-cum-historical in nature. The investigation is depended on the reports of the Commissions and Committees published by the Government of India from time to time for the educational purposes. Secondary sources like encyclopedia and history textbooks were used for study.

The study concluded that, Tagore was a naturalist and an idealist. He wants things ofbeauty and nice virtues to be taught in the curriculum. He also wants children to appreciate truth, beauty and goodness. Subjects recommended by him to be taught are History, geography, nature study, language, and science. Activities or finer subjects will include music, art, poetry, dancing, and dramatics. He was very particular about music and drama. He rejected mechanical methods of teaching which were uninspiring. Tagore wanted the boys to progress at their own rate without being guided by others. His approach is

Gestalt approach. He believes that children learn their lessons with the aid of their whole body andmind, with all the senses fully active and eager. Tagore says that if the atmosphere is good,discipline problems will not arise. It is only control that breeds in scandals and indiscipline so where there is freedom, there is no question of indiscipline. He also believes in self- discipline. Tagore discovered that the secret of maintaining discipline lies in the development of integrated personality. A key concept in Tagore's model is that of promoting a "narrative imagination" – the nurturing of creativity, empathy and diversity. The basic objectives of any worthwhile national education system should be promotion of creativity, freedom, joy and awareness of country's cultural heritage as proposed by Tagore.

Kumar, P. (2018) carried out a research under the title "Educational Thoughts of J Krishnamurti and Rabindranath Tagore- A comparative study"

The researcher feels that innumerable experiments in policy making as well as programme implementation have been done in last 68 years but the analysis doesn't give very positiveindication but the ideas of Tagore are still relevant as they are used as a base in the formulatio of

National Curriculum Framework 2005. The objectives of the research are tocritically examine the educational ideas and philosophical explanation of Rabindranath Tagore and J. Krishnamurti on several dimensions of education, to examine the deviation of modern schooling system from the ideas of both the educationists, to examine the similarities and differences of educational ideas of J. Krishnamurti and R. Tagore with reference to present education system and to compare educational practices in the institutions established by KFI and Rabindranath Tagore. The methods applied for the accomplishment of the first three objectives are philosophical, historical, analytical and comparative method whereas the fourth method was fulfilled through the fieldwork method and descriptive method. Qualitative content analysis and critical analysis of available literature including philosophical, educational and relevant literary thoughts available in the form of books, letters, articles and speeches was done. Field observation of practices in their institutions Rishi Valley School of Krishnamurti and Visva Bharati of Tagore was done. An open ended questionnaire was used verbally for students.

The findings of the research are, Jiddu Krishnamurthy and Tagore both developed an innovative as well as an alternative education system to seek truth by clarifying its development as well as its philosophical nature. Tagore talks about harmony with all existence through education and Krishnamurti talks about developing right relationship through education among all existence, which further leads harmony. The childhoodexperience of both prompted them to think about a new school system. Both represented the global consciousness of humanity in their ideologies. Tagore's model was based on Ashrama system where the teachers and the taught lived together and worked together for material welfare and spiritual well-being. Both were naturalist. Both prescribed holistic growth through union with nature. Tagore put more emphasis upon direct experience. Tagore was formidably logical and he didn't accept the truth of others. Tagore advocated self-governance, which is prerequisite to get rid of any authoritative trap, jointly between the students and the teachers in his school. Tagore was heavily influenced by old Indian scripture especially Upanishadas. Tagore always advocated that education should be provided through mother tongue but today's policy doesn't make any effort to provide education through local languages. Tagore pleaded that the twin powers of thinking and imagination should receive free and joyous exercise through child's mother tongue from very beginning. Tagore was totally against the classroom arrangement in which children have to sit inertly whilst lessons are pelted at them like hailstones on flower. He said that body and mind are vitally connected, so more understanding takes place if both are active. Tagore dreamed that type of tapobona model of institute which could create inner space ineach individual so that each individual could reflect on his own values and could understand about his role in this world.

Bandyopadhyay, S. (2017) carried out a study under the title "Educational ideas andpractices of Rabindranath Tagore and Maria Montessori a comparative analysis"

The study is historical and philosophical in nature. It is a comparative study of two philosophies. Educational philosophies of Rabindranath Tagore and Maria Montessori are explored in this study first. Later a comparative analysis is conducted of the educational ideas and practices of Rabindranath Tagore and Maria Montessori. Main objectives of the study are,

a) To analyse the similarities and differences in the educational philosophies of Rabindranath Tagore and Maria Montessori.

b) To study the aims, curriculum and methods of

education as propounded by Rabindranath Tagore and Maria Montessori.

c) To find out the relevance of the educational doctrines of Maria Montessori and Rabindranath Tagore in the present day education system.

It is a deep conviction of this study that the knowledge and implementation of the ideals and practices of Rabindranath Tagore and Maria Montessori will pave the way forfructification of a better and a more humane and altruistic human society. Some of the conclusions of the study are as follows:

Rabindranath Tagore's Idealism was based on Vedanta. His thoughts of Idealism found its reflection in his educational institution of Santiniketan. The first objectiveof the school was to give spiritual culture to the students.

Rabindranath Tagore as a Naturalist envisaged that nature is the best teacher of thepupil. So he established his educational institution Santiniketan in a natural settingat Bolpur. In his institution, the main principles of education were based on freedom, training of senses and creative activities. Tagore's Naturalism was a poet's perspective while Maria Montessori's Naturalism was a scientific one.

Aims of education as pointed out by Rabindranath Tagore includes the developmentof personality, enrichment of freedom of thought, development of men of culture, cultural synthesis of the East and the West, development of national values,development of scientific attitude and the spiritual development of the personality. Rabindranath Tagore gives importance to spiritual, intellectual, social, cultural aspects of the individuality. So he believed in integral development of the child.

Modern day education is child centric. Education gives priority to the needs and interests of the child. Rabindranath Tagore cried for the freedom of children in education. At Santiniketan the main principle of education was freedom, and activity.

Mondal, J. (2017) performed a research study under the title, "Tagore's Education System in Santiniketan: A Geographical Approach for Survival of Mankind."

The objectives of the study are as under:

a) To identify different types of social hazards those impede the socialsustainability.

b) To make a framework of Tagore's education system as an approach for socialsustainability.

c) To manage social development and mitigate social hazards through realisticessence of Tagore's education system.

The study being a qualitative research is confined within Literature survey related to Tagore's education system, and Perception study of people (ethnography) about Tagore'seducation system from view point of social sustainability.

He found in his study that, Tagore felt about a new education system in collaboration of ancient and modern time education system. Tagore's education system have been evolved due to two concerned manners:

a) Ancient vedanthic tradition from Indian scriptures like the Gita and theUpanishads.
b) Western classical & modern educational thought and scientific attitude.

The findings of the study are:
a) Tagore had very strong and modern perceptions and extended it throughintroducing Brahmacharya-Vidyalaya.
b) Rabindranath Tagore is a pioneer of the intellectual union of the spiritual East and the materialistic West.
c) Education system of Brahmacharya Vidyalaya made strong relationship between traditional past

and modern Indian education.

d) He had tried to develop the society by various techniques (like- simplicity, universal hood, rural reconstruction, cultural upliftment and preservation,afforestation etc.) within the flowing channel of education system.

He concluded that Tagore's education system is developed in a particular situation to improve the quality of education as well as to solve the problems that was seen in those days. With over-increasing demand of the society, the movement of economy has also changed. But according to Tagore, his invented education system is not rigid. Brahmacharya-Vidyalaya is the body of Tagore's education system (soul). We can preserve Tagore education system through the conservation of Brahmacharya-Vidyalaya and its proper utilization.

Mukherjee, D. (2017) studied "The Impact of Drama and Theatre Arts on AcademicPerformance -An Objective Assessment of Tagores Principle of Education Target area Birbhum"

The study was done with the aim to find out the academic performance of the students of secondary schools prior to instruction through two selected approaches i.e., Traditional Approach and Dramatic Approach, To estimate the academic performance of two paper ofstudents after conducting instructions through two different approaches, To compare the academic performance of two groups of students in different subjects treated through twodifferent approaches, To compare the academic performance of two groups of students in different subject groups within & between schools, To compare the achievements of two groups of students in language &co-curricular activities between Tagorean schools & the schools under other boards and To compare the achievements of students in co-curricular activities prior and after the experimentation between Tagorean schools & the schools under other boards.

For conducting the study, with a view to the objectives of the research, traditional approach and Dramatic approach were selected as the strategies for experimentation. It was conducted on the students of classes VI to IX and XI of Secondary and Higher SecondarySchools under three different Boards (WBBSE & Council, CBSE and Visva-Bharati University Schools). The tools of the study were entry level tests on all subjects of secondary schools with reference to the selected classes,

Learning materials for instructions through two different strategies on the selected units, Achievement Tests (Post Tests) on the selected units, A comprehensive achievement test on the subjects mathematics, science, social-science, and work education based on the units of respective classes and Opinionnaire for theatre personalities and the teachers of secondary schools havingexperience about theatre.

The comparison between the achievements of students of Tagorean School and the schoolsof West Bengal Board was made. It was observed that the relative performance of the students of Tagorean school in language and co-curricular subjects were significantly betterthan that of the students of the schools under West Bengal Board. The study suggests that,Tagorean Approach could be used for classroom instructions in the schools under West Bengal Board of Secondary Education. If it is required to use Tagorean Approach for classroom teaching, then the emphasis should be given on creating the proper school environment; but it is contrary to the recommendations of the Education Commissions thatthe medium of instruction should be the mother tongue or regional language. It should always be kept in mind that a conductive teaching-learning environment helps to improve the quality of academic performance of students in the subject.

Sharma, B. (2017) carried out a research under the title "A comparative study of theeducational philosophy of JJ Rousseau and RN Tagore in present situation".

The objectives of the study were,

a) To study and compare the different aspects of educational philosophies of J.J. Rousseau and Dr. Ravindranath tagore

b) To compare the contributions ob the both Rousseau and Tagore

c) To compare the importance of Rousseu's and Tagore's educational philosophy in the present context

The study is historical in nature where the original works of Rousseau and Tagore, Encyclopaedias in Education, Educational abstracts, Bibliographies and Directories, Biographical references and Quotation sources were used as tools to carry out the research.The important conclusions of the study are as follows:

Jean Jacques Rousseau and Rabindranath Tagore were of Naturalist philosophers. Rousseau's concepts of naturalism are quite near to William Wordsworth. Although Tagore's ideas were of his own yet Rousseau and Wordsworth influenced him.

J.J. Rousseau is the forerunner of new education. For him the aim of the education was the natural development of child. Tagore also wanted an which can develop natural potentialities of the child.

Both the natural educationists had advocated that Nature needs freedom to educate the child in natural surroundings.

a) Knowledge should come through personal experiences and senses, this idea has been forcibly emphasized by both the naturalistic educationists.

b) Bookish knowledge was ignored by both the naturalists.

c) Both had emphasized the slogan of 'Back to Nature', but human nature was also included in it.

d) Tagore felt greatly for the need of women's education, whereas Rousseau was not so serious about it as Tagore was.

e) Tagore was a practical naturalist while Rousseau was only theoretical.

f) Both the educationists had recommended the book of Nature.

g) Both the philosophers denied any kind of restrictions during child education. Child-centred education was the main theme of both the educationists.

Bose, A. (2016) carried out a study on "Rabindranath Tagore's Philosophy of Education and Development in India."

The aim of the study was to understand the philosophical groundings of the journey of the universal man that Tagore aspires for through education and development. It is revealed in the study that Tagore was a humanist as his philosophies are centred on man. The ideal education system in accordance with Tagore is the one that aims at man's perfection and development of all the aspects of human personality physical, intellectual and spiritual. Tagore is a naturalist who believes that the teaching of different subjects may be made natural through the utilisation of the various elements in the child's environment. He was not in favour of rigid classroom structures with buildings, furniture and books. Tagore's Siksha Satra experiment in Sriniketan promoted vocational education for the villager, teaching them methods and techniques for better farming practices and other vocations. The ideals of Sriniketan were literacy, social reform and rural welfare as Tagore believed that no education in India can be complete without the knowledge and understanding of the patterns of rural living. Tagore believed that mother tongue should be adopted as a medium of instruction as it will lead education to enter into the deeper strata of the society and bring about a permanent impact. Tagore's philosophy focuses too much on the spiritual education of the child. Bose feels that although we see reflections of Tagore's philosophy in our system but in certain aspects there is a need to reconsider his philosophy.

Ghosh, P. (2016) carried out a study to find "Ideals of education as envisioned by Tagore and Vivekananda Relevance in the contemporary society"

The objectives of the study were to identify the contributions of Swami Vivekananda and Tagore with respect to Indian philosophy and its influence on Indian education, Spiritual and Cultural background of education and its impact on education, National integration and its relevance in education, Patriotic viewpoints and its educational relevance and Morals and values in education. The study also aimed to find out the relevance of educational ideals of Swami Vivekananda and Tagore and their impact on the present educational scenario with respect to some selected dimensions like

    a) Aims of education,

    b) value education,

c) Woman education,

d) Technical and vocational education,

e) Mass education,

f) Education for international understanding,

g) To analyze the opinions of educationalists and philosophers regarding the educational vision and mission of Swami Vivekananda and Tagore,

h) To identify how their educational ideals will inculcate spiritual and cultural values among the students and

i) To find out how to spread international understanding through their educational ideals.

The study is comparative and philosophical where the investigator has taken into account the writings of Tagore and Vivekananda as primary sources whereas the opinion and comments of other thinkers and philosophers regarding Swami Vivekananda and Tagore'sphilosophy as secondary sources.

As mentioned in the study, Tagore, a modern Seer who belonged to the category of modernRishis had taken inspiration from ancient Vedic literature and analysed, interpreted and understood modern issues in its light. The study concludes that both Vivekananda and Tagore were Idealists, contemporaries, naturalist and pragmatists. Both of them believed that the soul of India rested on spiritualism. They were social reformers and viewed education as an instrument for social change. Both were rooted in the philosophy of Indiaand they were proud of India's Vedic culture. Both obtained Western education and lived in a period of conflict brought about by the struggle for Independence. They dreamed of spreading Indian culture throughout the world and through that they wanted a new sublime world order. Both of them were uncompromising nationalists who dreamed of the sovereignty and independence of India and believed that the prevalent educational system during their period was meant to serve the interest of the colonial masters and were harmfulto the Indian Nation.

Das, D. (2014) did a study of "Educational Philosophy of Rabindranath Tagore."

The objective of the paper was to analyze the

educational thoughts of Tagore, his basic conception of education and its process. The study is primarily based on secondary sourceslike the Books, Journals and Articles etc. The method used is historic-analytic method.

As discussed in the study, Tagore was influenced by the Christian conception of the fatherhood of God and by Shakespeare, Goethe, Wordsworth, etc. But the roots of his intellectual creativism and emotional make-up lie in the Upanishads, in the poetry of kalidas, in the lyrics of Vaisnavas, in the mystic poems of Kabir and the religiousatmosphere of the Brahmo Samaj. Rabindranath gave birth to "Santiniketan" (abode of peace), an Ashrama style educational institution in which he provided education based on the principle of freedom, natural trust, co-operation and joy. In his opinion child'seducation would be more effective if teachers and pupils live and work far away from dinand bustle of the city, like the teachers and students of the past. Rabindranath discarded thenotion of text-books. He put the responsibility of educating the students in a joyful manner upon the guru. He said the relationship between the student and the guru should be of companionship. Rabindranath was not happy with the prevailing state of education in his time, which robbed the child of his creative ability and natural potentialities.

Rabindranath introduced some cultural subjects in his educational institution like singing, dancing, painting, acting etc. because he believed that education is a process of upholding the creative abilities of children and not a process which merely concerned with bookish learning. Tagore was a great champion of education for international understanding. His patriotism and nationalism leads to internationalism.

Sengupta, S. (2014) studied "Upanishadic influence on educational thoughts of Rabindranath Tagore, Swami Vivekananda and Sri Aurobindo"

The study is historical in nature, which studies Upnishadic texts on educational idea and searches the educational thoughts and methodologies of Rabindranath Tagore, Swami Vivekananda and Sri Aurobindo. The researcher has prepared his thesis on the basis of data available in the books and journals. Original Upanishads and original works of Tagore, Vivekananda and Aurobindo. The objectives of the study are,

a) To study the methods and practices of the Upanishadic education system which may still have some bearing even today.

b) To bring into view the educational philosophies of these three educators viz. Rabindranath Tagore, Swami Vivekananda and Sri Aurobindo along with the impact of the Upanishadic system of education on them.

c) To investigate how the three great educators are influenced by the educational ideas of the Upanishadic education in respect of creating their respective centres of education and their congenial environment.

d) To evaluate how the three great educators are influenced by the educational ideas of the Upanishadic education in respect of the attitudes and the relationship of the teacher and the taught.

e) To trace out the living influence of Brahmacharya of the Upanishadic education system on the educational ideas of these three great educators

f) To find out the outlines of the writings of Rabindranath Tagore, Swami Vivekananda and Sri Aurobindo for reconstructing of contemporary Indian systemof education in the light of the Upanishads.

Some of the findings of the study are mentioned below:

a) While Rabindranath sets up a centre of learning at Santiniketan he has been deeply absorbed in his personal study and inclination towards the ideals of the Tapovan of the Upanishadic age as the comprehensive idea contained in the Upanishadic education serves the purpose.

b) Rabindranath makes sincere attempt to awaken and develop the innate cognitive disposition of the learner than he loads the unwilling mental frame like Svetasvata Upanishad since genuine thirst for knowledge alone leads to the real growth of knowledge.

c) Rabindranath brings back the ancient Upanishadic system of Brahmacharya. Rabindranath also like the seer-teachers of the Upanishadic age sets up shram Vidyalaya at Santiniketan to create congenial surroundings and favourable conditions in view of inspiring the learners to grow in the light of higher consciousness by practising 'Brahmacharya-Vrata'.

d) Following the ideals of the Upanishadic

Tapovan Rabindranath wants to see that the learners also lead a simple and unsophisticated and restrained life all along for their total individual growth.

Pushpanathan, T. (2013) conducted a research under the title "Rabindranath Tagore's philosophy of education and its influence on Indian Education."

As concluded in the study, Rabindranath Tagore believed that the aim of education is self-realization. He himself was a poet and a saint, who had, through his imagination and insight, realized the universal soul in himself and in nature. He believed that this realizationwas the goal of education. Because the universal soul is the root of our own soul, man's aim in life is to reach that universal soul of which all human beings are parts. The evolutionof nature is consciously or unconsciously driving us towards this universal soul, a process that can be assisted by education. Rabindranath's Educational philosophy is an adjunct ofhis general philosophy of life. He believed that every human being is one who has potentialities of progressing towards the Super human being, the universal soul. His conception of the universal soul bore clear imprint of the Gita and Upanishadic philosophies. Rabindranath believed in complete freedom of every kind for the students, the freedom of intellect, decision, heart, knowledge, action and worship. But in order to attain this freedom, the educand had to practice equanimity, harmony and balance. Rabindranath's pattern of education is independence, perfection and universality. In the process of education, the educator creates an environment in which the child's personality undergoes a free, perfect and unrestricted development. He believes in an inner harmony between man and Nature and God.

Saha, G. (2013) did a study on "Implicit scientific vision and values in educational experiments of Rabindranath Tagore an analysis"

The study was done with the following objectives:

a) To make a conceptual analysis of scientific vision and values,

b) To study the development process and crystallization of scientific vision and values of Tagore,

c) To make a critical analysis of curriculum and teaching learning process in Ashram vidyalaya now known as Patha Bhavana,

d) To study the scientific vision and values behind the formation of Sriniketan and

e) To suggest for necessary changes in policy and practice with regard to pedagogy in the light of scientific vision and values of Tagore.

The research sheds light on the questions like what kind of personality Tagore was, apart frombeing a genius poet and artist, what kind of scientific vision and values Tagore had, behind his educational experiments and how Tagore combined his Humanism and scientific vision in different activities at Santiniketan and Santiniketan.

The study followed descriptive survey method and the data collected was qualitative in nature and qualitative data analysis was done. The tools used for the study were

a) Analysis of the Text, Data, Letters,

b) Documents, Reports, etc taken from both Primary and Secondary sources,

c) Interview of selected experts in Tagorean Thought and closely associated with Santiniketan and Sriniketan

d) Observations of academic ambience of Ashram Vidyalaya and Siksha Satra, combining Nature and Nurture,

e) Co-Curricular activities of Santiniketan and

Sriniketan,

f) Art & Craft in Patha Bhavana and Siksha Satra,

g) observation & celebration of Festivals, Rituals and Exhibition of Achievements, Agricultural Produce and Craft products.

As concluded in the study, Tagore was not a man of science, neither a theorist nor an experimentalist but he embraced scientific temper in his life and creativity. Tagore was scientifically argumentative in all his writings through every phase of creativity. Rabindranath Tagore stands unique even today as possibly the greatest poet of nature andbeauty; science and mathematics coming up in poetic imaginations often too frequently asprofound yet common knowledge of nature and her laws, in a very exquisitely natural butyet in a very unique way. He invited Western teachers to come to Santiniketan to teach science to his student; he encourage students to go West in search of science. The poet wanted to unite education with applied science for developing community and for this, a need of an educational institution was felt which resulted in the birth of Santiniketan. This study has traced the various scientific vision that shaped Rabindranath's educational ideas and how the growth of his own personality was reflected in the development of his educational experiment at Santiniketan as well as Sriniketan.

Satyanarayana, P., Kumar, A. & Janardhanreddy, K. (2013) carried out a research on "Rabindranath Tagore as a Novelist."

The aim of the research was to shed light on the novels of Tagore. They concluded that thenovels of Tagore have not been paid due attention as his poetry has been but his novels are remarkable from every point of view. His claim in Bengali fiction is most predominant andnow in free India they are being read and revived with great gusto. Had Rabindranath Tagore written nothing but novels, he would still be the most predominant figures in the literary history of Bengal and English literature.

Shukla, S. (2013) carried out a research on "The Philosophy of Education in the Works of Rabindranath Tagore"

The study discusses about Education in India during Tagore's times, Tagore's experiencesand experiments in Education, Tagore's philosophy of Education with respect to man, universe and religion, Creativity, joy and freedom, Child psychology, Adolescent world, Atmosphere,

Simplicity, etc and Tagore's philosophy and education in contemporary India.

As found in the study, there was a constant change in the ideals of Tagore as a result of hisexperiences. This is why his experiments had dynamism in them. Tagore started experimenting in his school in Bolpur with the attempts of rural reconstruction and later on expanded it to the University of global-excellence. Tagore's philosophy not only talked ofabstractions like joy, freedom, love, man in relation with the universe, religion, culture, values, nature but also of concrete issues like language, childhood/ adolescent psychology,gender, discipline, science, teachers and, pedagogy at various levels of growing-up.His concept of freedom was intertwined with love and responsibility and enmeshed in his ideal of unity. He extolled the ancient Indian system of education focusing on spiritual growth and man's relatedness with the universe around. In his view both the spiritual and the scientific went beyond the individual to realise the truth and the universal in man. Religionfor him was something connected to humanity at large and, man, idealized as the exponentof God, was a natural concept of his religious beliefs. Tagore's works show his deep understanding of child and adolescent psychology. He wanted his teacher to understand his students, take interest in the life and ideas around and felt that human relationship betweena teacher and student is more important than pedantic communication. What makes Tagorean philosophy of education stand out is the fundamental fact that Tagore thought interms of man, not in terms of resources, as is being done in today's era of economics.

Policepatil, B. (2011) conducted a research under the title "A Study of Educational Thoughts of Dr. Rabindranath Tagore and their Relevance to Present Education System".

The study deals with Tagore's educational thought and practice his conception of man; hisviews on functions and aims of education, different stages of education, different kinds ofeducation, ideal teacher, community and parents; methods of teaching he advocated and put into practice, institutions he organized for putting his ideals to practice, his views on evaluation in education.

The objectives of the study are to make an analytical study of the evolution of Rabindranath Tagore's thought process on education, to make an assessment of Tagore's contribution tothe theory of Indian education, to make an appraisal of Tagore's contribution to the practiceof Indian education, to identify the areas where Tagore's view points on education may befound relevant for the modern Indian setting and to make suggestions for the improvementof the contemporary Indian educational system. He discussed the principles of education based on Tagore's philosophy. The study is philosophical and historical. The data is collected by the method of documentary survey from various primary sources like works written by Tagore himself –books, articles, speeches, pamphlets etc. and also books, articles, criticisms, monographs, biographies, etc written by various authors.

He found that Tagore emphasizes on freedom in different areas like freedom in activities,freedom to think, freedom to express emotions and freedom in education, which can be achieved through including many activities in education like fine arts, music, drama, etc. Education is not only about the intellectual development but also about creative self- expression. Active communication with nature and man is very important as it leads to theclose proximity with God, which is the ultimate goal of human life; therefore, Tagore insisted that education should be imparted in the atmosphere of nature with all its beauty, colors, sounds and all the forms of its manifestations.

Internationalism is very significantas the idea of separation among the nations is unnatural and international collaboration is necessary for the spiritual unity of humankind. Talking about the aims of education in the view of Tagore, he categorized the aims into various categories like moral and spiritual aims, intellectual aim, physical development, International understanding, Universal love and Harmonious life and Harmony between individual and social aims where the ultimateaim is 'Life in harmony with all existence'.

Singh, P. (2011) conducted a study under the title "Ravindra Nath Tagore aur SwamiVivekanand ke siksha darshan ka tulnatmak adhyayan ebam vartaman paristhitionme uski prasangikta"

The research was conducted to investigtate educational philosophies of Rabindranath and Vivekananda, to compare the thoughts of both the philosophers and find its relevance with the current scenerio. The research is carried out in Hindi language. The objectives of the study are to compare revolutionary educational thoughts of Tagore and Vivekananda with respect to its relevance in present time, to study the importance of the thoughts of these philosophers, to study moral and spiritual thoughts and provide suggestions to make the present educational system life oriented, to study how theories of these philosophers can be implemented practically and to evaluate their thoughts with respect to practicability keeping in mind the present situations.

As concluded in the study, both the philosophers gave due importance to cultural progressin Indian tradition. Nature was the source of inspiration for both of them and they proposedinternationalism for peaceful relations in the world. International journeys have played very significant role to shape new perspectives in education in Tagore's life. Rabindranathtried to implicate his thoughts in practical life for the integral development of children in Santiniketan. Rabindranath had taken important steps for the rural development. Shiksha Satra was established as an ideal institute in order to create ideal villages. Educational experiments done by him in Shiksha satra have been successful which replicates the practicality of his thoughts. According to Tagore, the best education does not just focus onpersonal development, rather it is for the upliftment of the whole society. His attempt wasto make students good citizens and to improve their social life through not just intellectual development, but also the development of aesthetic values. He focused on the developmentof external as well as internal development and create a full manhood.

Gurunathrao, K. (2010) carried out "A comparative study of philosophical and education views of Maharshi Aurobindo Rabindranath Tagore and Sarvepalli Radhakrishnan with reference to values of life"

The study is descriptive in nature where researcher has studied various relevant books on the educational ideas of the trio-philosophers namely Maharshi Aurobindo, Rabindranath Tagore and Sarvepalli Radhakrishnan and those published on them and their thoughts andviews. The tools used for the study are Auto-biographies, Writings and Speeches, RelevantLiterature, Visit to places, Web-site and Internet.

Objectives of the study are to explain the educational views which reflect the values of lifecherished by these trio-philosophers such as personal, moral, social, spiritual, cultural andaesthetic, to compare and contrast critically the educational ideas and views of these trio-philosophers of India, to study in detail the educational and philosophical thoughts of thesetrio-philosophers belonging to the British India, namely Maharshi Aurobindo, Rabindranath Tagore and Sarvepalli Radhakrishnan, in order to find out the relevance of their ideas in the present day context, to acquire knowledge about Maharshi Aurobindo's Integral Education, Rabindranath Tagore's Education for Fullness and Sarvepalli Radhakrishnan's Religious Education, to evaluate their work as the educationists and to say in what line did they make an advance over the past educators, to compare the educational implications and thoughts of these trio philosophers with the thoughts of other modern thinkers of India, to trace the influence of these eminent philosophers on modern educational thought and practice and to discuss the merits and demerits of the educational and philosophical thoughts of these trio-educational philosophers.

The study reveals that, According to Rabindranath Tagore a man can share his possessionswith others but not his soul. The discovery of inwardness is the essential basis of spirituallife. His educational, personal, moral, spiritual, cultural, and aesthetic beliefs were all colored by his deep religious faith. He says that teaching of religion or morals can never be imparted in the form of lessons. He puts more faith in an individual than in any institution. Therefore, he stands for individualism in education. He does not want the childto be crushed into the hearsay traditional methods of instruction. He finds music as an aidto the development of spiritualism. He emphatically states that while starting the school inthe natural surroundings of Bolapur his principal object was to give spiritual culture to the boys. He was always in favor of cultural unity. He always stressed on the three values namely Truth, Goodness and Beauty in educational endeavor.

Sengupta, S. (2010) studied "Thoughts of Swami Vivekananda and Rabindranath Tagore and their relevance to education"

The study is aimed to find the relevance of thoughts of Vivekananda and Tagore in presenteducational scenerio. It discusses about the past education system in India in the first chapter. Second chapter deals with the educational philosophy of Vivekananda whereas third chapter deals with the educational philosophy of Tagore. Present day education and its crisis are discussed in the fourth chapter. The fifth chapter talks about Aims of proper education and finding its gaps.

As discussed in the study, Rabindranath realizes the urgency of making the education to reach within one and all of the countries. He uses to think that when a part ofthe country is present educationally enlightened and the remaining parts are deprived of educational enlightenment, it increases self-deception and separation within the man, which is a great malediction on the part of the society. Rabindranath thinks that in a country where a basicidealism that has been created in human mind since long desirably should also be given equal importance with the subjects considered to be taught. The co-ordination between eastern and western education is very much essential. Ravindranath gives prime importance towards manifestation of student's mind, he thinks it proper for the students tokeep themselves away from all sorts of luxuries during the student life under educational atmosphere. Both of Vivekananda and Rabindranath believe that 'Brahmacarya' life is based on purity, simplicity, devotion and morality in character. It is known to all that, a strong moral character can boldly face any situation and is able to eliminate the suffering and can generate the necessary impulse in man to be sympathetic to the people around him rather than to be apathetic to him. Thus the system of education as conceived by Swami Vivekananda and Rabindranath Tagore is quite relevant to modern world and such systemof education only is able to pave the way to make this earth a happy place to live in. Where'Millennium Goals' of peace, prosperity and security will then be achieved bringing universal brotherhood a bond of relation among men and men of the whole world then onecan boldly say, ' Whole world is my friend'.

O'Connell, K. M. (2003) conducted a study under the title "Rabindranath Tagore onEducation."

In the article, he discussed about Tagore's contribution in Education. The article states thatTagore's experiences at Jorasanko provided him with a lifelong conviction concerning the importance of freedom in education. He also realized in a profound manner the importance of the arts for developing empathy and sensitivity, and the necessity for an intimate relationship with one's cultural and natural environment. He saw education as a vehicle forappreciating the richest aspects of other cultures, while maintaining one's own cultural specificity. In Tagore's philosophy of education, the aesthetic development of the senses was as important as the intellectual–if not more so–and music, literature, art, dance and drama were given great prominence in the daily life of the school. In keeping with his theory of subconscious learning, Rabindranath never talked or wrote down to the students,but rather involved them with whatever he was writing or composing. To encourage mutuality, Rabindranath invited artists and scholars from other parts of India and the worldto live together at Santiniketan on a daily basis to share their cultures with Visva-Bharati. In terms of curriculum, he advocated a different emphasis in teaching. Rather than studyingnational cultures for the wars won and cultural dominance imposed, he advocated a teaching system that analysed history and culture for the progress that had been made in breaking down social and religious barriers. His vision of culture was not a static one, butone that advocated new cultural fusions.

Purandare, P. (1982) carried out "A critical study of Rabindranath Tagore's educational philosophy"

The purpose of the study was to shed light on the educational thoughts and experiments of Rabindranath Tagore who was a versatile personality, who kept on learning throughout hislife and set an example of a novel educational system not just by giving the philosophy but also by implementing it in his life and experimenting it successfully. The study suggests that, the main principles of Tagore's philosophy are freedom, company of nature and revival of ancient Indian culture. Tagore introduced different arts in education and gave aesthetic approach to it. Tagore stood for all round development of child and therefore didnot give importance to examination. Being a staunt naturalist, he believed that nature's ownpurpose is to give the child fullness of growth. Tagore talked about the freedom of mind, heart and will. Tagore interprets freedom of heart as unrestricted human relationship. It was his considered opinion that the atmosphere in an educational institute and in human society in general should breathe sympathy, understanding and sensitiveness of soul ensuring freedom of communication with one another and inspiring largeness of heart. He often criticised bookish learning strongly. Tagore stressed the universal character of human knowledge to which all nations have been contributing since the dawn of the civilization. According to Tagore, Constant curiosity and alertness of mind and the emancipation of theintellect from inertia and dead habits should constitute a real element in the intellectual make up of an individual. He advocated cosmopolitan outlook on life. Vastness of forest life in the midst of nature induces a proportion and a relative sense of values. Tagore attached special importance to cultivation of the intellect to counter balance emotional immaturity and instability when it exists. Tagore's ideal was the development of all the innate faculties of an individual leading to an all-round harmonious development of his personality. The establishment of a proper harmony in our life as a whole was his goal in every field.

Jalan, R. (1976) undertook a study under the title "Tagore- His Educational Theory and Practice and its impact on Indian Education."

The research was conducted with the aim to determine the nature of Tagore's educationaltheory and its practice in his institute. It also intended to estimate the impacts of his program on Indian education. The material collected during a trip to Visva-Bharati and from other sources was used as reference for the study.

A description of educational readings on Tagore and selected works from Tagore'svoluminous writing on education, showing gradual development in his thinking is presented in the second chapter. The third chapter deals with educational theory of Tagore.Chapter 4 shows how Tagore tried to put his theory into practice in his institution.

As concluded in the fourth chapter, Tagore did not have any academic degree in education,but he was a great educator of his time as stated in the study. Tagore's thoughts on education are not formulated in any systematic treatises. He brought the Eastern and Western cultures together through his institution. Tagore contributed to the field ofaesthetic education by including music, art and dance in Visva-Bharati. The core of Tagore's educational theory puts greater emphasis on the complete harmonious development of individual personality. Tagore believed that education should help an individual to attain complete manhood, so that all his powers may be developed to the fullest extent for his own individual perfection as well as the perfection of human society. Education can become dynamic and vital only when it is in constant touch with any complete life. He wanted the boys and girl to be fearless, free and open-minded, self-reliant, full of the spirit of inquiry and self-criticism. Tagore's success lies in the fact that he did not try to control directly the ideas, feelings and values of his children but imaginatively designed an environment and a program of activities and experiences which evoked the desired responses. The researcher realized that Tagore's impact on education in India has not been well recognized and educational work of Tagore deserves more scrutiny. His impact on Indian education has been felt more, but it has not been articulated by researchers or educationists.

Periaswamy, A. (1976) conducted a study on "Rabindranath Tagore's Philosophy on International Education".

The study was done to investigate the concept of Tagore's International Education which was designed to facilitate international understanding and by this understanding peace and prosperity of mankind. His research work is qualitative and philosophical in nature. He hasreferred the literature of Tagore and other literary works done on Tagore's philosophy. Healso visited Visva Bharati University in Shantiniketan where he met professors who had worked with Tagore.

He found in his study that the main objective of Tagore's International Education was to develop relations among people and nations which is essential to achieve the goal of peace and brotherhood. This understanding is helpful not only to the common people but also tothe men who make foreign policies as policy makers cannot have the real picture of the problem without understanding the social, cultural and economic problems of people. Genuine international relations would help eradicate ethnocentrism. Tagore's ideal was the development of whole human personality in an atmosphere of freedom and fellowship. He was a practical idealist and not a dreamer. He was more an idealist than a naturalist. He devoted his entire life to the cause of education of the child to develop into a whole humanpersonality and as a citizen of the world. Tagore felt that the failure to recognize the central fact of inter-relations among people would lead to more conflict and misconceptions. Only international education would eradicate such misconceptions and misunderstanding among people. Tagore's love for humanity extended all political boundaries. He was consistent in the fact that there could be no more possibility of isolation of nations. All nations must work together for the happiness of all mankind. Tagore was admired and respected all over the world for not only as a great poet and philosopher, but also for his great love and affection for humanity regardless of race and religion.

Jana, M. (1974) studied "Educational philosophy of Tagore and its relevance to current educational thought".

The study aimed to study Tagore's philosophy of life, his thoughts on education and its relevance to present scenario. Relevant biographical elements are discussed in the first chapter. In the second chapter, Tagore's philosophy of life is described whereas Tagore's philosophy of education and his educational experiments are discussed in the third and fourth chapter respectively. The fifth chapter talks about Tagore's educational ideas in relation to current Educational thoughts. The views of Educational commissions of current time are compared with Tagore's views in the sixth chapter.

As concluded in the study, Tagore's philosophy of life-was shaped by the three main factors, namely, nature, man and Brahma and developed through three stages of his life athis ancestral residence in Calcutta, at his Zamindari at Silaidaha and lastly at the ashrama at Santiniketan. Tagore insisted so much on living a simple life in the heart of nature and observing, the rules of Brahmacharya in his ashrama. His educational programmes made such atmosphere that the individual man was able to realize the universal man in him. Tagore's educational programs in the heart of nature giving due importance to natural instincts and impulses of the children and attaching equal importance to the social serviceand spiritual upliftment had checked the injurious growth of individuality without giving the scope of sharpening the ego and produced a better balanced personality for a progressive society. His aim was to impart such education in such an atmosphere that willliberate man from ignorance, from superstition and from poverty, poverty of mind and heart or from narrowness because he believed that true happiness and real peace and prosperity are lying in immensity, in greatness of mind and heart and never in narrownessof mind and heart.

Tagore understood, that an individual must be physically sound, mentally alert and accomplished and spiritually elevated. Nevertheless, he must be socially adjusted and emotionally well-balanced. He must be educated in such a way that he might represent the true culture and tradition of the country where he was born and brought up and at the same time extend the spirit of cooperation and friendship to the world as a whole and work for the spiritual unity of mankind. The aim of education, according to Tagore was not to produce a good clerk or an efficient farmer, an able administrator, or a legislator; a renowned scientist or a technician, it is to develop complete manhood. By complete manhood Tagore understood a whole man, a balanced personality like a full bloomed lotusa man should exhale and exhibit all the best elements that are in him. His methods were based on the principles of freedom and joy, love and affection, artistic outlook and creative activity, cultivation of national tradition and international culture. His medium was purely national and even regional. The world will long remember Tagore for the signal contribution of universal humanism to the field of educational thought. He will hold the unique position as a precursor of the movement of international understanding, the most significant trend in modern educational thought.

Research Gap

The researcher has studied a number of literature on the Educational thoughts and Philosophy of Rabindranath Tagore which included books, journal articles, essays, PhD Thesis as well as Master's degree Dissertation. The educationists and the researchers have gone into minute details of the literary works of Rabindranath Tagore and have analyzed them with reference to the Education system or have compared with the Educational Philosophy any other remarkable Educationist or Educational philosopher. However, none of the researcher has conducted research as per the selected criteria that the researcher has selected in this dissertation, namely, Aims of Education, Methods of Education, Role of a Teacher, Qualities of a Teacher and Problems of Education. Keeping this Research Gap in mind, the researcher has tried to analyze the selected literary works of Rabindranath Tagore with reference to the selected criteria of Education in the context of Indian Education system.

Implication of the present study

The reviewed studies have shed light on the educational philosophies of various philosophers, similarities between the thoughts of other philosophers and Tagore, as well as the differences between the same. It has been found after the review of related literaturethat Tagore's views are far more broad and practical as compared to other philosophers. The reviewed studies have been proven very significant in context of the present studies asthey have helped the researcher to modify and finalize research questions and objectives, to decide the research methodology and have also provided knowledge basis related to thepresent study. It has also helped in the method of content analysis and derive the conclusions based on that. Review of related studies have also backed the findings and conclusions drawn out by the researcher.

CHAPTER 3
FUNDAMENTALS OF RESEARCH AND RESEARCH DESIGN

Introduction

In Chapter 3, Research methodology followed by the researcher for the research work is discussed. Primary and Secondary sources used to carry out this research work are discussed in detail in this chapter.

Present research work aims to find out answers to the research questions mentioned in chapter 1 through the study of selected Essays, Lectures and letters of Rabindranath Tagore. Qualitative data was collected from various primary and secondary sources including original works of Tagore, biographies, autobiography, previous researches, books related to Rabindranath Tagore written by other authors, various other materials like online articles, etc. Relevant historical data on Tagore's Educational philosophy was collected, sorted, analyzed, evaluated and arranged in order.

Origin of the Study

Identification of the proper theme is the first step of any research inquiry. The theme that has been chosen should be capable of producing ideas or series of ideas and thought system, which are justifiable. It is concerned with the problems and areas where assessment of knowledge is done and relationships are established among different concepts related to the field of education. Here the Research theme is Education in the Indian context in terms of five vital concepts of Education and Teaching, namely aims of Education, Method of Teaching, Role of a Teacher, Qualities of a Teacher and Problems of Education.

Research Methodology

After the theme is finalized, primary questions are identified based on the theme for which the researcher collects the data. The researcher collects maximum possible data according to the theme from the available primary and secondary sources available. The data are found in the form of literary works by the philosopher, opinions of other people on the literary works, reflections of other philosophers, etc. which is available in the form of books, philosophical texts, memoirs, diaries, letters, speeches, treatises, journals, thesis, research papers, etc. Data collection in a qualitative research is a time consuming process where theresearcher has to collect data by reading a lot of related literature. This stage is a very important stage, as the researcher has to identify the relevant data from the available material and the way of collecting it. Researcher also has to define the nature of data. Researcher has to check the authenticity of the available data sourcesand use only after confirming the authenticity. A lot of literature may be available related to the study, but the researcher has to be very clear about what kind of data should be collected and whether it is going to be useful for the study or not. For the present study, data was collected by the researcher from various primary and secondary sources which will be discussed later in this chapter.

Population of Research and Sampling

Out of the vast collection of Rabindranath Tagore's literary works, only those works are selected who have direct relation with Education. No particular sampling technique other than sticking to Educational theories and concept is followed. Tus the selected literary works belong to different decades of Tagore's lifetime and are of varying length. The tentative list is as follows:

Table 2

List of selected Literary works of Rabindranath Tagore

Serial No	Title	Category	Year of Publication
1	My School	Lecture	1915
2	Sikkhar Herpher	Lecture	1893

	(The vicissitudes of Education)		
3	Sikkhar Bikiron (Radiation of Education)	Lecture	1933
4	Vishwavidyalayer Roop (Shape of University)	Lecture	1932
5	Shikkhar Swangikaran (Privatization of Education	Lecture	1936
6	Strisiksha (Women Education)	Essay	1915
7	Swadhin Sikkha (Independent Education)	Essay	1905
8	Chatroder Nitisikkha (Moral Education of Students)	Essay	1892

9	Sikkhar Songskar (Educational Reforms)	Essay	1906
10	Sikkha aru Sanskriti (Education and Culture)	Essay	1935
11	Letters from Russia	Letter	1930-31
12	On Some Educational Questions	Letter	1919
13	Vernaculars for the M.A. Degree	Letter	1918

Tools and Techniques of Data collection

The Research Tool employed in the present study is in the form of a Table where the data collected are classified in the categories of the Research Questions raised in the study, namely Aims of Education, Methods of Education, Role of a Teacher, Qualities of a Teacher and Problems of Education. The data collected are organized in the categories of Essay, Letters and Lectures delivered by Rabindranath

Tagore in different points of his Lifetime. The original date and time of delivery of the lecture, time of writing of the letter as well as the date and details of the publisher of the writings are clearly mentioned in the beginning of each Table. Initially, a brief overview of the lecture/Essay/Letter is produced, then the excerpts of the writing supporting the research questions in the form of the above mentioned five criteria are presented under quotation mark.

The research tool is consulted with three experts from the Educational field (Faculty members in Indian institute of Teacher Education) for suggestions and required modifications. The inclusion of the fifth criteria of analysis (Problems of Education) is incorporated to the study following the suggestion of one of the Experts. The original research tool and the details of the experts are included in the Appendix.

Data collection

Collected data is classified under different titles based on the theme of the study. Analysis and synthesis of the data is done by the researcher where the researcher churns and filters the ideas first which are later synthesized in a series of ideas appropriate to the theme which can help in drawing the conclusion. Data interpretation is done logically and appropriate comments and judgments are given along with the references, which support the comments. Comparison, assessment and description of the ideas can be done while data interpretation which can supportthe arguments done by the researcher in the study. In the philosophical research, the researcher basically presents his/her on point of view on the point of view of the philosopher also considering the other people's point of views on the same philosopher. This makes it difficult for the researcher to be bias free. Researcher needs to be very careful before coming to any conclusion and make sure that the study is not biased or influenced by any other factors.

Data analysis technique

Data analysis is done through arrangement of in logical sequence of ideas, which can lead towards the conclusion of the study. Appropriate headings are selected for each segment of ideas, which are presented precisely. The care is being taken to maintain the clarity and continuity of ideas and concepts. Researcher takes care that the ideas do not go out of the context of the research theme. All the ideas presented under different headings should be capable of ultimately leading to the conclusion of the research and should support the conclusion.

References and are mentioned properly and are cited appropriately which play very important role in the case of qualitative research as they support the conclusions done by the researcher.

Researcher's Experience during Research

The overall experience of the researcher during the study is an enthralling as she went through one text to another from the vast writing of Rabindranath Tagore included in 27 volumes of "Rabindra Rachanabali". After filtering of the vast volumes of the writings for only those which have direct implication to Educational thoughts, concepts and processes, the intended study could be decreased to some extent. However, only those literary texts which have commendable number of contexts with reference to the selected criteria of study are included in the analysis. The researcher is positively surprised to observe that how these writings almost a century old, still hold specific relevance to the Indian system of Education and its problems. Specifically, regarding the recruitment of teachers in schools and universities along with the requirement of constant professional development of the teachers are clearly mentioned in one of the writing of Rabindranath Tagore which are extremely relevant these days. It is also of the observation of the researcher that many of the policies of the Indian Government regarding Education are based on Tagore's Educational philosophy, even including the latest National Education policy 2020. However, the researcher also believes that some of the sentence structures and phrases used by Tagore in his writings are not used by many in this era and some of the words used by Tagore need Dictionary consultation, as those words are not much used these days. In totality, the researcher is in awe of the writing caliber and depth of thinking of the Nobel Laureate and the great son of the soil Rabindranath Tagore.

CHAPTER 4
DATA ANALYSIS AND INTERPRETATION

Introduction

In this chapter, discussion on various lectures, Essays and Letters written or delivered by Gurudev Rabindranath Tagore at various points of his lifetime are presented with reference to the five selected criteria, namely Aim of Education, Role of a Teacher, Qualities of a Teacher, Methods of Education and Problems of Education. Only those Lectures, Essays and Letters are chosen which have direct inference to Education and Education system of India. Most of the content are studied in its original Bangla format and some have originally been delivered or written in English.

Nature of Data

Here, the nature of data is mostly primary data. Due to the extraordinary efforts of Publication Department of Vishva Bharati, all the writings of Rabindranath Tagore are preserved in an online archive in the nature of 'Rabindranath Rachanabali' in a total of 27 volumes. Moreover, some writings are published by Indian Culture Department of Government of India and well-known publishers like MacMillan and Oxford University Press in the original format. As far as secondary data are concerned, some PhD thesis and articles published by well known researchers on Tagore's writing are consulted.

Classification and Presentation of Data

To select number of related literary works from a plethora of writings from a Nobel Laureate like Rabindranath Tagore with such a high quality of literary skill and vocabulary is an elaborate task. Therefore, within the limited time frame allotted for the Dissertation work of Master in Education, the researcher could limit herself to the study and analysis of 5 lectures, 5 Essays and 3 Letters written by Rabindranath Tagore at different points of time. The length of the literary works are varied, particularly, the letters are in different parts, viz, Letters from Russia is a collection of 15 letters published in a single volume later. The important excerpts from the literary works in accordance with the selected criteria Aim of Education, Role of a Teacher, Qualities of a Teacher, Methods of Education and Problems of Education are presented in Tabular form within inverted comma. An overall analysis of the selected Essay or Letter or Lecture is also presented here keeping in mind the perspective of Education and Indian system of Education. The original Title of the Esaay/ Leture/Letter in Bangla is also presented in italics.

Data Analysis and Interpretation

Analysis of lectures

<u>Lecture 1</u>

Title of Lecture: My School

Date and Place of delivery: America, 1915

Publisher Details: This Lecture was published first in "The Modern Review" in and later included in <u>Personality</u>

'Personality' is a collection of six lectures delivered in America, was first published by Macmillan, New York, in 1917. The book is dedicated to C.F. Andrews.

In this lecture, Tagore explains the circumstances in which he started his school in Bengal in the early 1900s and had named it Shanti Niketan. His idea of the school was based on the pattern of the ancient Indian schools based on Guru Shishya Tradition. He wanted to bring up his students in the atmosphere of living aspiration. He wanted his students to lead simple lives and learn the lessons of life from Nature and their teachers. Tagore started his school to provide his students with an intimate vision of eternal life. According to him, the purpose of education must be the fullest growth and freedom of soul. Education should free man's soul from the bondage of any kind. It should give us the wealth of inner light and love. It should give us spiritual wisdom. The object of education should be the eternal welfare. He pondered over it and found that the whole country was in need of such education. Tagore chose a place for his school in Bengal, which was dedicated by his father to the seekers of peace. Thus, he started his school in the lap of nature with ten boys. In his ashram, there were disciples from all religions. It was free from any religious creed or dogma. In Shantiniketan, Tagore carried out his theory of education. It was based upon his experience of children's minds. He believed in the power of the subconscious mind of children. As Tagore was nourished in the free atmosphere, he tried various experiments at his school. He was of the opinion that during the early period of education children should learn their lessons through natural processes. His students learnt singing, dramatic performances, drawing, painting and music directly through persons and things. To cultivate the spirit of 'self-help' and self-control was the motto of his school. It was totally a different school than any formal school.

Table 3

Excerpts from the Lecture 'My School'

Serial No	Page No	Excerpt	Criteria
1	142	"The highest education is that which does not merely gives us information but makes our life in harmony with all existence."	Aim of Education
2	145	"The growth of experience leads to forming instinct which is the result of nature's own method of instruction"	Method of Education
3	148	"During their period of education, the children should be given to know that the world is not all drawing room, but there is such a thing as nature to which their limbs are made beautifully to respond"	Method of Education
4	151	"Children are not born ascetics, fit to enter at one into the monastic discipline of acquiring knowledge. At first, they must gather knowledge	Method of Education

| | | through their love of life, and then they will renounce their lives to gain knowledge, and then again they will come back to their fuller lives with ripened wisdom" | |
| 5 | 153-154 | "The object of Education is to give man the unity of truth. Formerly when life was simple, all the different elements of man were in complete harmony. But, when there came the separation of the intellect from the spiritual and the physical, the school education put entire emphasis on the intellect and on the physical side of man. We denote our sole attention to giving children information, not knowing that by this emphasis we are accentuating a break between the | Aim of Education |

		intellectual, the physical and the spiritual life."	
6	157	"For us to maintain our self-respect which we owe to ourselves and to our creator, we must make the purpose of our education nothing short of the highest purpose of man, the fullest growth and freedom of soul."	Aim of education
7	157	"In an ideal 'Chatuspathis', Sanskrit name for University, the students live in their master's home like the children of the house, without having to pay for their board and lodging or tuition. The teacher prosecutes his own study, living a life of simplicity, and helping the students in their lessons as a part of his life and not of his profession.	Role of Education

| 8 | 178 | "The object of education is the freedom of mind which can only be achieved through the path of freedom- through freedom has its risk and responsibility as life itself has. Children are living beings- more living than grown up people, who have built their skills of habit around them. Therefore, it is absolutely necessary for their mental health and development that they must not have mere schools for their lessons, but a world whose guiding spirit is personal love. It must be an 'ashram' where men have gathered for the highest end of life, in the piece of nature, where life is not merely meditative, but fully awake in its activities, where boys' minds are not being | Aim of Education |

| | | perpetually drilled into believing that the ideal of the self-idolatry of the nation is the truest ideal for them to accept, where they are bidden to realize man's world as God's kingdom to whose citizenship they have to aspire, where the sunrise and the sunset and the silent glory of stars are not daily ignored, where nature's festivities of flowers and fruit have their joyous recognition from man and where the young and the old, the teacher and the student, sit at the same table to partake of their daily food and the food of their eternal life." | |

Lecture 2

Title of the Lecture: Radiation of Education (*Sikkhar Bikiron*)

Time and Place of delivery: Calcutta University, Feb 1933

Published by: Calcutta University Press, Calcutta

Source: National Library of India

In this lecture delivered to the students of Calcutta University in February 1933, Rabindranath Tagore talks about the rich Educational Heritage of India right from the ages of the Ramayana and the Mahabharata through the rulings of different kings who supported the teaching and spreading of knowledge of various scripts to the citizens of the country. He specifically mentioned the Great Indian Universities like Nalanda and Takshshila and urged the students to get inspired by them. He explained in detail, how the religious scriptures like the stories of Dhruva-Prahlada, Sita's exile, Karna's armouring, Harishchandra's sacrifice formed the psychological basis of the Indian children and contributed a lot to the moral education of the child.

Tagore also compared the progress of education in the countries like Japan, USA and some parts of Europe and urged the students to take the positive notes from the growth of Education in those countries. While expressing his concern about lack of good quality textbooks in the native language, Tagore also stressed on the leaning of English as a second language, as the lack of understanding in English language would hinder the progress of the students because most of the good quality literature are in English. He also requested the learned community of teachers to come forward with more translation work from English to Bengali.

Table 4

Excerpts from the Lecture 'Radiation of Education'

Serial No	Page No	Excerpt	Criteria
1	1	"The word 'Education' we are happy to recite in our hearts has the appearance of a barn, but looking outside we see a smouldering courtyard."	Aim of Education
2	1	"High lanterns are hung in schools and colleges for the light of education, but if it is a light trapped in a closed wall, then we will say that it is an invisible evil. When we conquer our country with our countries regarding education, we pay attention to the visible part and	Role of a Teacher

		do not take into account of the invisible part."	
3	3	"Knowledge is not the property of scholars; it is the wealth of the entire society."	Role of a Teacher
4	3	"Western learning in Japan is shorter than in India, but there it is not a clapped-out patchwork. There the power of thinking is continuously transmitted to the minds of all countries under the influence of the knowledge that pervades there. This thinking is not one-size-fits-all. According to the signs of modern times, there is diversity in this thought but also unity, that unity is the unity of reason."	Method of Education
5	4	"The knowledge veiled in the English language cannot naturally accompany our minds. That's why many of us don't get as much education as we do.	Problems of Education

		This science is separated from the weather of the four directions; Tram runs between our house and school, mind doesn't. Our country is out of school; In that country, there is a lot of school protest, it is said that there is no cooperation. In that separation, our language and thoughts are mostly like schoolboys."	
6	14	"At the beginning of all, we want an educated mind. Literature is a way of imparting education outside the school-college. But that literature must be the source of all-encompassing education; It should be seen that the way to accept him is paved everywhere."	Method of Education
7	18	"Interdisciplinary degrees are awarded in universities; In this	Aims of Education

| | | case, there is no need for such largeness on the occasion of conferring title. Individuals often have predilections for particular subjects. If he can show his special rights in that regard, he is entitled to get his special place in the society. I see no reason to deprive him of that right." | |

Lecture 3

Title of the Lecture: The Vicissitudes of Education (*Shikkhar Herpher*)

Time and Place of delivery: 1893, At Rajsahi College, Calcutta

Publisher: Vishva Bharati (Rabindra Rachanabali, Vol VI, Page 567-572)

As a young landlord managing his family's rural estates, Tagore came to realize the possibilities of introducing education and co-operation to transform rural life. Thus, he began to turn his thoughts towards the problems of education. He spoke publicly on 'The Vicissitudes of Education' in which he made a strong plea for the use of the mother tongue. His first experiments in teaching also date from this period. He expressed his concern about quality textbooks in this lecture. He also stressed upon 'learning with pleasure' for permanent learning in the children. In this era where the Nation was facing the introduction of British policies of Education to the Education system, this lecture is path breaking as it gives a glimpse to the Grass root level problems of the Education system of India and the concerns of the common people.

Table 5

Excerpts of the Lecture 'The Vicissitudes of Education'

Serial No	Page No	Excerpt	Criteria
1	567	"As long as the children are confined to education only, i.e., the essentials, their minds will never be sufficiently occupied. A boy cannot become a good man unless independent study	Aim of Education

		is mixed with essential education- even when he reaches adulthood, he remains to a large extent a boy intellectually."	
2	567	"But unfortunately we don't have much time. As soon as possible, I have to study the language abroad and pass and enter the work. Therefore, there is no time for anything other than reading and memorizing without looking left or right. So, if you see any hobby book in the hands of boys, you have to snatch it immediately."	Problems of Education
3	568	"As much as we B. A. M. A. Passing, devouring books, the intellect is not so strong and mature. I can't grasp anything like that, I can't roll anything like that, I can't make anything stand up with that much force.	Problems of Education

		Our opinions, speech and rituals are not exactly the same as those of a child. That is why we try to cover up our emotional wretchedness with pomp and circumstance."	
4	569	"The main reason for this is that we do not enjoy learning from childhood. Voicing only what is absolutely necessary. By doing so, the work goes on somehow, but no progress is made. Eating air does not fill the stomach, eating food fills the stomach, but in order to properly digest the food, it is necessary to eat air. To properly digest such a textbook requires the help of many other books. Reading with pleasure the power of reading increases imperceptibly; Perceptiveness Conceptuality The power of	Methods of Education

		thinking speaks quite easily and naturally."	
5	569	"If the children are taught Grammar and Dictionary of foreign languages only in which there is no life, no joy, no leisure, no innovation, can the boy ever get mental nourishment, expansion of mind, strength of character in this? Can he come up with something when he reaches puberty? Can he overcome obstacles with his own strength, he can keep his head elevated with his natural brilliance? Doesn't he just learn to memorize, copy and share?"	Problems of Education
6	570	"If you do not practice thinking and imagination from childhood, you will not be able to find at hand during work."	Problems of Education

| 7 | 571 | "Of you want to make a boy a man, you have to start making him a man from childhood, otherwise he will remain a boy and not a man. From the childhood, instead of relying only on the memory, we should give free time to independent management of thinking and imagination." | Method of Education |
| 8 | 572 | "If, from our childhood, language education is accomplished by thought education, and of all the ways of life are regularized with thought, then only a proper harmony can be established in all our lives, we can be quite simple and can take a proper measure of all things." | Role of a Teacher |

Lecture 4

Title of Lecture: Shape of University [*Vishwavidyalayer Rup*]

Time and Place of delivery: December, 1932, Calcutta University

Publisher: Calcutta University Press

This lecture was delivered by Tagore in the later stage of his life, when he was already an established poet, writer and a Nobel Laureate. Everyone in the Academic Fraternity looked upon to him for advice and guidance in various fields of growth that the country was in the need of. In this lecture, Tagore tried to explain the very meaning of University, its structure and the expected way of working, to the audience who consisted of the renowned Academicians of the city, Professors, students and Staff members of Calcutta University. Tagore explained the rich heritage of Indian universities like Nalanda, Taxshila and cited the works of the famous travellers like Hiuen Sang on these universities.

Table 6

Excerpts from the Lecture 'Shape of University'

Serial No	Page No	Excerpt	Criteria
1	3	"University is a specialized field of pursuit. Generally speaking, the pursuit or the pursuit of knowledge. But that doesn't make it clear, because the meaning of the word 'Vidya' is wide and its pursuits are diverse."	Aim of Education
2	7	"Indian Universities like Nalanda, Vikramshila originated in the earnest impulse of the Indian mind, in the inexorable impulse of nature. It is certain that the pursuit of knowledge and education spread in different ways."	Aim of Education
3	10	"The first university was established in India years ago. The chronology of Nalanda, Vikramsila, The school of Taxsila has not yet been	Role pf a Teacher

| | | established with definite accuracy, but it can be assumed that it predates the European universities. They originate in the earnest impulse of the Indian mind, in the inexorable impulse of nature. It is certain that the pursuit of knowledge and education spread in different ways and in different ways in the country before him. The all-pervading pursuits of the society appeared at one time and place in an accumulated and concentrated form." | |
| 4 | 11 | "The true life-spring of the native university was the genuine respect which everyone had for their greatest learning, which was unshakable by great self-sacrifice." | Role of Teacher |

| 5 | 12 | "It is easy to imagine that in all these great sacrificial fields of knowledge, what kind of great and intense conflict of mind with human mind was going on, how the fire of Dhisakti was constantly burning. Not giving notes from a printed textbook, but imparting untiring enthusiasm from heart to heart. Those who are the best of the country in education, intelligence and knowledge are gathered here from far and wide. The students are also intelligent, respectful, privileged; But they got the right of entry by passing a tough test to the Dwarpandit." | Method of Education |
| 6 | 15 | "At that time (time of Nalanda), great civilizations emerged in other parts of the world; But, nowhere else has such a great | Method of Education |

		cooperation of the human mind been heard on the penance of knowledge. The main reason for this is deep respect for universal humanity, a sense of pride in learning, and a strong sense of responsibility to donate those resources to all of the world and abroad with the absolute joy of having and creating intellectual resources. Today it is time for us to remember, especially in this day of indolence and disrespect to ourselves, to people, to our pursuits, that, In the history of mankind, it was in India that the universal gift of knowledge was introduced with the liberal South."	
7	17	"University was naturally the first creation to protect and propagate the knowledge for which a particular country, a	Role of Teacher

		particular race felt a special love, glory and responsibility. The will that is at the root of all creation, originates from the will of all nations. At the root of this desire is an abundance of energy."	

Lecture 5

Title: 'Privatization of Education' [*Sikkhar Swangikaran*]

Year: February 1936

Published by: Vishva Bharati

Retrieved from https://www.tagoreweb.in/Essays/shikkha-73/shikkhar-angikoron-6278

Privatization of Education has been an issue of concern from the time of British rule. The objectives of privatization of education in India is to provide quality education, to promote technological advancement, to achieve widespread private ownership in the society and reduce the burden of Government as well as to provide education in remote area and small urban area. In this lecture, Tagore speaks exclusively about the pros and cons of Privatization of Education in India. According to him, Education for masses was the most important thing for the growth of the underprivileged people of a developing country like India. He was of the opinion that instead of depending solely on the Government for providing Education facilities for the citizens, the industrialists, the academicians and the well-wishers of the country should come forward with proposals for establishing schools for the needy and make arrangements for providing better infrastructure and educational facilities for them.

Table 7

Excerpts from the Lecture 'Privatization of Education'

Serial No	Page No	Excerpt	Criteria
1	1	"The most recognised and most overlooked thing about education is that education is organic, not mechanical."	Method of Education

| 2 | 2 | "A society where the light of education falls on one part of the society, while the other large part is uneducated, that society is cursed with the curse of self-mutilation. There is a vast gap of darkness between the educated and the uneducated, their difference of mind is stronger than two different people. Civilized society alone knows that the unity of mind is absolutely essential in the unity of education." | Aim of Education |
| 3 | 3 | "The practice of expressing thoughts and feelings in words is a major part of education." | Aim of Education |

Analysis of Essays

Essay 1

Title: Independent Education (*Swadhin Sikkha*)

Year: 1905 (Bengali Year 1312)

Published by: Vishva Bharati

[Retrieved from www.Tagoreweb.in/Essays/shikkha-73/swadhin-shikkha-6290]

Rabindranath Tagore was concerned about the education of not only the regular children of the Nation, but also the unconventional students of the country. By unconventional, it is meant that those students who had to drop out from studies due to various reasons like poverty, not being able to pay the school fees, not having enough working members in the family, famine, victims of natural disaster like flood, earthquake etc. There was lack of awareness in the country about Education too at that period of time. But for the overall growth of Education in the country, every person needs to be educated. So, Tagore thought of including everyone in the Education process and get them the minimum qualifications, not only for getting a job or establishment in life, but in order to lead an well informed and scientific way of life. He proposed vocational Education and Education in Life skills for those unconventional students too.

Table 8

Excerpts from the Essay 'Independent Education'

Serial No	Page No	Excerpt	Criteria
1	1	"There is a group of students who rise above this elementary school but do not reach college, usually they also cannot claim Government jobs. Many of them try to get employed in the apis of Sadagar, in the seresta of the zamindar, in the office of the wealthy, in the household market-government etc. But their education system is not very good in the country."	Problems of Education
2	2	"Therefore, those who study up to school and those who can expect to study only a little further than that due to various shortages and difficulties, if the country takes the burden of their education in its own hands, there is no reason for hindrance."	Problems of Education

3	2	"If you count them, their number will be much more than the students who have passed the college. There is no doubt that if we can provide proper education to this wide range of lower classes, then the country will return to its glory."	Problems of Education
4	2	"Their education should be imparted from the beginning in such a way that they can know well what is called philanthropy and can be prepared in every way to earn a living. All the ideas, knowledge and habits that can be imparted in the classroom in childhood, are never possible through speech in adulthood."	Method of Education
5	3	"But we will have to take the burden of such a large country-wide work in our own hands. But they also know that if this	Method of Education

		work is handed over to the government, it will be child's play and the Macmillan company will be satisfied in the profits. However, this education will not be as we want it to be, rather it will be the opposite in some parts."	
6	4	"Elsewhere, I have seen that some persons are voluntarily setting up schools for its community. If such an effort is made in our country, then it will be doing great to these disadvantaged people of the country."	Method of Education

Essay 2

Title: Women's Education (*Stree Sikkha*)

Year: 1915 (Bengali Year 1322)

Published by: Vishva Bharati

Rabindranath Tagore through his numerous novels and short stories emphasized women education which has paved the way of women emancipation. He portrayed such bold characters in his stories, which was rare and even inconceivable at that time he wrote them because they have questioned the traditional role of women, defying the customs in their own way in search of freedom to live a normal life which was denied and ultimately in pursuit of greater freedom of inner self.

Tagore was one of the greatest supporters of women education. He viewed that man and women were complimentary to each other leading to the concept of mutual respect and need. He was one of the strongest champions of the cause of women. Therefore, he gave his views regarding different aspects to woman education. Through education, he wanted to bring harmony between man and nature and man and God. He recommended harmonious development of women's personality. That means, there should be physical, mental, moral and spiritual developments of girls through education. Similarly, he wanted that girls should be economically independent. He also wanted to attain the freedom of mind and give importance to individual and social development of girls. As an internationalist, Tagore was in favour of developing international understanding and world citizenship among boys and girls. Apart from this, he also suggested that education could also bring about cultural and character development of girls.

Tagore's ideas reveal that women should be equal partner of men in all fields, neither subordinate nor superior. He expressed definite opinion towards women education. He wanted women of the country to come forward and lead in promoting women education. He wanted women to be true to their nature, real companions of men, standing by their side in movements of crises, sharing their anxiety and lending company in their grief. Such were his views on women's education. There was perhaps no stronger champion of the cause of women like him. He strongly advocated education for girls and equal status with them. But at the same, he held that women had their own sphere and their deeds were complementary to men as their competitor.

Tagore recommended same curriculum for girls and boys. He thought that girls should be taught different sciences like natural science, social sciences and especially domestic science must be compulsory for girls. To widen mental horizon of pupils, he wanted to include mathematics in curriculum. Tagore wanted to develop aesthetic sense among girls; therefore, he also introduced music, painting, dance and craft in curriculum. To make girls financially independent, Tagore also recommended agriculture and technical education for girls. Regarding medium of instruction he wanted that mother tongue should be adopted but he also did not deny the importance of foreign language. He also favored that religious education should be given to girls for their spiritual development.

In order to meet the aims of education for girls, Tagore had given different methods of teaching. He adopted realistic approach, activity principle and teaching while walking. He also suggested some teaching methods to teach girls, for example, he laid stress on discussion and questioning methods.

Therefore, his methods of teaching were activity centered. In spite of all these aspects, Tagore also wanted that girls should be aware of their rights. He wanted to educate girls so that they could get knowledge about their rights which are equal to men.

Table 9

Excerpts from the Essay 'Women's Education'

Serial No	Page No	Excerpt	Criteria
1	1	"If Education is the means of attaining humanity and if education has the inherent rights of human beings, then I cannot understand why women cannot be deprived of that right on account of any policy."	Aim of Education
2	1	"But by saying that there will be no difference between men and women in the education system, if you say this, you are disrespecting God. Vidya has two categories. One of pure knowledge, one of use. Where there is pure knowledge there is no difference between men and women, but where there is practice there is a difference. We want education of pure knowledge to teach girls to be human beings, but on top of that	Role of a Teacher

		practical education to teach girls to be girls has a specialty, what is wrong with accepting this?"	
3	3	"The part of love is more in women's nature--if not for this, the child would not be human, the family would not survive. A mother serves her child out of love, there is no responsibility in her; A wife serves her husband because there is love, there is no responsibility in her. But the liability comes when the relationship of affection is not a normal relationship. If all wives could naturally love all husbands, it would not be possible. But as long as there is a substance called society, then people will have to follow a rule in many respects and to a large extent.	Role of a Teacher

| | | But, while creating those rules, the society keeps following its inner nature. Society has made you believe that girls are easy to fall in love with. So the rule about girls is the rule of love. Society therefore demands from girls that they act as if they love the world. They will serve father, mother, brother, sister, husband and children. Their work is a work of love, this is their ideal." | |

Essay 3

Title: Moral Education of Students *(Chatroder Nitisikkha)*

Year: 1892 (Bengali Year 1299)

Published in: Sadhana (Rabindra Rachanabali, Volume 17, Page 340-344)

Moral education may be defined as helping children and young people to acquire a set of beliefs and values regarding what is right and wrong. This set of beliefs guides their intentions, attitudes and behaviors towards others and their environment. Moral education also helps children develop the disposition to act in accordance with such beliefs and values. More fundamentally, it encourages children to reflect on how they should behave and what sort of people they should be. For many people, these questions are linked to religious belief, but moral education programs treat religion and morality as conceptually distinct (Halstead, J.M, 2010). Moral education in school helps students imbibe virtues and moral habits that build their personalities outside the classroom. While children can be good at math, science and literature, if they lack basic humanity or human interaction skills, their talents are of no value.

Education for social empathy and values are usually considered to be the task of ethical education; yet for Tagore they are spiritual education. According to him, one needs to be connected to a higher reality and be free from one's limited ego to acquire and develop ideals and values. Tagore is convinced that we cannot support children's ethical development through mere teaching or preaching, e.g. religious education, as he does not believe in a fixed moral code or ideals that could be passed on.

He argues that values cannot be directly taught and that this is only possible to do with sectarian dogma or tradition. Direct passing on of "value" might therefore only lead to piety but never to spiritual and proper ethical development (Tagore R., *Religious Education*, 1911). Instead, spiritual development requires widening one's consciousness, filling it with love and truly comprehending the world (Tagore, R. *The Philosophy of Our People*, 1926). This very often happens only through intense moments of enlightenment and inspiration and it demands patience (Tagore, R. *Letters to a Friend*, 1928)

Tagore does not believe that religious education should be a separate subject. He argues that spirituality will only be separate from life and education in general, if children acquire "our incessant habit of ignoring" the spiritual world. He is convinced that children's spirituality will develop on its own if they are not discouraged from this and if they are surrounded by the right atmosphere of art, music, nature and the inspiration through teachers who are themselves trying to develop their spirituality.

Table 10

Excerpts from the Essay 'Moral Education of Students'

Serial No	Page No	Excerpt	Criteria
1	340	"Before determining the method of policy education, it is necessary to determine the basis on which the policy is based. Before starting to build a wall, it is good to think about what is the foundation, what is the material and how will the wall stay straight and not fall down. It is logical to investigate the cause of the fault before attempting to remove the character fault. Without knowing the cause of the disease, there is a possibility of getting opposite results."	Role of a Teacher
2	341	"Human nature, especially child-nature, is imitative and appreciative. All the reforms that are ingrained in the mind at a young age by the examples of others, especially elders and loved ones, and their praise and	Role of a Teacher

		criticism, are in fact driven by those reforms in our lives."	
3	344	"Moral education should be the way to inculcate the beauty of duty and purity in the mind at an early age. If purity, truth, kindness, non-violence, etc. are to be rooted in the heart in the form of reformation, then the beauty of all these qualities must be displayed and then the mind will be attracted towards it by itself. Impurity, anger, hatred, and jealousy must be shown how ugly they are. And character should be formed in such a way that, just as we feel shyness and abhorrence even at the thought of touching an impure or hideous substance, so we should feel abhorrence at the thought of coming in contact with impurity, and feel shyness at committing wrongdoing. Just as	Quality of a Teacher

		we teach boys to avoid the joy of wallowing in the mud and enjoy the joy of being clean, so we should teach them to avoid impure and unjust actions. But this kind of education is not the work of two or four dry monotonous maxims; It is the act of keeping an eye on thousands of small details from house to house. The beauty of purity and justice cannot be seen in the bound bowl of the motto, if you want to feel how beautiful purity is and how ugly impurity is in your heart, let me read good novels and poems. The heart has nothing to do with moral textbooks."	

Essay 4

Title: Educational Reforms *(shikkhar songskar)*

Year: 1906 (Bengali Year 1313)

Published in: Rabindra Rachanabali Volume 10, 573-576 (Vishva Bharati)

In this article, Rabindranath Tagore has made analogies from Irish, English and Russian Educational System to suggest the reforms required in the Educational system of India. He suggested the importance of character building, inquisitiveness in children for the success of educational system of India. As this article was written in the time when people of India were fighting for independence from the British rule, Tagore was of the opinion that the control of the Government over the Education system is not good for the growth and development of Education. So, he opined that if people want to see success and development of the Education system in India, they should take control of the system to their own hands and make necessary reforms by themselves.

Table 11

Excerpts from the Essay 'Educational Reforms'

Serial No	Page No	Excerpt	Criteria

| 1 | 1 | "The Englishman in his native country understands well that boyish emotions are natural and healthy among boys. They know that if this impulse can be nurtured regularly without suppressing it, it will one day be stored as strength of character and intellect. The main means of creating cowardice is to completely suppress this sensation. Boys who are true benefactors, who recognize nature's good intentions in this sensation, do not regard it as a nuisance. That is why the various sources of 'Balochita Chapalya' are protected by the learned people. In England this virtue of forgiveness is fairly practiced--even, to us, it seems excessive." | Qualities of a Teacher |

| 2 | 2 | "There is one way to create such people who will think for themselves, search for themselves, work for themselves, and obey the orders of the next, do not protest against the opinion of the next, and be a provider for the next, but the law of creating such a person is different. It goes without saying that we would naturally want to prepare the nation for independence. When England had its heyday, England did not interfere with this ideal on any racial basis-- Meckl's comments on educational policy in India are a proof of this. Times have changed now; This is why the conflict between the patriots and the authorities over the ideals of education has become inevitable. We cannot at all | Methods of Education |

		agree to lay the permanent foundation of Tabedari in this country with the help of schools. So, the time has come, now we have to take education into our own hands."	
3	3	"It is not at all difficult for the government to improve the welfare of the country especially with the people, otherwise what is the problem of this country. Therefore, if we focus on being worthy of human rights and not the right to a job, then there is no doubt that the day has come for complete individualization of education. If we do not invent and take the initiative to educate the people of the country from childhood, then we will be destroyed in every way - we will die in food, we will die in health, we will die in intelligence.	Problems of Education

		Dying in character -- that's for sure. In fact, we are dying all the time without making the proper effort to remedy it, the thought of which does not properly arise in our minds, that deep-seated indifference and depravity-- there is no way to cure it by any program or institution except real education from childhood."	
4	3	"It seems to me that it is now especially important to do what is right quietly and persistently, not only without asking permission from the government, but consciously avoiding its participation. The strength of the government lies in the people's ignorance, and the government knows this, and will therefore always oppose true enlightenment. It is time we realized that fact. And it is most	Role of a Teacher

| | | undesirable to let the government, while it is spreading darkness, pretend to be busy with the enlightenment of the people. It is doing this now by means of all sorts of pseudo educational establishment which it controls; schools, high schools, universities, academies, and all kinds of committees and congresses. But good is good and enlightenment is enlightenment, only when it is quite good and quite enlightened." | |

<u>Essay 5</u>

Title: Education and Culture (*Sikkha ebong Sanskriti*)

Year: 1935

Published by: Vishva Bharati

Culture and education are two inseparable parameters and they are interdependent. Any educational pattern gets its guidance from the cultural patterns of a society. For instance, in a society with a spiritual pattern of culture, the educational focus would be on the achievement of moral and eternal values of life. On the contrary, if the culture of a society is materialistic, then its educational pattern will be shaped for the attainment of materialistic values and comforts. A society which does not follow any culture definitely has no definite educational organization. So, the culture of a country has a very powerful impact on its educational system.

Today while human lives continue to live in local realities, the lives and experiences of youth growing up will be allied to, social processes, economic realities, technological and media innovations, and cultural flows that go across international borders with ever greater momentum. These worldwide transformations will involve youth to adapt to new skills that are well ahead of what most educational systems can now distribute.

Rabindranath Tagore's views were in support of non-dogmatic defence of harmony and principles of unity, and he tried to achieve this in his education models by going beyond the realms of collapsing of cultural differences and without sacrificing local/individual ties and that admits to no artificial boundaries – political, ideological or geographic.

Table 12

Excerpts from the Essay 'Education and Culture'

Serial No	Page No	Excerpt	Criteria
1	1	"Culture succeeds the entire human psyche from a deeper level. Under its influence, people automatically get all-round success from the heart. Under his influence, the passion for pure knowledge and the enthusiasm for selfless activity became natural. True culture values genuine courtesy more than passive compliance. It is not his percept that politeness is useful	Qualities & Role of a Teacher

		for dealing with people, a cultured man can harm himself, but cannot degrade himself. He feels shy to promote himself flamboyantly or to advance himself by selfishly pushing everyone. All that is hypocrite or hypocrite pains him in this grief. He delights in honouring excellence of all kinds, in sincere identification with all, that is best in art, literature and human history. He can judge, he can forgive, he can break through the barriers of discord where he sees what is good."	
2	3	"Culture makes the deep layer of people's mind veritable. Thus, the entire mind of man has become successful. It develops the fondness for deep knowledge and modest act. The actual culture has focussed on genuine	Qualities & Role of a Teacher

		courtesies, not on trivial rituals. The culturally enriched man can harm himself but cannot be exacerbating. He does not like to show off much. Whatever is abominable or illusory generates pain to his heart. He delights in showering respect to all excellent things in art, literature and even in the history of humanity because he is cordially tied to their mastery. He has the ability to judge, to pardon, he does not consider disagreements. The person can see only the goodness in people. He does not envy the people around him. It shows his broadness of mind."	

Analysis of Letters

<u>Letter 1</u>

Title: Letters from Russia [*Russiar sithi*]

Published by: Vishva Bharati (Rabindra Rachanavali, Volume 10, 557-616)

This is a series of letters (Total 15 letters, one conclusion and two appendices) written by Rabindranath Tagore on his visit to Russia in the year 1930-31. Tagore was invited to Russia in 1926 and 1929 as well, but could not travel due to health reasons. Finally he could sail to Europe with four companions, Ms Margot Einstein (sculptor and stepdaughter of scientist Albert Einstein), Saumyendranath Thakur (grand-nephew of Rabindranath Tagore), Arium Williams and Amiya Chandra Chakravarty (literary critic, academic, poet, literary secretary to Rabindranath Tagore and a close associate) and reached Russia on September 11, 1930. Playwright, critic and journalist, Anatoly Lunacharsky, who was also involved with the Ministry of Education, was the one who invited Tagore to Russia in his personal capacity. There was enthusiasm about Tagore's visit amongst certain people including Russian orientalist Sergei Oldenburg, who specialised in Buddhist studies. The 1st letter was addressed to Rathindranath Tahkur (son of Rabindranath Thakur), 2nd and 4th letter were addressed to Nirmalakumari Moholanobish, 3rd and 5th letter were addressed to Prasantachandra Moholanobish, 6th letter was addressed to Asha Adhikari, 7th, 10th, 11th and 12th letters were addressed to Surendranath Karke, 8th and Appendix were addressed to Ramananda Chattopadhyay, 9th letter was addressed to nandlal Basu, 13th letter was addressed to kalimohan Ghosh and the 14th letter was addressed to Sudhindranth Dutta. All these persons were close associates to Rabindranath Tagore in Shanti Niketan.

Through the letters, he elaborately explains the key points observed by him regarding the culture, administration and Education system of Russia and points out the things that should be adopted by India for the growth and development of the country. He appreciated the efforts made by the Russian Government and the people of Russia to take Education to the masses and the enthusiasm with which Education is spreading throughout the country. The could feel "all people are equal" when he saw the agricultural farm workers enjoying good quality drama in the theatres along with the creamy layer of the society. He also explains how Russia was dealing with space exploration ideas along with the establishments of Museums as early as in the 1930s.

Table 13

Excerpts from the letters 'Letters from Russia'

Serial No	Letter No	Excerpt	Criteria
1	Letter 1	"Education is the biggest solution to all our problems. For so long most of the people in the society have been deprived of the full opportunity of education--India is almost completely deprived. Here it is surprising to see the wonderful enthusiasm with which the education is spreading throughout the society. The extent of education is not only in numbers, but in its completeness, in its intensity. What a lot of arrangements and what a lot of enthusiasm so that no people are helpless and idle. Not only to White-Russia-- they are spreading education like a flood among the half-civilized races of Central Asia;	Role of a Teacher

		There is no end to the effort to get them to the final harvest of science. Here the theaters are crowded with good operas and big dramas, but the people who see them are agricultural and workers. They are not insulted anywhere. In the meantime, I have noticed the awakening of their minds and the happiness of their self-esteem everywhere that I have seen their institutions."	
2	Letter 1	"The tireless enthusiasm, courage, intelligence and self-sacrifice that I see in the education system here, I would be grateful even if I had a very small amount of it. The less sincere energy and genuine enthusiasm, the more money has to be sought."	Methods of Education

| 3 | Letter 6 | "I was very surprised. Within eight years, education has changed the minds of people in all countries. Those who were dumb got language, those who were stupid got their hearts uncovered, those who were disabled were awakened to their self-power, those who were under humiliation came out of the dungeon of society and got equal seat with everyone. It is hard to imagine that such an idea could happen so quickly to so many people. It is mind-blowing to see that there is a flood of education in their once dead gang. From one end of the country to the other end is aware. In front of them a new path of hope is open across the horizon; Life is in full swing everywhere." | Role of a Teacher |

| 4 | Letter 6 | "Come here and see, they have made education come alive. That is because they didn't separate the school from the world. They do not teach to pass or to make scholars -- they teach to make people entirely." | Qualities of a Teacher |
| 5 | Letter 7 | "After returning from Russia, I went to the American port today. But the memory of Russia still occupies my mind. The main reason is that - in other countries that I have visited, they do not move the mind as a whole, they have enthusiasm for various actions in their own circles. Somewhere there is politics, somewhere there is a hospital, somewhere there is a university, somewhere there is a museum - experts are working on it. But here the | Role of a Teacher |

		whole country with one purpose in mind has made a great body into a great person by entwining all the departments into one nervous network. Everything has come together in a single pursuit."	
6	Letter 7	"They are spreading education in various ways. One of them is the museum. They have entangled all the villages and towns in the network of various museums. That museum is not passive like our Santiniketan library, but active."	Methods of Teaching
7	Letter 7	"Russia's space exploration initiative is widespread. There are about two thousand such educational centers, with a membership of over seventy thousand. In all these centers the past history of the place and the past and present financial	Methods of Teaching

		condition are explored. Apart from that, what kind of productive power of those places or whether any minerals are hidden there or not, it is sought. All these centers have a serious duty to educate the general public along with the museums. This new era of public education in the Soviet state, the extensive practice of spatial information and the associated museum, is a major mechanism."	
8	Letter 10	"In science education, the reading of books should be combined with the observation of the eyes, otherwise it becomes a double-edged evasion of education. Why only science, this applies to most education. That education is aided by the addition of	Methods of Teaching

| | | museums of various subjects in Russia. This museum is available not only in big cities, but also in small rural villages." | |
| 9 | Letter 10 | "Another method of visual learning is travel. You know that I have been carrying the idea of traveling school for a long time. India is so vast a country, so varied in all respects, that it cannot be fully understood by reading Hunter's Gazetteer. Pilgrimages on foot were once common in our country--our tirthas are also spread over all parts of India. This was the way to experience India as fully as possible. If students can be taken all over India for five years focusing only on education then their education is ripe." | Methods of Teaching |

| 10 | Letter 10 | "When the mind is active it can easily absorb and digest the subject of education. It is also necessary to feed the stomach with solid food--just like that solid education is essential for the mind. Being trapped in a stagnant school, the food of a stagnant class girl does not have mental health. The need for mannequins cannot be denied at all--people have so much knowledge that there is no way to extract them in the field, they have to collect most of them from the storehouse. But if students can be brought out through nature schools along with Bookish schools, then there is no shortage." | Methods of Teaching |
| 11 | Letter 12 | "Beginning with October 1st, 1930, the new budget year, a number of new scientific | Role of a Teacher |

		institutions and Institutes will be opened in Turkmenistan, namely :	
		1. Turkmenistan, Geological Committee	
		2. Turkmenistan, Institute of Applied Botany	
		3. Institute for study and research of stock breeding	
		4. Institute of Hydrology and Geophysics	
		5. Institute for Economic Research	
		6. Chemico-Bacteriological Institute and Institute of Social Hygiene.	
		The activity of all the scientific institutions of Turkmenistan will be regulated by a special scientific management attached to the	

		Council of People's Commissions of Turkmenistan."	

Letter 2

Title: On Some Educational Questions

Published Year: 1919

Publisher: First published in the Mysore Economic Journal under the title "Sir Rabindranath Tagore's Views on Some Educational Questions", was reprinted in The Modern Review in April 1919, 1011-1016

This open letter was written by Rabindranath Tagore to the Mysore Economic journal on the burning questions of Indian Education System prevailing at that time. This was the time where people were fighting for setting up a revolutionary educational system in India, which would focus on Education for the masses. Many universities were established at that time but their functioning was not streamlined. All the academicians were working together to form guidelines for the working of these universities. At the same time, people were also thinking seriously for the use of only mother tongue in the elementary and the secondary level of education. As a senior Academician and Nobel laureate, everyone in the Academic fraternity looked upon Rabindranath Tagore for his valuable suggestions and remarks in the Educational scenario of India in this pre-independence era.

Many of his views on University System of Education are still relevant in the present era. He was very vocal on proper selection criteria professors in the universities and the quality of facilities as well as scholarships the Professors should receive from the authorities. His views on the selection of subjects in the college and university education are still followed in the 21st century. His liberal idea about women's Education is also seen in this interview.

Table 14

Excerpts from the Letter 'On some Educational Questions'

Serial No	Page No	Excerpt	Criteria

| 1 | 1011 | **Universities:**

"While the routine work of the University classes, men may be appointed, as Assistant Professors, in consideration of their academical titles and diplomas, it would be a most serious blunder to select Professors for higher work on the same principle. For the latter have to be the leaders and directors of thought. And none but such as have given unquestionable proof of originality and genius should be placed in such positions. It is because of this defect in our Universities that most of them have not been the success that they would otherwise have been

The right method of appointing Professors is to invite the leading writers and thinkers | Qualities of a Teacher |

		available, on any subject, irrespective of race, colour, creed or caste to deliver courses of lectures and to select the best from such lecturers. Next, such Professors, when appointed, should be bound by a condition that within three years they should produce some original work and that in every three years succeeding, they should continue to give evidence of thought on original lines."	
2	1012	"The system of 'Exchanging' professors of different Universities for short periods, as in America, should also be adopted."	Qualities of a Teacher
3	1012	"High salaries must necessarily be paid. But that will be cheaper than the present system, which is more costly, in that it does not	Qualities of a Teacher

		bring a corresponding return for the large sums spent."	
4	1012	"There should be travelling scholarships to enable the students to visit different provinces in India collecting materials for their special studies from observation and submitting them to proper authorities."	Qualities of a Teacher
5	1013	"Professors, engaged in research work, should select students to collaborate with them. The mechanical portions of their work, such as collecting data from different sources, collating different versions of texts, drawing up concordances, and other such tasks, should be left to these students to carry out with the guidance of their professors."	Qualities of a Teacher

6	1013	**<u>Subjects of Study:</u>**	Methods of Teaching
		"Another chief reason for the paucity of original thought and production in the existing Universities is the viciousness of dividing the pupil's energies and attention in the Collegiate stage. A grounding in general knowledge ought to be provided for upto the entrance. But in the University, pupils should be allowed to bring up, for a degree, only one subject, in which the standard might be raised. Such a graduate will have greater depth, consequently greater love of his subject, greater aptitude for research work and better scope for manifesting originality, if he have any. The universities will then turn out a superior type of graduates,	

		which alone could make for real advancement of knowledge in the land."	
7	1013	**<u>Medium of Instruction:</u>** "As a general rule, the mother tongue, if it be one of the leading vernaculars of India, should be made the medium of instruction, but the adoption of this principle should be gradual. The sciences cannot be immediately taught in the vernacular. It is, therefore, necessary to bifurcate the courses of study in the University. Pupils desirous of bringing up humanistic subjects like History, Economics, Sociology and Philosophy, should be made to get their education in the vernacular. Pupils seeking to gain degrees in Science subjects should be	Method of Teaching

		instructed through the medium of English. The necessary books for the humanistic subjects may be translated at once. In the course of ten or fifteen years, all the courses mau be given in the vernacular and the 'bifurcation' abolished. Englidh should be universally taught as a second, but compulsory language."	
8	1014	**<u>Fine Arts:</u>** "Instruction in Fine Arts is an urgent necessity. For, these arts develop a province of the mind, which remains untouched by modern Indian Education. This defective development of the mind of our times has seriously stunted the growth of national life. The first step must be to organize, under the direction of Experts, a 'Museum' on the	Methods of Education

		most scientific lines. Articles indicative of the life and culture of all the people of India, must be secured and then similar articles of other races and the cultures of the world, as far as possible. They must be classified according to the purposes they were or are intended not only from economic, historical or ethnological standpoints, but also from the ethical and aesthetical."	
9	1014	**<u>Sanskrit Education:</u>** "There is a false notion that Buddhistic culture is either antagonistic or alien to Hindu culture. But they are, in fact, more closely related than Aryan and Dravidian cultures, The study of the Buddhistic and the Pali literature should be	Methods of Teaching

| | | combined with a study of Sanskrit literature. The Pehlavi literature should also be associated with it, for the same reason. Else, a comprehensive idea of Sanskrit culture cannot be attained." | |
| 10 | 1014 | **<u>Women's Education:</u>**

"Women's education cannot be the same as men's for the reason that women have a special duty to discharge towards society and humanity. It is not that every woman should be made to learn the culinary art or that she should have no higher ambition than to be a cook or a house-manager. Woman has a right to learn the sciences and arts that man learns and to enter, as far as practicable, the walks of life that man usually seeks. But it must not be forgotten that to her alone | Methods of Teaching |

		belongs one of the greatest privileges of life. Of nature's endowments to man the most valuable is his 'individuality'. Its preservation and development is one of humanity's foremost concerns. This can be done best only by women. She must, therefore, be first trained for discharging this great duty of rearing up the real man of the future, and her studies must be subordinated to this end. Else, the very object of creation will have failed. The courses that have such an aim can be best given in the Vernacular."	
11	1015	**<u>Primary and Secondary Education:</u>** "So far as the Primary stage goes, there is something to be said in favour of the old. Hindu	Methods of Education

| | | method of teaching pupils one subject after another. It does not mean that the child should learn nothing of history or geography for months or years when it is engaged in the study of Language of Arithmetic, when language is taken up, it should be the one subject of special and direct instruction. But the teacher and the parents may give the child talks on various topics or subjects incidentally in the garden, on the road, at dinner or elsewhere. Task work must be confined only to one subjects. The talks should prepare the child for receiving instruction in other subjects, later on. In the high school or lower secondary stage, however a number of subjects may be taught simultaneously. | |

| | | The mother tongue should be the medium of instruction. The fewer the textbooks, the better in the Primary and the Lower Secondary Stage. In the High School Stage, vernacular textbooks for all subjects should be prepared, without any further delay." | |
| 12 | 1015 | **<u>Education in General:</u>**

"All educational developments must proceed from within outwards. It isreally a spiritual process, not merely an intellectual or a mechanical one. The spirit being greater than the body and even the individual mind, education is process covering the widest area. Education is, in a real sense, the breaking of the shackles of individual narrowness. The aim must, therefore, be to develop | Aims of Education |

not only the individual aspect of the mind but also the universal or the spiritual, which is the chief characteristic of the Hindu system. It is therefore necessary to bring together in every educational organization, all the different cultures found in India, and as far as possible, all the cultures of the world, all the phases of religion and art, in which the universal mind has expressed itself in different ages and countries, i.e., to co-ordinate these various cultures without attempting the suppression of the natural differences. The highest aim of education should be to help the realization of unity, but not of uniformity. Uniformity is unnatural. And, in fact, its attainment is not possible. A sound educational system

		should provide for the development of variety without losing the hold on the basic or spiritual unity. Hence the idea underlying the Bolepur school is to bring together pupils of all creeds and cultures and to help them to realize their spiritual brotherhood and to develop, freely and fully at the same time, their individual and racial characteristics."	
13	1016	**<u>A Real Indian University:</u>** "There must be a place, if not in every province, at least in one centre in this vast country, to which the best intellects of India and even of the world outside, could be induced to resort, where they could meet, stay temporarily or permanently and impart their knowledge to the	Role of a Teacher

public. It will help to kill racial, sectarian, caste and other prejudices and be a real fountain of universal light. It is only Hindu states, whose rulers have in their veins flowing the ancient Aryan spiritual culture, based on 'unity' and 'universality' can realize its importance and organize a real university of this type, which will be India's educational contribution to the world's progress."

<u>Letter 3</u>

Title: Vernaculars for the M.A. degree

Published Year: November, 1918

Published by: The Modern Review, 1007-1009

This open letter was written by Rabindranath Tagore in response to Sir Ashutosh Mukherjee's proposal for introducing Indian vernaculars in Calcutta university for

M.A. Education programme. Tagore was always in favour of teaching in vernacular medium or in the mother tongue for the young children. But for the higher classes, he stretched upon the idea of learning the English language as well. This is because of the reason that not a large amount of good quality reference books was available in the vernacular languages which would be beneficial in the Masters level. According to him, the students should be allowed to think freely in their studies in the Masters level. He also suggested a lot of travel for the students, particularly those who were doing research on folk literature and stressed on outside the classrooms and not limited to one institution.

Table 15

Excerpts from the Letter 'Vernaculars for the M.A. degree'

Serial No	Page No	Excerpt	Criteria
1	1007	"Our language, the principal instrument for shaping and storing our ideals, should be allowed to remain much more plastic than it need be in the	Aims of Education

		future when standards have already been formed which can afford a surer basis for our progress."	
2	1008	"In the modern European Universities, the medium of instruction being the vernacular, the students in receiving, recording and communicating their lessons perpetually come into intimate touch with it, making its acquaintance where it is not slavishly domineered over by one particular sect of academicians. The personalities of various authors, the individualities of their styles, the revelation of the living power of their language are constantly and closely brought to their minds- and therefore all that they need for their final degrees is a knowledge of the	Methods of Education

history and morphology of their mother tongues. But our students have not the same opportunity, excepting in their private studies and according to their private tastes. And therefore, their minds are more liable to come under the influence of some inflexible standard of language manufactured by pedagogues and not given birth to by the genius of artists. I assert once again that those who, from their position of authority, have the power and the wish to help our language in the unfolding of its possibilities, must know that in its present stage freedom of movement is of more vital necessity than fixedness of forms."

| 3 | 1009 | "The University should not make any attempt, by prescribing definite textbooks, to impose or even authoritatively suggest any particular line of thought to the students, leaving each to take up the study of any prescribed subject,- grammar, philology, or whatever it may be, along the line best suited to his individual temperament, judging of the result according to the quantity of conscientious work done and the quality of the thought process employed." | Methods of Teaching |

Thus, a comprehensive analysis of the selected Literary Text of Rabindranath Tagore are presented in a Tabular Form with reference to the selected five criteria of Education namely Aim of Education, Methods of Education, Qualities of a Teacher, Role of a Teacher and Problems of

Education. The Summary of this analysis is presented in the
next Chapter.

CHAPTER 5

SUMMARY, FINDINGS

AND IMPLICATIONS

"The highest education is that which does not merely give us information but makes ourlife in harmony with all existence".

(Rabindranath Tagore)

Introduction

Rabindranath Tagore is one of the earliest thinkers and pioneers in the field of Education in India who worked tirelessly to build the Education system in India during the British Rule. All the policies of education and acts that came into being during and after the British rule had major contribution from Tagore's thinking and Educational Philosophy. Rabindranath Tagore's Educational Philosophy touches all the aspects of human life including Education, Religion, Spirituality, Politics, Nationalism, etc. All these aspects seem to be separate but are intervened with each other. His philosophy is reflected in his literary works   like poems, novels, articles, letters written to different people at different points of his lifetime and his lectures. After a careful assessment and extensive study of his works as well as other literature focusing on his philosophy, some key principles can be derived.

Summary of Research

The educational implications reflected in Tagore's philosophy are as follows:

- Physical Development of the child
- Intellectual Development of the child
- Development of Moral and Aesthetic values of the students
- Spiritual Development of the students
- Self –Realization of the citizens
- Internationalism of Education
- Humanity
- Creativity, Art and Craft in the Curriculum
- Importance of Mother Tongue in Education
- Freedom in Education
- Harmony with Nature
- Individual Harmony
- Social Harmony
- Universal Harmony

Physical development

Rabindranath Tagore gave utmost importance to physical health of the children, as the saying goes 'a healthy mind resides in a healthy body'. Physical health can be nurtured by allowing the children to play freely in the natural environment. Training of different body partsand the senses through exercises is important for the physical well-being of the children. He emphasized on the art of movement of the body to build appreciable body language. The function of the body is not just to carry out the vital activities, but to express ourselves using not only the facial expressions but through all the parts of the body.Bodily expressions help to perform the task in a better way.

According to him, students should be encouraged to dance and perform other physical activities, which involve the movement of all the muscles. Such activities maintain the harmony between body and the mind. He does not support the classroom education in which the students have to just sit and keep on receiving information, which does not involve any physical activity. The students should be allowed to jump, climb the tree, run off, chase the animals or pick the fruits from the tree during the class. It is the need of the child to use the whole body and express through it.

Intellectual development

Tagore believed that intellectual development can never take place with bookish knowledge but can happen in the environment around and through the real life situations. Storing a lot of information in mind is not intellectual development but developing rationaland independent thinking ability in the child will make the child logical and will lead to the intellectual development of the child. Rather than controlling the child by imposing pre-established ideas, allowing the child to think and explore on his own is necessary for the intellectual development. Tagore gave importance to science education. Scientific attitude is necessary for the intellectual development of the child, which can be achieved through real experiences and not through mere theoretical bookish knowledge.

Tagore believed that the subconscious mind of the children is more active than the conscious one, and so it is important to surround them with all kinds of activities, which could stimulate their minds and gradually arouse their interest.

Development of Moral and Aesthetic values

Tagore's emphasis was on the basic human moral values like love and kindness for others.He did not believe in imposing any disciplinary rules but rather gave importance to self- discipline, which comes naturally by giving such free environment. Tagore was the most aesthetic person who could see the beauty in everything. His poetry and other writings reveal the same. Development of aesthetic values is very much important for enjoying thelife and living it to its fullest potential. In Santiniketan, the atmosphere was so full of the beauty of nature. Playing the music, dancing, drama and celebration of the festivals is the routine in the institute. Aesthetic values can be developed in the children by allowing themto express themselves without any resistance or hindrance.

Tagore emphasized that, the curriculum must provide enough opportunities for pupils to enjoy the beauty of nature and to feel wonder at its marvels, to practice painting, sculpture,drama, music, etc., and to participate in purposeful activities beyond the area of fine arts. Aesthetic enjoyment is as important as intellectual and physical pleasure according to Tagore.

Spiritual development and self realization

Rabindranath's book like Sadhana and Gitanjali reflect the depth of his spiritual mind. Forhim, spiritual development is the ultimate goal of life that can be achieved through the development of inner self. Education should lead to the spiritual satisfaction of the person. Direct interaction with nature is very much important for the achievement of spiritual goalsof life. A student should be able to look within, examine and talk with the inner self and ultimately know the true self. Teaching strategies that stimulate meta-cognition can empower the spiritual development. Self-expression is also very important in this process. Education should enable the person to differentiate between the inner self, which is not physical and the outer self that is physical. In 'Sadhana', Tagore says,

"In the night we stumble over things and become actually conscious of their individual separateness, but the day reveals the great unity which embraces them. And the human being, whose inner vision is bathed in an illumination of his consciousness, at once

realizesthe spiritual unity reigning supreme over all differences of race, and his mind no longer awkwardly stumbles over individual facts of separateness in the human world; accepting them as final, he realizes that peace is in the inner harmony which dwells in truth, and notin any outer adjustments, that beauty carries an eternal assurance of our spiritualrelationship to reality, which waits for its perfection in the response of our love."(p.39)

Tagore believed in the spiritual world which is not separate from this world but it is its innermost truth, which should be felt by the individual with every breath. One should not finish the life like a dreamer without any awakening. The object of education is to give man the unity of truth. In older times, life was simple, all the elements of human were in harmony naturally, but later on, education separated all the elements and put emphasis only on physical and intellectual development. Such education is harmful for the spiritual development of the person which needs to be changed.

Internationalism

Internationalism or the international

harmony was one of the core characteristics of Tagore's educational philosophy. He always wanted the unity of east and west. International collaboration was must for the development of humanity in the world. He refuted the idea of shallow nationalism that ultimately brings violence but supported the idea of universal peace and harmonious relations among countries. Separation of the world in parts can never bring prosperity and peace. Accepting the cultures of other people in theworld is very important as all the cultures have their own specialties. A person has to become a universal being and should not limit himself to any boundaries. Physical boundaries are created by men and are not natural according to Tagore. He believed in India as an idea with its great heritage of divine knowledge and not as a mere a piece of land with geographical boundaries. Nature has never created any boundaries. He wanted the boys and girls to be fearless, free and open- minded, self- reliant, full of the spirit of inquiry and self- critical, with their roots deep in the soil of India but reaching out to the world in understanding, neighborliness, cooperation and material and spiritual progress. Actually Tagore's success lies in t he fact that he did not try to control directly the ideas, feelings, and values of children but imaginatively desi gned an environment and a program of activities and experiences which evoked the desired responses. He also believed that the education of a country acquires shape and substance only against the entire background and it is important that there is a strong relationship between education and society.

Viswa Bharati is the university founded by Tagore on the principle of Internationalism as he had realised that the problems of the present civilization was the misunderstanding among various cultures which can be solved by the cultural collaboration. This universityhas students and educators from all over the world. Tagore says,

"Geographical boundaries have lost their significance in the modern world. Peoples of theworld have come closer. We must realize this and understand that this closeness must be founded on love. I don't deny that nations are hurting one another, that they are exploitingone another. Still, the East and West must join hands in the pursuit of truth."

This thought is quite relatable in the present

era of information technology where geographical boundaries have been broken by the digital world.

Humanity

Humanity is the most necessary value, which should be developed in the pupils. They should be able to practice love in their life. Children should be provided with theopportunities to come in intimate contact with others and feel the empathy for others. All the worldly problems which are aroused due to hate can be solved by the humanity. Tagorehad great faith in humanity. Children should be taught the lessons of humanity which willlead to the harmonious life with others in future. Tagore said (as cited in My Life in My Words),

"I have great faith in humanity. Like the sun it can be clouded, but never extinguished. I admit that at this time when the human races have met together as never before, the basicelements appear predominant. The powerful are exulting at the number of their victims. They take the name of science to cultivate in the school boy superstitions that they have certain physical signs indicating their eternal right to rule, as the explosive force of the earthquake once might have claimed, with

enough of evidence, its never-ending sway over the destiny of this earth. But they in their turn will be disappointed."(p.97)

He saw education as a vehicle for appreciating the r richest aspects of other cultures, while maintaining one's own cultural specificity. As he wrote: *"I was brought up in an atmosphere of aspiration, aspiration for the expansion of the human spirit. We in our home sought freedom of power in our language, freedom of imagination in our literature, freedom of soul in our religious creeds and that of mind in our social environment. Such an opportunity has given me confidence in the power of education which is one with life and only which can give us real freedom, the highest that is claimed for man, his freedom of moral communion in the human world.... I try to assert in my words and works that education has its only meaning and object in freedom from ignorance about the laws of the universe, and freedom from passion and prejudice in our communication with the human world."*

Creativity, art and craft

Gurudev believed that in all creative

activities, the complete personality of man finds its expression; and particularly, the sub-conscious mind, which is almost fathomless in its depth, is revealed in arts, music and dance. Tagore himself was creative and his creativity was limitless which excelled in all the areas including literature, music, painting and other fine arts. Creativity is the expression of God present in every human.

Siksha Satra was the experiment done by Tagore which provided the experience in dealing with this overflowing abundance of child life, its simplicity, to provide utmost liberty within surroundings that are filled with creative possibilities. He believed in giving education to the children between six and twelve not only through gathering impressions through sight, smelling, hearing and taste, but more especially through touch and the use of the hands. The children should be taught handicraft as well as housecraft. In the workshop, the child becomes a producer and a creator, will acquires skills and wins freedom for its hands. The child deserves such opportunities of creating rather than depending on the elders to gain the self confidence in life. In Siksha Satra, the children were taught the activities like Cotton wick, tape and band making, Straw-sandal making, Dyeing with simple vegetable dyes, Wool work, Pottery, carpentry and carving, smithy and tool making, tailoring, bamboo construction, cycle cleaning and repair, Musicalinstrument making, Food preparation, Wheat grinding, etc.

In carrying out of the crafts, some art, some science, some element of business enters in. These crafts offer an approach to self-preservation and self-confidence to achieve economic stability in future. Without such feeling of confidence in the power to face the fight for livelihood through the trained fingers and hands, it is impossible to achieve that freedom of spirit upon which the fullest enjoyment of life is dependent. Creative expressionleads the child in the world of abstraction and ultimately in the world of spiritual truth. When a man of genius produces his works primarily for the purpose of expressing some ideal of perfection be it in forms, in ideas or in service, he gives expression to his own deeper consciousness of the infinite within.

Importance of mother tongue in education

Tagore believed that education must be done in the mother tongue as it is the language in which the pupil thinks which makes the education process natural and long lasting. Minds are quickened if the children are taught in their own language. The process of learning should be as simple as the process of eating which is possible only when it is done in mothertongue. In the words of Tagore (as cited in My Life in My Words) , *'Learning should as far as possible follow the process of eating. When the taste begins from the first bite, the stomach is awakened to its function before it is loaded, so that its digestive juices get full play. Nothing like this happens, when the Bengali boy is taught in English.'(p. 148)*

Shedding the light on the difference between the processes of learning the language naturally and learning another language in an artificial manner, Tagore says,

"The child joyfully learns to speak, because from the lips of father and mother it gets glimpses of language as a whole. Even while it understands but little, it is thereby continually stimulated and its joy is constantly at work in order to gain fullness of utterance. If,

instead of having before it the exuberance of expression, the child had been hemmed in with grammar texts, it would have to be forced to learn its mother tongue at thepoint of the cane, and even then could not have done it so soon." (p.147)

Freedom in education

"Where the mind is without fear and the head is held high; Where knowledge is free;
Where the world has not been broken up into fragments by narrow domestic walls; Where words come out from the depth of truth;
Where tireless striving stretches its arms towards perfection;
Where the clear stream of reason has not lost its way into the dreary desert sand of dead habit;
Where the mind is led forward by thee into ever-widening thought and action –
Into that heaven of freedom, my Father, let my country awake." (Tagore, 1913, p.31)

In this poetry, Gurudev reveals what freedom means to him. Freedom is not any shrunk idea but he believed in the freedom in true sense and byall means. He believed that freedom in the mere sense of independence is meaningless. Perfect freedom lies in the perfect harmony of relationships, which we realize in this world, ntthrough our response to it in knowing but in being. Objects of knowledge maintain an infinite distance from us who are knowers. For knowledge is not union. Therefore, the farther world of freedom waits us what we reach truth, not through feeling it by our senses,or knowing it by reason, but through the union of perfect sympathy. He said, *'We have our own freedom of will which can only find its true harmony in the freedom of other wills.'*

Pupils must be given the freedom to think, freedom to act and freedom to express their emotions. The object of education is the freedom of mind that can be achieved through the path of freedom. Freethinking can happen only in mother language. Education in foreign language will resist the development thinking ability of the child. Children should be given the freedom to think on the academic and social problem that cannot be done through imposing rigid curriculum or authoritative teacher. He also talks about the freedom of expression through the art and creativity. Talking about the liberation or freedom of mind, he believed that emotions are liberated from undesirable sentiments when one becomes conscious of the supreme soul.

He strongly had the belief that the schools must provide free environment to the children the present school system was so torturing according to him. It was an arrangement for giving lessons that was not suitable for the children. The children must gather their loveof life and then they will renounce their lives to gain knowledge. He said,

'My idea is that the mind should find its freedom in every respect, and I am sure that our children have, through early training, freedom from the barriers of country and race, creeds and sects.'

He was aware of the fact that life has its risks and freedom has its responsibility and yet they are preferable for their immense value and not for any other ulterior results. The founding of his school had its origin in the memory of that longing for freedom during thechildhood.

Harmony with nature

Tagore was a naturalist who insisted that education should be imparted in an atmosphere of nature with all its beauty, colors, sounds, forms and other manifestations. According to Tagore, nature is the manifestation of God. Closeness to the nature leads to the expansionof thoughts. He believed that the mind has hunger for the ministrations of Mother Nature. One can grow into full manhood only if nursed by earth and water, sky and air and nourished by them as by our mother's breasts. He founded the school in Santiniketan which was far away from the city in the natural environment. In his words, *'I selected the spot where the sky is unobstructed to the verge of horizon. There the mind could have its fearless freedom to create its own dreams, and the seasons could come withall their colours and movements and beauty into the very heart of the human dwelling. Andthere I got a few children around me and I taught them.' (Dasgupta, 2006, p.144)*

The association with nature has great influence on the mental development of pupils. It facilitates the formation of instincts. The mind acquires knowledge through direct relationship with nature. The radiance of the rising sun, the quietness of the evening and the beauty of the stars safeguard the mind from disturbing forces, clashes, conflicts and the complexities of the outside world.

Children have their active sub-conscious mind, which, like the tree, has the power to gatherits food from the surrounding atmosphere. For them the atmosphere is a great deal more important than rules and methods, building appliances, class teachings and textbooks. Children need to work in a perfect collaboration with nature, in a passive relationship of sympathy with atmosphere.

Individual, social and universal harmony and joy

Individual harmony refers to the harmony of the body, mind and soul of the individual. Tagore talks about the all-round development of an individual personality through the harmonious union of the spirit with the environment. For Tagore, education is something that brings harmony with the whole existence. Harmony within the self, harmony with the society and the universal harmony among all the cultures of the world. Tagore experiencedthe fact that the man is always seen within his racial limits and not as a part of humankind wherever we go. He wanted his Ashram in Santiniketan to be one place in the world where all can mingle without the differences of religion, language and race.

He believed that education should help an individual to attain complete manhood, so that all his powers may be developed to the fullest extent for his own individual perfection as well as the perfection of the human society in which he was born. He believed that education was not merely a means for the growth and fullness of the individual, but it was also concerned with t he whole physical and social milieu in which his life was lived. Tagore believed that the lack of wealth is not the most important, but the problem of unhappiness is the great problem. Wealth, which is the synonym for the production and collection of things, men can make use of ruthlessly. They can crush life out of the earth and flourish. However, happiness, which may not compete with wealth in its list of materials, isfinal, it is creative; therefore, it has its source of riches within itself. His scheme of village reconstruction 'Sriniketan' had the objective to bring the stream of happiness in the village life with the collaboration and contributions of the scholars, the poets, the musicians and the artists. According to Gurudev, multiplying materials intensifies the inequalities between those who have and those who have not, and this yields a fatal wound to the social system. That is why he wanted shift the focus from the material wealth to the inner wealthand happiness to bring the individual and social harmony.

Applications of Research (Visva-Bharati: A distinguished contribution of Tagore in the field of Education)

"Visva-Bharati represents India where she has her wealth of mind which is for all. Visva-Bharati acknowledges India's obligation to offer to others the hospitality of her best culture and India's right to accept from others their best."

-Rabindranath Tagore

Rabindranath started his experiments in education in 1901 by founding a school in Santiniketan with only five students which later on turned to the university named 'Visva- Bharati University'. The motto of this institute is "Yatra Vishwam Bhavati Eka Nidam" which means *"Where the world makes a home in a single nest"*. Tagore founded this institute with the vision of establishing peace and harmony among different cultures and nations which can be achieved through understanding and accepting different cultures with open minds. People tend to condemn other cultures when they evaluate them as per their own social standards. This ethnocentrism can be removed through harmoniousinternational relations.

Santiniketan

Santiniketan was a dream project of Tagore for which he sold all his books, his belongings and his copyrights to make the ends meet. He wanted this school to be like an ancient Ashrama (hermitage), which welcomes all the kind of people, be it rich or poor. He believed that English education had failed to produce dedicated workers as it overlooked the poverty while paying attention only to the worthless pleasures. The roots of asceticismshould be established during the young age as said by Tagore. He wanted a school with thecompleteness of the world and not a mere setup to give lessons. The aim was to make it grow through a creative spirit and not based on some pre -established religion. Tagore wasa naturalist who believed that the education should take place in the natural environment away from the interruption of artificial urban life where there is very less scope for childrento express their true inner self and live with the purest joy. The place he chose to found theschool was also a natural place with peaceful environment. As Tagore says (cited in My Life in My Words),

"I selected a beautiful place, far away from the contamination of town life. I knew that themind has its hunger for the ministrations of mother-nature, and so I selected the place where the sky is unobstructed to the verge of the horizon."(Dasgupta, 2006, p.144)

Tagore wanted to free the minds of the students from the blind beliefs and let them welcomeand respect the whole humanity irrespective of which caste or creed they belong or whichplace they have come from. The students in his school were encouraged to do their own work, like sweeping own place, making the beds, etc. They used to wake up early in the morning and join physical exercise followed by bath and prayer. The subjects taught in the school included Mathematics, English, Bengali, Sanskrit, History, Geography and Science along with the craft activities like carpentry, bookbinding, weaving and other vocational crafts. Singing, drawing, drama, arts, dance, etc. were given importance in education. Otherthan that, literary meetings to develop students' taste in literature used to be arranged everyweek. Games were also the part of education in Santiniketan. Tagore encouraged community service by making children do the activities like helping the poor, fixing the roads, gardening, etc. Freedom and joy should never be compromised in life or in the process of education as Tagore believed and he also practiced it in his school. Gurudev said (as cited in My Life in My Words),

"My idea was that education should be part of life itself, and must not be detached from itand be made into something abstract. And so when I brought these children around me, I allowed them to live a complete life. They had perfect freedom to do what they wished, asmuch liberty as was possible for me to give them. And in all their activities, I tried to put before them something which would be interesting to them." *(Dasgupta, 2006, p.145)*

The infrastructure of Santiniketan contained various buildings with their unique names based on their locations and purpose. These buildings are as follows:

- Uttarayana (As it was situated in the northern part of the Ashrama)
- Konark (Rehearsals of Tagore's plays took place here)
- Udayana (Dance, drama, literary meetings,

etc. was held here, Tagore's lastbirthday was also celebrated here)

- Shyamali (Mud hut, dignitary guests like Gandhiji, Lal Bahadur Shastri, VinobaBhave, Mother Teresa, etc. stayed here when they visited Santiniketan)
- Punascha (The last house of Tagore)
- Udichi (One of the houses of Tagore)
- Chitra-Bhanu Guha Ghar (workshop of Rathindranath)
- Bichitra- Rabindra Bhavana (Rabindra Museum)
- Chatimtala
- Mandir (Prayer hall)
- Teen Pahar
- Taladhwaj
- Amrakunja
- Dehali
- Nutan Bari
- Saal Bithi
- Singha Sadan
- Vidya Bhavana
- Purvatoran and Paschimtoran

- Patha Bhavana
- Gour Prangan
- Samindra Sishu Pathagar
- Bell tower
- Dija Biram
- Hindi Bhavana
- Cheena Bhavana
- Mukut Ghar
- Santoshalaya
- Benu Kunja
- Dinantika
- Chaiti
- Naba Nandan
- Sangeet Bhavana
- Kalo Bari
- Natya Ghar
- Central Library
- Nippon Bhavana

Tagore believed and also propagated the idea that the life should be celebrated and not be carried like a burden. Celebrations should be the part of education as they enable the persons to be free from the tensions and let them live a fulfilled life. It encourages social collaborations and enhances love and bonding amid the individuals. Children learn to consider and respect each other's feelings and develop harmonious relations. Celebrationsalso make the individuals express themselves fully and whole heartedly which is necessary for the holistic development of the children. It makes them to be one with their surroundings and love the whole existence. Festivals were the part of the educational process in Santiniketan. Many seasonal, religious as well as commemoration festivals are celebrated in Santiniketan. Seasonal festivals made the children understand and value the nature and its patterns. Religious festivals inculcated the cultural values in children. Commemorating festivals made the children understand the value of good deeds ofsomeone and encouraged them towards contributing something to the society. The festivals celebrated in Santiniketan are as follows:

> Hala Karshan Utsava (Festival of ploughing during monsoon)

> Varsha Mangal (Celebration of monsoon)

> Rakhi Bandhan

> Silpo Utsav (The festival of Technology celebrated on the day of Viswakarma Puja)

- Saradotsava (Natya Utsav during pre-autumn season)
- Ananda Bazar (The Mart of Joy where students would arrange fairs)
- Nandan Mela (Shilpacharya Nandalal Bose's birthday)
- Poush Utsava (The festival of Poush)
- Maharshi Smaran (In memory of Maharshi Debendranath)
- Maghotsava (Festival of Magh for establishment of Brahmo Samaj)
- Magh Mela (The fair of Magh- foundation day of Sriniketan)
- Basanta Utsava (The Spring Festival)
- Gandhi Punyaha
- Rabindra Saptaha
- Rammohan Smarana (Cpmmemorating Raja Rammohan Roy)
- Dharma Chakra Pravartana (In memory of Lord Buddha)
- Birth Anniversary of Rabindranath and New year's festival
- Death Anniversary of Tagore and tree plantation

(Vriksha Ropan Utsava)

> Independence day and Republic day

Sriniketan

Sriniketan was the scheme of village reconstruction undertaken by Rabindranath for the betterment of the life of rural people after observing the miserable conditions of rural people in Silaidah, Patisar and Kaligram. He established the 'Institute of Rural Reconstruction' in a village named Surul that was named as 'Sriniketan' which literally means 'An abode of well-being'. The aim was to educate village people in order to make them self-reliant. Leonard K. Elmhirst was the first director of Sriniketan.

Research and experiments were conducted here for the development of the village in a scientific manner. It also exhibits the scientific temper of Rabindranath Tagore. They did research in agricultural field and cultivated the crops. A medical dispensary was opened in Sriniketan to provide free medical treatment to village people and the youth of the village was encouraged to run it. A scout group was formed to carry out such activities which was named as 'Brati Balak Samgathan'. Sriniketan also had a Maternity

Home-cum-Child welfare which was set up with the help of state government then. Vocational training, Health education, Production, Agriculture, Animal husbandry, etc. activities were the part of Rural Reconstruction Department in Sriniketan to train and educate people for being able to earn their livings. Vocational education was at the core of Sriniketan under which various craft activities like leather craft, wood craft, clay craft, lacquer works, embroidery weaving, carpet weaving, bookbinding, printing, block making, etc. trainings were given. Tagore encouraged the openings of Cooperative societies in villages that can provide loans to farmers. Other educational institutions established in Sriniketan are as follows:

- ❖ Siksha- Satra (School for village children)
- ❖ Lok Siksha Samsad (For informal education)
- ❖ Siksha Charcha (Training for primary school teachers)
- ❖ Institute of Rural Reconstruction (Diploma program in Rural reconstructionprojects)

Visva- Bharati University- Institutional Structure and Educational Practices

Visva-Bharati is the central university

situated in Santiniketan, West Bengal. The university was founded by Gurudev Rabindranath Thakur who had dreamt of a unique educational institute where the whole humanity will stay unitedly irrespective of gender, cast, religion, creed and nationality. This dream university was named as 'Visva-Bharati' where the whole world unites with India. This institute was Tagore's voice of internationalism against extreme nationalism. Tagore dedicated himself to this university and utilised all his Nobel Prize money as well as royalty money for this institute. Jawaharlal Nehru passed the bill in the parliament to give recognition to Visva- Bharati University as a Central University. Visva- Bharati has also been given the status of 'An Institute of National Importance'. Visva- Bharati is the only university in India where the Prime Minister of India is appointed as a chancellor by the president of India. Professor Bidyut Chakrabarty is the current Vice- Chancellor of this university. It is a co-educational institute where the education is provided starting from kindergarten to Ph.D.

The vision and mission of Visva- Bharati as mentioned on the university website are as follows:

- ✓ To study the mind of man in its realisation of different aspects of truth from diverse points of view.

- ✓ To bring into more intimate relation with one another, through patient study and research, the different cultures of the East on the basis of their underlying unity.

- ✓ To approach the West from the standpoint of such a unity of the life and thought of Asia

- ✓ To seek to realize in a common fellowship of study the meeting of the East and the West, and thus ultimately to strengthen the fundamental conditions of world peace through the establishment of free communication of ideas between the two hemispheres.

- ✓ With such ideals in view, to provide at Santiniketan, a centre of culture where research and study of the religion, literature, history, science and art of Hindu, Buddhist, Jain, Islamic, Sikh, Christian and other civilizations may be pursued along with the culture of the West, with that simplicity in externals which is necessary for true spiritual realization, in amity, good fellowship and co-operation between the thinkers and scholars of both Eastern and Western countries.

Institutes in Visva- Bharati

1. School of Higher Secondary Education (Uttar-

Siksha Sadana)

2. Institute of Language, Literature and Culture (Bhasha Bhavana)

3. Institute of Humanities and Social Sciences (Vidya- Bhavana)

4. Institute of Science (Siksha Bhavana)

5. Institute of Dance, Drama & Music (Sangit Bhavana)

6. Institute of Fine Arts (Kala Bhavana)

7. Institute of Education (Vinaya Bhavana)

8. Institute of Tagore Studies and Research (Rabindra- Bhavana)

9. Institute of Rural Reconstruction (Palli- Samgathana Vibhaga)

10. Institute of Agricultural Science (Palli- Siksha Bhavana)

11. Institute of Primary & Secondary Education in Santiniketan (Patha Bhavana)

12. School of Secondary Education in Sriniketan (Siksha Satra)

13. Granthana Vibhaga (To manage Tagore's publications)

Various Centres for Studies

1. Centre for Buddhist Studies

2. Centre for Endangered Languages

3. Centre for Comparative Literature

4. Centre for Modern European Languages, Literatures and Culture Studies

5. A.K. Dasgupta Centre for Planning and Development

6. Nippon Bhavana

7. Indira Gandhi Centre

8. Computer Centre

9. Rural Extension Centre

10. Centre for Mathematics Education under Siksha Bhavana

11. Siksha Charcha (Centre for training of primary school teachers)

12. Agro- Economic Research Centre

13. Department of Environmental Studies under Siksha Bhavana

14. Centre for Journalism and Mass Communication under Vidya Bhavana

15. Rathindra Krishi Vijnan Kendra

16. Rabindra Charcha Prakalpa

17. Centre for Women Education

Findings of Research

Rabindranath Tagore's views on Aims of Education

Self Realization

Tagore puts a lot of emphasis on spiritualism and states that personal development relies on spiritual knowledge and the self-Realization of an individual.

Physical Development

Tagore also focused on the sound and healthy physical development of children by stressing the importance of activities like yoga, sports, and more.

Intellectual Development

Tagore also focused on the intellectual development of children such as imagination, creativity, free-thinking, curiosity, and the like.

Development of Moral and Aesthetic values

Tagore's emphasis was on the basic human moral values like love and kindness for others.He did not believe in imposing any disciplinary rules but rather gave importance to self- discipline, which comes naturally by giving such free environment. Tagore was the most aesthetic person who could see the beauty in everything. His poetry and other writings reveal the same. Development of aesthetic values is very much important for enjoying the life and living it to its fullest potential. In Santiniketan, the atmosphere was so full of the beauty of nature. Playing the music, dancing, drama and celebration of the festivals is the routine in the institute. Aesthetic values can be developed in the children by allowing them to express themselves without any resistance or hindrance.

Tagore emphasized that, the curriculum must provide enough opportunities for pupils to enjoy the beauty of nature and to feel wonder at its marvels, to practice painting, sculpture,drama, music, etc., and to participate in purposeful activities beyond the area of fine arts. Aesthetic enjoyment is as important as intellectual and physical pleasure according to Tagore.

Relationship between man and God

Tagore stressed that one must be dedicated to sacredness and spiritualism to establish a perfect harmony between man, nature, and God.

Social Development

Tagore believed that individuals should treat all human beings equally and stated, "man service is service to god".

Freedom

Tagore stated, "Education has learning only when it is imparted through the path of freedom".

International Brothehood

Being a lover of humanity, Tagore wanted to make a synthesis between Eastern culture and Western culture by education. He wanted to promote inter-cultural and inter-social understanding for the unity and harmony of mankind. He believed in the dictum that "Service to man is service to God".

Rabindranath Tagore's views on Methods of Education

Teaching through Tours and Trips

Tagore believed that the subjects like history, geography, economics and other social sciences can be effectively taught through excursions and tours to important spots. By this students will get an opportunity to observe numerous facts and gain firsthand knowledge through direct experience.

Learner Centred Education

The education system is heading towards being Learner centered in present times which was Teacher centered earlier and the educator used to the controlling authority. Rabindranath has always talked about the child's freedom in education. He mentioned that he used to act as a companion of the children rather than behaving like a senior authority. He also talked about the interests of children and making the teaching-learning process as interesting as possible to keep the childrenengaged.

Activity based Learning

Tagore was always against the bookish knowledge and believed in the training of senses through different activities. Rabindranath Tagore said that for the development of child's body and mind, learning through activity is essential. Therefore he included activities like climbing tree, drama, jumping, plucking fruits, dancing etc. in his educational programmes. He planned to provide maximum activities to the students in natural environment in his school in Santiniketan. Thus, it is relevant to the concept of Activity based Learning prevailing in current times.

Narration-cum-discussion and debate method

Narration-cum-discussion and debating activities were organized Tagore's education centre to develop oratory abilities of the students. Students were encouraged to solve problems of various areas through rational debate and thorough discussion.

Heuristic Method

Rabindranath Tagore introduced Heuristic method as an important method of teaching in his educational institution. In this method first, the students, are asked questions to clarify their doubts on topics and teachers try to satisfy them by their correct answers. Then the teacher asks the questions to students to evaluate how far the students are able to comprehend the topic discussed in the class.

Play way method

Playing games was a compulsory activity in Tagore's school that allows childrento grow fully and also maintains physical health.

Importance of Co-curricular activities

Many co-curricular activities were the part of education in Santiniketan. The importance of co-curricular activities has been accepted widely in present times.

Informal Education

Tagore had introduced informal education in 1936 and had established an institute for it called Lok Siksha Samsad. This concept was introduced in National Policy of

Education 1986. The importance of informal education is discussed and accepted widely in present times.

Teacher training

Tagore had founded an institute called 'Siksha Charcha' for the training of primaryschool teachers in 1937 where the learner's psychology and pedagogy was taught to the prospective teachers. Teacher training has been given very much importanceworldwide to improve the teaching learning process which Tagore had speculated way before time.

Mother Tongue as a medium of instruction:

Tagore has always given importance to mother tongue in education as it comes verynaturally to children. It allows children to express themselves better and flourish with grace. School education in Santiniketan is still given in Bengali medium. New Education Policy -2020 has also proposed mother tongue as a medium of instruction in during primary education.

Community Service:

Tagore has dedicated his whole life for community service. He encouraged studentsfor community service by providing various activities like repairing the roads, planting the trees, helping the poor, etc. In recent times, many community service activities take place in educational institutions like NCC, NSS, Blood donation camps, tree plantation, etc.

Vocational Education:

Vocational education is the need of the hour in present times. Tagore gave importance to vocational education by giving the training of various craft activitiesas discussed earlier, agriculture, etc. Various diploma courses and industrial trainings focusing upon a specific vocation are open today that shows how Tagore's educational practices are applicable in present.

Importance of Technology:

Although Tagore has given importance to natural environment, he has not overlooked the importance of ever changing technology. The festival of technologycalled 'Silpo Utsava' celebrated in Santiniketan backs this statement where the Hindu God of Technology Lord Viswakarma was worshipped and students could exhibit their creations. The importance of technology is obvious in present times which Tagore had speculated and accepted in his times.

Research and Scientific Approach:

Siksha Bhavana is the Institute of Science established by Tagore which representshis scientific temper despite being spiritual. He carried out research activities in theagriculture field and cultivated crops in Sriniketan in a scientific manner using chemical fertilizers. Science education and research are given very much importance in today's times.

Soft Skills in Education:

Tagore had introduced drawing, painting, music and various other art activities in his educational institute. The importance of soft skills is realised in present times.

Co-education and Inclusive Education:

Visva- Bharati was a co-educational institute where all the type of students and people were welcomed irrespective of their background. This practice coincides with the present concept of inclusive education.

Experiential Learning:

Experiential is the current approach to education where students construct their ownknowledge rather than just grabbing pre-established information. Rabindranath also encouraged such practices where students used to get maximum experiences of reallife rather than just lessons in a limited set up.

Rabindranath Tagore's views on Role of a Teacher

1. Rabindranath Tagore believed that the teacher's own life, his own search for truth should be such that encourages the student to respect truth and nature. Teaching lessons in the class and giving lectures on ideals and principles is not real education.

2. Education can be successfully imparted by understanding childhood and giving oneself totally in love and union with it. The best education a child can get is in the atmosphere of love, trust and joy. Tagore gave a *mantra* to teachers – "Don't try to preach your principles to children, instead give yourself completely in love" (*Rabindranath Tagore: Philosophy of Education and Painting*, ed. Devi Prasad (New Delhi: National Book Trust, 2007) p. 36).

3. Rabindranath Tagore remarks that a teacher can never truly teach unless he is still learning himself. A lamp can never light another lamp unless it continues to burn its own flame. The teacher must be dedicated to learning regardless of the teaching profession

4. Tagore adds that the teacher who has come to the end of

his subject, who has no living traffic with his knowledge, but merely repeats his lessons to his students, can only load their minds; he cannot quicken them.

5. The teacher is believed to be a true Guru. The teacher must be a guide and a true mentor who motivates the students for life.

6. .A teacher must be dedicated and self-motivated to motivate the students.

7. The teacher must teach moralistic and ideal ethics to the student.

8. A teacher must be pure-hearted only then the teacher can enlighten the students.

Rabindranath Tagore's views on Qualities of a Teacher

1. The teacher should believe in the children with great love and affection, sympathy, and empathy.

2. Instead of emphasizing on bookish learning, the teacher should provide a conducive environment to the child so that he/she engages himself/herself in useful and constructive activities and learn from his/her own experiences.

3. The teacher should always be busy motivating the creative capacities of the children so that he remains busy with constructive activities and experiences.

4. The teacher should be celibate, solitary, knowledgeable, thoughtful, unique personality and great.

5. The teacher should have the qualities of service, renunciation, cooperation, bliss, dutifulness, etc.

6. Tagore termed harsh teachers as Jail wardens.

7. The teacher should try to acquaint a child with the real situations, social conditions, and environment of life and to enable him/her to adjust to them.

8. The teacher should inspire the students for development of social qualities, so that he/she can contribute to the progress of society.

9. The teacher should try to enhance the values of patience, peace, self-discipline, and inner freedom in the students.

10. The teacher should work towards training of different organs and senses of the students alongside a healthy body and natural development.

Rabindranath Tagore's views on Problems of Education

1. Tagore reviewed education is surrounded by walls, locked by gates, guarded by doorman, stung by punishment, hurried by bells; this type of education can never bring happiness in human life

2. The medium of Education in the primary level, other than mother tongue can cause serious problems to the learning

of students. Tagore always advocated learning in the mother tongue.

3. According to Tagore, Mass illiteracy is the greatest threat to the Education system of the Nation.

4. According to Tagore, book Centered Education would destroy all the natural instincts of students and the creative abilities.

5. Superstition ad undue cult of the people is also a problem of Education.

6. Poverty and suppression of the disadvantageous section of the society by the rich and influential section of the society also creates problem in education.

7. If the policies of education proposed by the Government does not cater to the needs of the society, then also it can be a problem to Education.

Discussion on Findings

Relevance of Tagore's Educational Philosophy in Current Scenario

Rabindranath's educational philosophy was not a system in the prevalent sense of the term system. A system formulated by modern day pedagogies with rules and regulations and ready-made methodology in which teachers are thought how to teach particular subjects and prepare lessons and text books within set paradigms. Rabindranath discarded the notion of textbooks. He put the responsibility of educating the students in a joyful manner upon the guru. He said that the relationship between the student and the guru should be of companionship. He said, *"The teachers heart continues to receive every moment of his life, and that is why he continuously gives himself totally."*

He finds the proof of his truth and honesty in the process of giving and from the joy, he receives from it. Joy emerges on its own when minds meet in a healthy spirit. That joy is the energy of creativity and it's result is transfer of knowledge. Those who are conscious of their duties, but do not experience joy, tread on a different path. I consider the person to person relationship between the guru and shishya the prime means of imparting knowledge. Being a naturalist Tagore was aware of the sensitivity of young children and he had a firm faith in the educative value of natural objects and events. According to him —The highest education is that which does not merely give us information but makes our life in harmony with all existence. Children have their active subconscious mind which like the tree has the power to gather food from the surrounding atmosphere

First important writing in this direction is "**Tapovan**" (Jan, 1910) — Forest. In this article for the first time Tagore introduced a new idea of the education of feeling (**Bodhersadhana**) and he distinguished it from the education of the senses and the education of the intellect. This education of feeling consists of the realization of man's bond of union with the universe through the spirit, through the soul, through the deeper intuition of feeling. Through his national system of education India should endeavor to discover and attain the characteristic truth of her civilization pursued through the centuries by her prophets, thinkers and saints and "that truth is not mainly commercialism, imperialism or nationalism; that truth is universalism"(Tagore, 1351 B. S., p. 100). The highly significant point here is that while Tagore is still talking in terms of nationalism and swearing by the ideals of Ancient India, he is interpreting the highest of these ideals in terms of internationalism.

.   As Rabindranath had very broad and open views about every aspects of life, his philosophy is found to be evergreen and relevant in any period of time. The relevance of his educational philosophy is discussed here by pointing out some of the prevailing concepts in education in present times which are as follows:

Implications of the Study

Glimpses of Tagore's Educational Thoughts on NEP 2020

Tagore's philosophy of education consisted of humanism, idealism and naturalism. He believed in establishing harmony with nature, surroundings and with international relations as well. Harmony along with freedom was the basic pillar of his educational belief. He believed teaching should be more realistic than decorated and theoretical. Keeping this in mind, he founded Viswa- Bharati in Shantiniketan that fulfilled his educational desire. Tagore's educational ideas were a blend of eastern and western cultures. In his early life, he had criticised the colonial form of education considering it to be incapable of providing holistic education but his mind-set changed during the First World War. Since then, he started accepting European culture and supported the concept of amalgamation of Indian and European cultures. Tagore believed that knowledge should not have any boundary; it must flow freely.

The National Educational Policy 2020 is believed to have followed the principles of Tagore. The NEP 2020 stresses on establishing multidisciplinary universities in the same way Tagore had established educational institutions like Pathabhavana, Siksha Shatra, Viswa-Bharati, where activity-based learning is the main mode. Moreover, NEP also talks about international collaboration that matches with the educational history of Viswa-Bharati where a number of international scholars have been involved. The common points of Tagore's educational curriculum and NEP 2020 includes -

- ❖ He stressed on the fact of making mother tongue as the major mode of education.
- ❖ He focused on self-realization.
- ❖ Intellectual development.
- ❖ Social Development.

He reformed education through emotion, spiritual aspect and less theory based.

He encouraged a multi-lingual, multi-cultural and multi-racial approach towards education giving full freedom to students to choose what they wanted to learn. Similarly, some of the significant moves in the NEP are choice between three- or four-year undergraduate courses, multiple entry and exit options in degree courses and adding 3.5 crore seats in higher education institutions with a single regulator to oversee them.

Just like Tagore envisioned, NEP 2020 ensures that every Indian becomes empowered.

Tagore used to say – "highest education is that which not only informs us, but brings our life in harmony with all existence. Certainly, the larger goal of the National Education Policy is linked to this, best education is not one that gives information, but makes us relevant, the National Education Policy has set the foundation for 21st century India."

Recommendations for further Research

The writings of Rabindranath Tagore is expanded over 17 large volumes as published by Vishva Bharati. These works have been translated to over 50 languages over the world. Still, the understanding of these scholarly works are being done by academicians at different stages. Many writings are even included in textbooks of many countries. In this dissertation, only 13 literary works of varied length could be analysed which have direct inference to Education. But the analysis and understanding of many other literary works are still needed from student's point of view as well as policy maker's point of view because of the reason that these literary works are evergreen, thought provoking and have relevance to each Education Policy that a nation need to make. Therefore, extensive study of the literary works of Rabindranath Tagore are utmost needed.

Conclusion

By the study of the mentioned literary works of Rabindranath Tagore which included 5 lectures, 5 Essays and 3 letters, it is found out that Tagore's writings reflected his thoughts and concerns about the existing Education policy of India. He wrote freely about the problems of the Education system of India and how the problems can be dealt with. He also visited many countries extensively and tried to incorporate the good things from their Education system to the way education system works in India. In this dissertation, from an extensive study of the selected literary works of Rabindranath Tagore, Tagore's views about Aims of Education, Methods of Education, Qualities of a Teacher, Role of a Teacher and Problems of Education are noted and discussed. Moreover, it is shown how his thoughts and Educational Philosophy are still relevant in India.

Bibliography

Bandyopadhyay, S. (2017). *Educational ideas and practices of Rabindranath Tagore and Maria Montessori a comparative analysis.* (Doctoral Dissertation, University of Calcutta) Retrieved April 24, 2020, from http://hdl.handle.net/10603/211595

Best, J.W. & Kahn, J.V. (2005). *Research in Education.* Prentice Hall of India Pvt. Ltd.

Bose, A. (2016). Rabindranath Tagore's Philosophy of Education and Development inIndia. *Researchpaedia, 3(1)*, 2347-9000, p.2

Chakraborty, A. (2018). The Educational philosophy of Ravindranath Tagore and Rishi Auravinda Ghosh. *International Journal of Research and Analytical Reviews (IJRAR), 5(3)*, 278-283 Retrieved from http://ijrar.org/papers/IJRAR1903289.pdf

Chaudhari, B. (2018). Tagore and Nationalism. *International Journal of Advanced Educational Research, 3(1)*, 345-347 Retrieved from www.educationjournal.org

Das Gupta, U. (2006). *My Life in My Words.* Penguin Books India Pvt. Ltd.

Das, D. (2014). Educational Philosophy of Rabindranath Tagore. *India: Department of Philosophy, Women's College.IMPACT: International Journal of Research in Humanities, Arts and Literature, 2(6),* 1-4. Retrieved April 22, 2020, from http://citeseerx.ist.psu.edu/viewdoc/download?doi=10.1.1.679.2323&rep=rep 1&type=pdf

Dasgupta, U. (2004) *Rabindranath Tagore: an illustrated life,* Oxford university Press, London.

Ghosh, P. (2016). *Ideals of education as envisioned by Tagore and Vivekananda Relevance in the contemporary society.* (Doctoral Dissertation, University of Calcutta) Retrieved April 25, 2020, from http://hdl.handle.net/10603/163914

Gurunathrao, K. (2010). *A comparative study of philosophical and education views ofMaharshi Aurobindo Rabindranath Tagore and Sarvepalli Radhakrishnan with reference to values of life.* (Doctoral Dissertation, Karnatak University Dharwad) Retrieved April 24, 2020, from http://hdl.handle.net/10603/96063

Guthrie. A. (1962), *Madam Ambassador, Life of Vijay Lakshmi Pundit,* Harcourt Brace and World Inc, New York, pp 16.

Halstead, J.M. (2010). Moral Education. In: Clauss-Ehlers, C.S. (eds) Encyclopedia of Cross-Cultural School Psychology. Springer, Boston, MA.

https://www.hindipanda.com/rabindranath-tagore-biography/ retrieved on 13th January 2021.

https://www.tagoreweb.in/Essays/shikkha-73/shikkhar-angikoron-6278

https://www.tagoreweb.in/Essays/shikkha-73/shikkha-o-songskriti-6276

Jalan, R. V. (1976). *Tagore- His Educational Theory and Practice and its impact on Indian Education* (Doctoral Dissertation, University of Florida). Retrieved Apr.22, 2020, from https://archive.org/details/tagorehiseducati00jala/page/n11/mode/2up

Jana, M. (1974). *Educational philosophy of Tagore and its relevance to current educational thought.* (Doctoral Dissertation, University of Calcutta) Retrieved Apr. 24, 2020, from http://hdl.handle.net/10603/158228

Janaiah, C. (2018). *S Radhakrishnan and Rabindranath Tagores Philosophical Perspectives on Education -A Comparative Study.*(Doctoral Dissertation, Osmania

University).Retrieved April 23, 2020, from http://hdl.handle.net/10603/209095

Kabir, H. (1962), *Rabindranath Tagore,* London University, London, , p 11, 56

Khanolkar, J.H. (1963) *The Lute and the Plough: A life of Rabindranath Tagore, translated by Thomas Gay,* The Book Centre Private Limited, Bombay, pp 179, 353.

Kripalini, K. (1962), *Rabindranath Tagore*, Grove Press Inc. New York, pp 19, 22, 90, 78, 64, 267.

Kumar, P. (2018). *Educational Thoughts of J Krishnamurti and Rabindranath Tagore-A comparative study.* (Doctoral Dissertation, Visva Bharati University) Retrieved April 26, 2020, from http://hdl.handle.net/10603/214336

Manjula R., Jeevan Kumar T. (2014). Novels of Rabindranath Tagore - A study. *International Journal of English Language and Literature, Vol.2 No.7* ISSN: 2321-1164 (Online), 2347-2642 (Print), p.267-277

Mondal, J. (2017). Tagore's Education System in Santiniketan: A Geographical Approach for Survival of Mankind. *Imperial Journal of Interdisciplinary Research, 3,* 1399-1404. Retrieved April 22, 2020, from https://pdfs.semanticscholar.org/3133/9d760bd85ff780026

Mukherjee, D. (2017). *The Impact of Drama and Theatre Arts on Academic Performance -An Objective Assessment of Tagore's Principle of Education Target area Birbhum.* (Doctoral Dissertation, Visva Bharati University) Retrieved April 26, 2020, from http://hdl.handle.net/10603/216460

O'Connell, K. M. (2003). 'Rabindranath Tagore on education', *The encyclopedia of pedagogy and informal education.* Retrieved April 22, 2020, from https://infed.org/mobi/rabindranath-tagore-on-education/

Osterling A, *Tagore and the Noble Prize*, Centennial Volume, p 207.

Patel, R. (2015). *Marite Chahi Na Aami.* Ahmedabad: Gurjar Prakashan.

Pathak, S. (2001). *The philosophical strands in Rabindranath Tagore's poetry.*

Periaswami, A (1976) *Rabindranath Tagore's Philosophy of International Education,* submitted to Loyola University of Chicago.

Periaswamy, A. (1976). "Rabindranath Tagore's Philosophy of International Education"

Dissertations.Paper1588.

http://ecommons.luc.edu/luc_diss/1588

Policepatil, B. B. (2011). *A study of education thoughts of Dr Rabindranath Tagore and their relevance to present education system.*(Karnatak University, Dharwad). Retrieved Mar.23, 2020, from http://hdl.handle.net/10603/95956

Purandare, P. (1982). *A critical study of Rabindranath Tagore's educational philosophy.* (Doctoral Dissertation, Savitribai Phule Pune University) RetrievedApr.26, 2020, from http://hdl.handle.net/10603/160388

Pushpanathan, T. (2013). Rabindranath Tagore's philosophy of education and its influence on Indian education. *International Journal of Current Research and Academic Review, 1(4)*, 42-45. Retrieved April 22, 2020 from
https://www.researchgate.net/publication/270791595_Rabindranath_Tagore's_
Philosophy_of_Education_and_its_influence_on_Indian Education

Rabindra Rachanabali, (Reprint 2003), Vol 6, Page 567-572

Rabindra Rachanabali, (Reprint 2003), Volume 17, Page 340-344

Rabindra Rachanabali (Reprint 2003), Volume 10, 573-576

Rabindra Rachanavali, (Reprint 2003), Volume 10, 557-616

Radhakrishnan S. (1919) *Rabindranath Tagore's Philosophy of Education*, MacMillan and Co Limited, London, Retrived Mar.1, 2020, from www.ijhssi.org

Rhys, E. (1916), *Rabindranath Tagore, a Biographical Study*, McMillan & Co, New York, pp 9.

Saha, G. (2013). *Implicit scientific vision and values in educational experiments of Rabindranath Tagore an analysis.* (Doctoral Dissertation, Visva Bharti University) Retrieved April 25, 2020, from http://hdl.handle.net/10603/242345

Satyanarayana P., Phaniraja A., Janardhanreddy K. (2013). Rabindranath Tagore as a Novelist. *International Journal of Humanities and Social Science Invention, 2(1),*18-21. Retrieved Mar.1, 2020, from www.ijhssi.org

Sengupta, S. (2010). *Thoughts of Swami Vivekananda and Rabindranath Tagore and their relevance to education.*

(Doctoral Dissertation, Tripura University) Retrieved Apr.24 2020, from http://hdl.handle.net/10603/202426

Sengupta, S. (2014). *Upanishadic influence on educational thoughts of Rabindranath Tagore, Swami Vivekananda and Sri Aurobindo.* (Doctoral Dissertation, University of Kalyani) Retrieved Apr.24, 2020, from http://hdl.handle.net/10603/63864

Sharma, B. (2017). *A comparative study of the educational philosophy of JJ Rousseau and RN Tagore in present situation* (Doctoral Dissertation, V.B.S. Purvanchal University). Retrieved April 22, 2020, from http://hdl.handle.net/10603/179222

Shukla, S. (2013). *The Philosophy of Education in the Works of Rabindranath Tagore.* (Doctoral Dissertation, University of Allahabad) Retrieved Apr.26, 2020, from http://hdl.handle.net/10603/249558

Singh, P. (2011). *Ravindra Nath Tagore aur Swami Vivekanand ke siksha darshan ka tulnatmak adhyayan ebam vartaman paristhition me uski prasangikta.* (Doctoral Dissertation, V.B.S. Purvanchal University) Retrieved Apr.25, 2020, from http://hdl.handle.net/10603/44904

Som R. (2010) , *Rabindranath Tagore: The Singer and His Song*, Penguin India.

Tagore R. (1961), *Centennial Volume,* Sahitya Akademy, New Delhi, pp 8.

Tagore, R. ((1911/1935) 'Religious Education.' The English Writings of   Rabindranath Tagore, Volume 4, A Miscellany. Ed. Nityapriya Ghosh. Delhi: Sahitya Akademi, 2006. 249-260, 253-257.

Tagore, R. (1915). *Sadhana: The Realization of Life*, The Macmillan   Company.   www.spiritualbee.com/spiritual-book-by-tagore/

Tagore, R. (1917). *Personality.* The Macmillan Company.

Tagore, R. (1921). *Glimpses of Bengal – A selection of Letters*   [e-book].   Retrieved   from http://www.spiritualbee.com/tagore-book-of-letters/

Tagore, R. (1928) 'Letters to a Friend,' The English Writings of Rabindranath   Tagore, Volume 3, A Miscellany. Ed. Sisir Kumar Das. Delhi: Sahitya Akademi, 2006, pp. 219-322

Tagore, R. (2019). *My Reminiscences*. Notion Press.

Tagore, R. (2019). *Nationalism.* Prakash Books India Pvt. Ltd.

Tagore, R. 'The Philosophy of Our People.' The English Writings of   Rabindranath Tagore, Volume 3, A Miscellany. Ed. Sisir Kumar Das. Delhi: Sahitya Akademi, (2006 /1926), 559-569.

Tagore, R. (1913).*Gitanjali*, [e-book]   Retrieved   from www.spiritualbee.com/gitanjali-poems-of-tagore/

Thompson, E. (1948), *Rabindranath Tagore, Poet and Dramatist,* Oxford University Press: London, pp 12, vii, 47.

Thompson, E. (2018) *Rabindranath Tagore, His Life and Work,* Franklin Classic Trade Press.

APPENDIX

(ORIGINAL BANGLA TEXT)

Retrieved from https://www.tagoreweb.in/Essays

শিক্ষার বিকিরণ (shikkhar bikiron)

ভোজ্য জিনিসে ভাণ্ডার উঠল ভরে, রান্নাঘরে হাঁড়ি চড়েছে, তবু ভোজ বলে না তাকে। আঙিনায় পাত পড়ল কত, ডাকা হয়েছে কতজনকে, সেই হিসাবেই ভোজের মর্যাদা। আমরা যে এডুকেশন শব্দটা আবৃত্তি ক'রে মনে মনে খুশি থাকি সেটাতে ভাঁড়ার-ঘরের চেহারা আছে, কিন্তু বাইরে তাকিয়ে দেখি ধূ ধূ করছে আঙিনা। শিক্ষার আলোর জন্য উঁচু লণ্ঠন ঝোলানো হয়েছে ইস্কুলে কলেজে, কিন্তু সেটা যদি রুদ্ধ দেয়ালে বন্দী আলোক হয় তা হলে বলব আমাদের অদৃষ্ট মন্দ। সমস্ত-পট-জোড়া ভূমিকার মধ্যেই ছবির প্রকাশ, তেমনি পরিস্ফুটতা পাবার জন্যে শিক্ষা চায় দেশজোড়া ভূমিকা। ব্যাপক-ভূমিকা-ভ্রষ্ট শিক্ষা কতই অস্পষ্ট, অসম্পূর্ণ, কেবল অভ্যাসবশতই তার দৈন্যের বেদনা আমাদের মন থেকে মরে গিয়েছে। এডুকেশন নিয়ে অন্য দেশের সঙ্গে স্বদেশের যখন তুলনা করি তখন দৃশ্য অংশটাই লক্ষ করি, অদৃশ্য অংশের হিসাব রাখি নে। মিলিয়ে দেখি যুনিভার্সিটি সেখানেও আছে, আমাদের দেশেও তার প্রতিরূপ দুটো-একটা দেখা দিচ্ছে। ভুলে যাই এমন কোনো ভাগ্যবান দেশ নেই যেখানে বাঁধা শিক্ষালয়ের বাইরে সমস্ত সমাজ জুড়ে আবাঁধা শিক্ষার একটা দিগন্তবিকীর্ণ বৃহত্তর পরিধি না আছে।

এক কালে আমাদের দেশেও ছিল। যুরোপের মধ্যযুগের মতো আমাদের দেশে শাস্ত্রিক শিক্ষাই ছিল প্রধান। এই শিক্ষার বিশেষ চর্চা টোলে, চতুষ্পাঠিতে, কিন্তু সমস্ত দেশেই বিস্তীর্ণ ছিল বিদ্যার ভূমিকা। বিশিষ্ট জ্ঞানের সঙ্গে সাধারণ জ্ঞানের নিত্যই ছিল

চলাচল। ওয়েসিসের সঙ্গে মরুভূমির যে বৈপরীত্যের সম্বন্ধ তেমন ছিল না পণ্ডিতমণ্ডলীর সঙ্গে অপণ্ডিত লোকালয়ের। দেশে এমন অনাদৃত অংশ ছিল না, যেখানে রমায়ণ মহাভারত পুরাণকথা ধর্মব্যাখ্যা নানা প্রণালী বেয়ে প্রতিনিয়ত ছড়িয়ে না পড়ত। এমন-কি, যে-সকল তত্ত্বজ্ঞান দর্শনশাস্ত্রে কঠোর অধ্যবসায়ে আলোচিত তারও সেচন চলেছিল সর্বক্ষণ জনসাধারণের চিত্তভূমিতে। গাছের খাদ্য যথেষ্ট-পরিমাণ জল দিয়ে তরল হলে তবেই গাছ তাকে শাখায় প্রশাখায় গ্রহণ করতে পারে, তেমনি করেই সেদিন কঠিন বিদ্যাকে রসে বিগলিত করে সর্বজনের মনে সঞ্চারিত করা হয়েছে। যে সময়ে আমাদের দেশে পূর্তকর্ম ধর্মের অঙ্গ ছিল তখন গ্রামে গ্রামে জলাশয়ের আয়োজন স্বতই ছিল বিস্তৃত, সর্বজনে মিলে আপনিই আপনার তৃষার জল জুগিয়েছে; রাজপরিষদের কোনো ব্যয়কুন্ঠ আমলা-সেরেস্তায় জলের জন্য মাথা খুঁড়তে হয় নি। তেমনি করেই সমাজ দেশের বিদ্যা আপনিই দেশময় বিতরণ করেছে। না যদি করত তবে সমস্ত দেশ আজ বর্বরতায় কালো কর্কশ হয়ে উঠত। বিদ্যা তখন বিদ্বানের সম্পত্তি ছিল না, সে ছিল সমস্ত সমাজের সম্পদ।

যেখানে খবরের কাগজেরও পত্রমর্মর শোনা যায় না এমন একটি সামান্য গ্রামে চাষিরা একদিন আমাকে নিমন্ত্রণ করেছিল। সেখানে প্রায় সকলেই মুসলমান। আমার অভ্যর্থনা উপলক্ষে চলছিল একটা গানের পালা। চাঁদোয়ার তলায় কেরোসিন-লণ্ঠন জ্বলছে, মাটির উপর ছেলে বুড়ো সকলেই বসে আছে স্তব্ধ হয়ে। যাত্রাগানের প্রধান বিষয়টা গুরু-শিষ্যের মধ্যে তত্ত্বালোচনা--দেহতত্ত্ব, সৃষ্টিতত্ত্ব, মুক্তিতত্ত্ব। থেকে থেকে তারই সঙ্গে নাচ গান কৌতুকের দ্রুতমুখরিত ঝংকার। এই পালার একটি বিশেষ অংশ আজও আমার মনে আছে। কথাটা এই, যাত্রী প্রবেশ করতে চলেছে বৃন্দাবনে, পাহারাওয়ালা আটক করলে তার পথ; বললে, "তুমি চোর, ভিতরে তোমাকে যেতে দেওয়া হবে না।' যাত্রী বললে, "সে কী কথা, কোথায় দেখলে আমার চোরাই মাল।' দ্বারী, বললে, "ঐ- যে তোমার কাপড়ের নীচে লুকানো, ঐ-যে তোমার আপনি, ওটা

ষোলো-আনা আমার রাজার পাওনা, ফাঁকি দিয়ে রেখেছ নিজেরই জিম্মায়।' এই বলতে বলতে মহা ঢাক ঢোল বেজে উঠল, চলল পরচুলো ঝাঁকানি দিয়ে ঘন ঘন নাচ। যেন ঐখানটা পাঠের প্রধান অংশ, অধ্যাপকমশায় পেন্সিলের মোটা দাগ ডবল ক'রে টেনে দিলেন। রাত এগোতে লাগল, দুপুর পেরিয়ে একটা বাজে, শ্রোতারা স্থির হয়ে বসে শুনছে। সব কথা স্পষ্ট বুঝুক বা না বুঝুক, এমন একটা-কিছুর স্বাদ পাচ্ছে যেটা প্রতিদিনের নীরস তুচ্ছতা ভেদ করে পথ খুলে দিলে চিরন্তনের দিকে।

এমনি কতকাল চলছে দেশে; বারবার বিচিত্র বিচিত্র রসের যোগে লোকে শুনেছে ধ্রুব-প্রহ্লাদের কথা, সীতার বনবাস, কর্ণের কবচদান, হরিশচন্দ্রের সর্বস্বত্যাগ। তখন দুঃখ ছিল অনেক, অবিচার ছিল, জীবনযাত্রার অনিশ্চয়তা ছিল পদে পদে, কিন্তু সেইসঙ্গে এমন একটি শিক্ষার প্রবাহ ছিল যাতে করে ভাগ্যের বিমুখতার মধ্যে মানুষকে তার আন্তরিক সম্পদের অবারিত পথ দেখিয়েছে, মানুষের যে শ্রেষ্ঠতাকে অবস্থার হীনতায় হেয় করতে পারে না তার পরিচয়কে উজ্জ্বল করেছে। আর যাই হোক, আমেরিকান টকির দ্বারা এ কাজটা হয় না।

অন্য সকল দেশে আবশ্যিক শিক্ষার প্রবর্তন হয়েছে অল্পদিন হল। আমাদের দেশে যে জনশিক্ষা তাকে আবশ্যিক বলব না, তাকে বলব স্বেচ্ছিক। সে অনেক কালের। তার পশ্চাতে কোনো আইন ছিল না, তাগিদ ছিল না; তার স্বতঃসঞ্চার ছিল ঘরে ঘরে যেমন রক্তচলাচল হয় সর্বদেহে।

তার পরে সময়ের পরিবর্তন হল। ইতিমধ্যে শিক্ষিতসমাজ যখন রাজদ্বারের দিকে মুখ ফিরিয়ে মন্ত্রিসভায় প্রবেশাধিকারের আবেদন কখনো-বা রুদ্ধকণ্ঠে কখনো-বা কৃত্রিম আক্রোশে পেশ করছিলেন তখন তাঁদের পিছনের দিকে গ্রামে গ্রামে পিপাসার জল এল পাঁকের কাছে নেমে, এ দিকে শহরে শহরে দ্বারে দ্বারে ঝরতে লাগল কলের জল। আমরা বিস্মিত হয়ে বললেম, একেই বলে উন্নতি। দেশের যেটা বৃহৎ রূপ সেটা লুকোল আমাদের

আগোচরে, যে প্রাণ যে আলো দেশের সর্বত্র বিকীর্ণ ছিল সেটা প্রতিসংহত হল ছোটো ছোটো কেন্দ্রে।

এ কালে যাকে আমরা এডুকেশন বলি তার আরম্ভ শহরে। তার পিছনে ব্যাবসা ও চাকরি চলেছে আনুষঙ্গিক হয়ে। এই বিদেশী শিক্ষাবিধি রেলকামরার দীপের মতো। কামরাটা উজ্জ্বল, কিন্তু যে যোজন যোজন পথ গাড়ি চলেছে ছুটে সেটা অন্ধকারে লুপ্ত। কারখানার গাড়িটাই যেন সত্য, আর প্রাণবেদনায় পূর্ণ সমস্ত দেশটাই যেন অবাস্তব।

শহরবাসী একদল মানুষ এই সুযোগে শিক্ষা পেলে মান পেলে, অর্থ পেলে, তারাই হল এন্‌লাইটেন্‌ড়, আলোকিত। সেই আলোর পিছনে বাকি দেশটাতে লাগল পূর্ণ গ্রহণ। ইস্কুলের বেঞ্চিতে বসে যাঁরা ইংরেজি পড়া মুখস্থ করলেন শিক্ষাদীপ্ত দৃষ্টির অন্ধতায় তাঁরা দেশ বলতে বুঝলেন শিক্ষিতসমাজ, ময়ূর বলতে বুঝলেন তার পেখমটা, হাতি বলতে তার গজদন্ত। সেই দিন থেকে জলকষ্ট বলো, পথকষ্ট বলো, রোগ বলো, অজ্ঞান বলো, জমে উঠল কাংস্যবাদ্যমন্দ্রিত নাট্যমঞ্চের নেপথ্যে নিরানন্দ নিরালোক গ্রামে গ্রামে। নগরী হল সুজলা, সুফলা, টানাপাখা-শীতলা; সেইখানেই মাথা তুললে আরোগ্যনিকেতন, শিক্ষার প্রাসাদ। দেশের বুকে এক প্রান্ত থেকে আর-এক প্রান্তে এত বড়ো বিচ্ছেদের ছুরি আর-কোনোদিন চালানো হয় নি, সে কথা মনে রাখতে হবে। আধুনিকের লক্ষণ বলে নিন্দা করলে চলবে না। কেননা কোনো সভ্য দেশেরই অবস্থা এরকম নয়। আধুনিকতা সেখানে সপ্তমীর চাঁদের মতো অর্ধেক আলোয় অর্ধেক অন্ধকারে খণ্ডিত হয়ে নেই। জাপানে পাশ্চাত্য বিদ্যার সংস্রব ভারতবর্ষের চেয়ে অল্প কালের, কিন্তু সেখানে সেটা তালি-দেওয়া ছেঁড়া কাঁথা নয়। সেখানে পরিব্যাপ্ত বিদ্যার প্রভাবে সমস্ত দেশের মনে চিন্তা করবার শক্তি অবিচ্ছিন্ন সঞ্চারিত। এই চিন্তা এক ছাঁচে ঢালা নয়। আধুনিক কালেরই লক্ষণ অনুসারে এই চিন্তায় বৈচিত্র্য আছে অথচ ঐক্যও আছে, সেই ঐক্য যুক্তির ঐক্য।

কেউ কেউ তথ্য গণনা করে দেখিয়েছেন, পূর্বকালে এ দেশে গ্রাম্য পাঠশালায় প্রাথমিক শিক্ষার যে উদ্যোগ ছিল ব্রিটিশ শাসনে ক্রমেই তা কমেছে। কিন্তু, তার চেয়ে সর্বনেশে ক্ষতি হয়েছে, জনশিক্ষাবিধির সহজ পথগুলি লোপ পেয়ে আসাতে। শোনা যায়, একদিন বাংলাদেশ জুড়ে নানা শাখায় খাল কাটা হয়েছিল অতি আশ্চর্য নৈপুণ্যে; হাল আমলের অনাদরে এবং নির্বুদ্ধিায় সে-সমস্ত বদ্ধ হয়ে গেছে বলেই তাদের কূলে কূলে এত চিতা আজ জ্বলেছে। তেমনি এ দেশে শিক্ষার খালগুলোও গেল বদ্ধ হয়ে, আর অন্তর-বাহিরে সমস্ত দীনতা বল পেয়ে উঠেছে। শিক্ষার একটা বড়ো সমস্যার সমাধান হয়েছিল আমাদের দেশে। শাসনের শিক্ষা আনন্দের শিক্ষা হয়ে দেশের হৃদয়ে প্রবেশ করেছিল, মিলেছিল সমস্ত সমাজের প্রাণক্রিয়ার সঙ্গে। দেশব্যাপী সেই প্রাণের খাদ্যে আজ দুর্ভিক্ষ। পূর্বসঞ্চয় কিছু বাকি আছে, তাই এখনো দেখতে পাচ্ছিনে এর মারমূর্তি।

মধ্য-এশিয়ার মরুভূমিতে সে-সব পর্যটক প্রাচীন যুগের চিহ্ন সন্ধান করেছেন তাঁরা দেখেছেন, সেখানে কত সমৃদ্ধ জনপদ আজ বালি চাপা পবে হারিয়ে গেছে। এক কালে সে-সব জায়গায় জলের সঞ্চয় ছিল, নদীর রেখাও পাওয়া যায়। কখন রস এল শুকিয়ে, এক-পা এক-পা করে এগিয়ে এল মরু, শুষ্ক রসনা মেলে লেহন করে নিল প্রাণ, লোকালয়ের শেষ স্বাক্ষর মিলিয়ে গেল অসীম পাণ্ডুরতার মধ্যে। বিলুপ্তসংখ্যক গ্রাম দিয়ে আমাদের যে দেশ সেই দেশের মনোভূমিতেও রসের জোগান আজ অবসিত। যে রস অনেক কাল থেকে নিম্ন স্তরে ব্যাপ্ত হয়ে আছে তাও দিনে দিনে শুষ্ক বাতাসের উষ্ণ নিশ্বাসে উবে যাবে, অবশেষে প্রাণনাশা মরু অগ্রসর হয়ে তৃষার অজগর সাপের মতো পাকে পাকে গ্রাস করতে থাকবে আমাদের এই গ্রামে-গাঁথা দেশকে। এই মরুর আক্রমণটা আমাদের চোখে পড়ছে না, কেননা, বিশেষ শিক্ষার গতিকেই দেশ-দেখা চোখ আমরা হারিয়েছি; গবাক্ষলন্ঠনের আলোর মতো আমাদের সমস্ত দৃষ্টির কেন্দ্রীভূত শিক্ষিতসমাজের দিকে।

আমি একদিন দীর্ঘকাল ছিলুম বাংলাদেশের গ্রামের নিকটসংস্রবে। গরমের সময়ে একটা দুঃখের দৃশ্য পড়ত চোখে। নদীর জল গিয়েছে নেমে, তীরে মাটি গিয়েছে ফেটে, বেরিয়ে পড়েছে পাড়ার পুকুরের পঙ্কস্তর, ধূ ধূ করছে তপ্ত বালু। মেয়েরা বহুদূর পথ থেকে ঘড়ায় করে নদীর জল বয়ে আনছে, সেই জল বাংলাদেশের অশ্রুজলমিশ্রিত। গ্রামে আগুন লাগলে নিবোবার উপায় পাওয়া যায় না; ওলাউঠা দেখা দিলে নিবারণ করা দুঃসাধ্য হয়ে ওঠে।

এই গেল এক, আর-এক দুঃখের বেদনা আমার মনে বেজেছিল। সন্ধে হয়ে এসেছে, সমস্ত দিনের কাজ শেষ করে চাষিরা ফিরেছে ঘরে। এক দিকে বিস্তৃত মাঠের উপর নিস্তব্ধ অন্ধকার, আর-এক দিকে বাঁশঝাড়ের মধ্যে এক-একটি গ্রাম যেন রাত্রির বন্যার মধ্যে জেগে আছে ঘনতর অন্ধকারের দ্বীপের মতো। সেই দিক থেকে শোনা যায় খোলের শব্দ, আর তারই সঙ্গে একটানা সুরে কীর্তনের কোনো-একটা পদের হাজারবার তারস্বরে আবৃত্তি। শুনে মনে হত, এখানেও চিওজলাশয়ের জল তলায় এসে পড়েছে। তাপ বাড়ছে, কিন্তু ঠাণ্ডা করবার উপায় কতটুকুই বা! বছরের পর বছর যে অবস্থা-দৈন্যের মধ্যে দিন কাটে তাতে কী করে প্রাণ বাঁচবে যদি মাঝে মাঝে এটা অনুভব না করা যায় যে, হাড়ভাঙা মজুরির উপরেও মন বলে মানুষের একটা-কিছু আছে যেখানে তার অপমানের উপশম, দুর্ভাগ্যের দাসত্ব এড়িয়ে যেখানে হাঁফ ছাড়বার জায়গা পাওয়া যায়! তাকে সেই তৃপ্তি দেবার জন্যে একদিন সমস্ত সমাজ প্রভূত আয়োজন করেছিল। তার কারণ, সমাজ এই বিপুল জনসাধারণকে স্বীকার করে নিয়েছিল আপন লোক ব'লে। জানত এরা নেমে গেলে সমস্ত দেশ যায় নেমে। আজ মনের উপবাস ঘোচাবার জন্যে কেউ তাদের কিছুমাত্র সাহায্য করে না। তাদের আত্মীয় নেই, তারা নিজে নিজেই আগেকার দিনের তলানি নিয়ে কোনোমতে একটু সান্ত্বনা পাবার চেষ্টা করে। আর-কিছুদিন পরে এটুকুও যাবে শেষ হয়ে; সমস্ত দিনের দুঃখধন্দার রিক্ত প্রান্তে নিরানন্দ ঘরে আলো জ্বলবে না, সেখানে গান উঠবে না আকাশে। ঝিল্লি ডাকবে বাঁশবনে,

ঝোপঝাড়ের মধ্য থেকে শেয়ালের ডাক উঠবে প্রহরে প্রহরে; আর সেই সময় শহরে শিক্ষাভিমানীর দল বৈদ্যুত আলোয় সিনেমা দেখতে ভিড় করবে।

এক দিকে আমাদের দেশে সনাতন শিক্ষার ব্যাপ্তি রুদ্ধ হয়ে জনসাধারণের মধ্যে জ্ঞানের অনাবৃষ্টি চিরকালীন হয়ে দাঁড়ালো, অন্য দিকে আধুনিক কালের নতুন বিদ্যার যে আবির্ভাব হল তার প্রবাহ বইল না সর্বজনীন দেশের অভিমুখে। পাথরে-গাঁথা কুণ্ডের মতো স্থানে স্থানে সে আবদ্ধ হয়ে রইল; তীর্থের পাণ্ডাকে দর্শনী দিয়ে দূর থেকে এসে গণ্ডুষ ভর্তি করতে হয়, নানা নিয়মে তার আটঘাট বাঁধা। মন্দাকিনী থাকেন শিবের ঘোরালো জটাজুটের মধ্যে বিশেষভাবে; তবুও দেবললাট থেকে তিনি তাঁর ধারা নামিয়ে দেন, ব'হে যান সাধারণভাবে ঘাটে ঘাটে মর্তজনের দ্বারের সম্মুখ দিয়ে, ঘটে ঘটে ভরে দেন আপন প্রসাদ। কিন্তু আমাদের দেশে প্রবাসিনী আধুনিকী বিদ্যা তেমন নয়। তার আছে বিশিষ্ট রূপ, সাধারণ রূপ নেই। সেইজন্যে ইংরেজি শিখে যাঁরা বিশিষ্টতা পেয়েছেন তাঁদের মনের মিল হয় না সর্বসাধারণের সঙ্গে। দেশে সকলের চেয়ে বড়ো জাতিভেদ এইখানেই শ্রেণীতে শ্রেণীতে অস্পৃশ্যতা।

ইংরেজি ভাষায় অবগুণ্ঠিত বিদ্যা স্বভাবতই আমাদের মনের সহবর্তিনী হয়ে চলতে পারে না। সেইজন্যেই আমরা অনেকেই যে পরিমাণে শিক্ষা পই সে পরিমাণে বিদ্যা পাই নে। চার দিকের আবহাওয়ার থেকে এ বিদ্যা বিচ্ছিন্ন; আমাদের ঘর আর ইস্কুলের মধ্যে ট্রাম চলে, মন চলে না। ইস্কুলের বাইরে পড়ে আছে আমাদের দেশ; সেই দেশে ইস্কুলের প্রতিবাদ রয়েছে বিস্তর, সহযোগিতা নেই বললেই হয়। সেই বিচ্ছেদে আমাদের ভাষা ও চিন্তা অধিকাংশ স্থলেই ইস্কুলের ছেলের মতোই। ঘুচল না আমাদের নোটবইয়ের শাসন, আমাদের বিচারবুদ্ধিতে নেই সাহস; আছে নজির মিলিয়ে অতি সাবধানে পা ফেলে চলা। শিক্ষার সঙ্গে দেশের মনের সহজ মিলন ঘটাবার আয়োজন আজ পর্যন্ত

হল না। যেন কনে রইল বাপের বাড়ির অন্তঃপুরে; শ্বশুরবাড়ি নদীর ও পারে বালির চর পেরিয়ে। খেয়া-নৌকাটা গেল কোথায়?

পারাপারের একখানা ডোঙা দেখিয়ে দেওয়া হয়, তাকে বলে সাহিত্য। এ কথা মানতেই হবে, আধুনিক বঙ্গসাহিত্য বর্তমান যুগের অন্নে বস্ত্রে মানুষ। এই সাহিত্য আমাদের মনে লাগিয়েছে এ কালের ছোঁওয়া, কিন্তু খাদ্য তো ও পার থেকে পুরোপুরি বহন করে আনছে না। যে বিদ্যা বর্তমান যুগের চিত্তশক্তিকে বিচিত্র আকারে প্রকাশ করছে, উদ্‌ঘাটন করছে বিশ্বরহস্যের নব নব প্রবেশদ্বার, বাংলাসাহিত্যের পাড়ায় তার যাওয়া-আসা নেই বললেই হয়। চিন্তা করে যে মন, যে মন বিচার করে, বুদ্ধির সঙ্গে ব্যবহারের যোগসাধন করে যে, সে পড়ে আছে পূর্ব-যুগান্তরে; আর যে মন রসসম্ভোগ করে সে যাতায়াত শুরু করেছে আধুনিক ভোরে নিমন্ত্রণশালার আঙিনায়। স্বভাবতই তার ঝোঁক পড়েছে সেই দিকটাতে যে দিকে চলেছে মদের পরিবেশন, যেখানে ঝাঁঝালো গন্ধে বাতাস হয়েছে মাতাল।

গল্প কবিতা নাটক নিয়ে বাংলাসাহিত্যের পনেরো-আনা আয়োজন। অর্থাৎ ভোজের আয়োজন, শক্তির আয়োজন নয়। পাশ্চাত্য দেশের চিত্তোৎকর্ষ বিচিত্র চিত্তশক্তির প্রবল সমবায় নিয়ে। মনুষ্যত্ব সেখানে দেহ মন প্রাণের সকল দিকেই ব্যাপৃত। তাই সেখানে যদি ক্রুটি থাকে তো পূর্তিও আছে। বটগাছের কোনো ডাল বা ঝড়ে ভাঙল, কোনোখানে বা পোকায় ছিদ্র করেছে, কোনো বৎসর বা বৃষ্টির কার্পণ্য, কিন্তু সবসুদ্ধ জড়িয়ে বনস্পতি জমিয়ে রেখেছে আপন স্বাস্থ্য, আপন বলিষ্ঠতা। তেমনি পাশ্চাত্য দেশের মনকে ক্রিয়াবান করে রেখেছে তার বিদ্যা, তার শিক্ষা, তার সাহিত্য, সমস্ত মিলে; তার কর্মশক্তির অক্লান্ত উৎকর্ষ ঘটিয়েছে এই-সমস্তের উৎকর্ষ।

আমাদের সাহিত্যে রসেরই প্রাধান্য। সেইজন্যে যখন কোনা অসংযম কোনো চিত্তবিকার অনুকরণের নালা বেয়ে এই সাহিত্যে

প্রবেশ করে তখন সেটাই একান্ত হয়ে ওঠে, কল্পনাকে রুগ্ণ বিলাসিতার দিকে গাঁজিয়ে তোলে। প্রবল পরাণশক্তি জাগ্রত না থাকলে দেহের ক্ষুদ্র বিকার কথায় কথায় বিষফোড়া হয়ে রাঙিয়ে ওঠে। আমাদের দেশে সেই আশঙ্কা। এ নিয়ে দোষ দিলে আমরা নজির দেখাই পাশ্চাত্য সমাজের; বলি, এটাই তো সভ্যতার আধুনিকতম পরিণতি। কিন্তু সেইসঙ্গে সকল দিকে আধুনিক সভ্যতার যে সচিন্ত সচল প্রবল বৃহৎ সমগ্রতা আছে সেটার কথা চাপা রাখি।

একদা পাড়াগাঁয়ে যখন বাস করতুম তখন সাধু সাধকের বেশ ধারী কেউ কেউ আমার কাছে আসত; তারা সাধনার নামে উচ্ছৃঙ্খল ইন্দ্রিয়চর্চার সংবাদ আমাকে জানিয়েছে। তাতে ধর্মের প্রশ্রয় ছিল। তাদেরই কাছে শুনেছি, এই প্রশ্রয় সুরঙ্গপথে শহর পর্যন্ত গোপনে শিষ্যে প্রশিষ্যে শাখায়িত। এই পৌরুষনাশী ধর্মনামধারী লালসার লোলতা ব্যাপ্ত হবার প্রধান কারণ এই যে, আমাদের সাহিত্যে সমাজে সেই-সমস্ত উপাদানের দিকে মনের ঔৎসুক্য জাগিয়ে রাখতে পারে।

এজন্যে অন্তত বাঙালি সাহিত্যিকদের দোষ দেওয়া যায় না। আমাদের সাহিত্য সারগর্ভ নয় বলে একে নিন্দা করা সহজ, কিন্তু কী করলে একে সারালো করা যায় তার পন্থা নির্ণয় করা তত সহজ নয়। রুচির সম্বন্ধে লোকে বেপরোয়া, কেননা ও দিকে কোনো শাসন নেই। অশিক্ষিত রুচিও রসের সামগ্রী থেকে যা-হোক-কোনো-একটা আস্বাদন পায়। আর, যদি সে মনে করে তারই বোধ রসবোধের চরম আদর্শ তবে তা নিয়ে তর্ক তুললে ফৌজদারি পর্যন্ত পৌঁছতে পারে। কবিতা গল্প নাটকের বাজারের দিকে যারা সমজদারের রাজপথটা পায় নি অন্তত তারা আনাড়িপাড়ার মাঠ দিয়েও চলতে পারে, কোনো মাশুল দিতে হয় না কোথাও। কিন্তু যে বিদ্যা মননের সেখানে কড়া পাহারার সিংহদ্বার পেরিয়ে যেতে হয়, মাঠ পেরিয়ে নয়। যে-সব দেশের 'পরে লক্ষ্মী প্রসন্ন, এবং সরস্বতীও, তারা সেই বিদ্যার দিকে নতুন

নতুন পথ পাকা করছে প্রত্যহ; পণ্যের আদানপ্রদান চলছে দূরে নিকটে, ঘরে বাইরে। আমাদের দেশেও তো বিলম্ব করলে চলবে না।

বিশ্ববিদ্যালয়ের রূপ (bishwabidyalayer rup)

অপরিচিত আসনে অনভ্যস্ত কর্তব্যে কলিকাতা বিশ্ববিদ্যালয় আমাকে আহ্বান করেছেন। তার প্রত্যুত্তরে আমি আমার সাদর অভিবাদন জানাই।

এই উপলক্ষে নিজের ন্যূনতা-প্রকাশ হয়তো শোভন রীতি। কিন্তু প্রথার এই অলংকারগুলি বস্তুত শোভন নয়, এবং তা নিষ্ফল। কর্তব্যক্ষেত্রে প্রবেশ করার উপক্রমেই আগে থাকতে ক্ষমা প্রার্থনা ক'রে রাখলে সাধারণের মন অনুকূল হতে পারে, এই ব্যর্থ আশার ছলনায় মনকে ভোলাতে চাই নে। ক্ষমা প্রার্থনা করলেই অযোগ্যতার ত্রুটি সংশোধন হয় না, তাতে কেবল ত্রুটি স্বীকার করাই হয়। যাঁরা অকরুণ তাঁরা সেটাকে বিনয় ব'লে গ্রহণ করেন না, আত্মগ্লানি বলেই গণ্য করেন।

যে কর্মে আমাকে আমন্ত্রণ করা হয়েছে সে সম্বন্ধে আমার সম্বল কী আছে তা কারো অগোচর নেই। অতএব ধরে নিতে পারি, কর্মটি আমার যে উপযুক্ত সে বিচার কর্তৃপক্ষদের দ্বারা পূর্বেই হয়ে গেছে।

এই ব্যবস্থার মধ্যে কিছু নূতনত্ব আছে--তার থেকে অনুমান করা যায়, বিশ্ববিদ্যালয়ের মধ্যে সম্প্রতি কোনো-একটি নূতন সংকল্পের সূচনা হয়েছে। হয়তো মহৎ তার গুরুত্ব। এইজন্য সুস্পষ্টরূপে তাকে উপলব্ধি করা চাই।

বহুকাল থেকে কোনো-একটি বিশেষ পরিচয়ে আমি সাধারণের দৃষ্টির সম্মুখে দিন কাটিয়েছি। আমি সাহিত্যিক; অতএব, সাহিত্যিকরূপেই আমাকে এখানে আহ্বান করা হয়েছে এ কথা

স্বীকার করতেই হবে। সাহিত্যিকের পদবী আমার পক্ষে নিরুদ্বেগের বিষয় নয়, বহু দিনের কঠোর অভিজ্ঞতায় সে আমি নিশ্চিত জানি। সাহিত্যিকের সমাদর রুচির উপরে নির্ভর করে, যুক্তিপ্রমাণের উপর নয়। এ ভিত্তি কোথাও কাঁচা, কোথাও পাকা, কোথাও কুটিল; সর্বত্র এ সমান ভার সয় না। তাই বলি কবির কীর্তি কীর্তিস্তম্ভ নয়, সে কীর্তিতরণী। আবর্তসংকুল বহুদীর্ঘ কালস্রোতের সকল পরীক্ষা সকল সংকট উত্তীর্ণ হয়েও যদি তার এগিয়ে চলা বন্ধ না হয়, অন্তত নোঙর ক'রে থাকবার একটা ভদ্র ঘাট যদি সে পায়, তবেই সাহিত্যের পাকা খাতায় কোনো-একটা বর্গে তার নাম চিহ্নিত হতে পারে। ইতিমধ্যে লোকের মুখে মুখে নানা অনুকূল প্রতিকূল বাতাসের আঘাত খেতে খেতে তাকে ঢেউ কাটিয়ে চলতে হবে। মহাকালের বিচারদরবারে চূড়ান্ত শুনানির লগ্ন ঘণ্টায় ঘণ্টায় ঘটে না, বৈতরণীর পরপারে তাঁর বিচারসভা।

বিশ্ববিদ্যালয়ে বিদ্বানের আসন চিরপ্রসিদ্ধ। সেই পাণ্ডিত্যের গৌরব-গম্ভীর পদে সহসা সাহিত্যিককে বসানো হল। সুতরাং এই রীতিবিপর্যয় অত্যন্ত বেশি ক'রে চোখে পড়বার বিষয় হয়েছে। এরকম বহুতীক্ষ্ণদৃষ্টি-সংকুল কুশাঙ্কুরিত পথে সহজে চলাফেরা করা আমার চেয়ে অনেক শক্ত মানুষের পক্ষেও দুঃসাধ্য। আমি যদি পণ্ডিত হতুম তবে নানা লোকের সম্মতি-অসম্মতির দ্বন্দ্ব সত্ত্বেও পথের বাধা কঠোর হত না। কিন্তু স্বভাবতই এবং অভ্যাসবশতই আমার চলন অব্যবসায়ীর চালে। বাহির থেকে আমি এসেছি আগন্তুক, এইজন্য প্রশ্রয় প্রত্যাশা করতে আমার ভরসা হয় না।

অথচ আমাকে নির্বাচন করার মধ্যেই আমার সম্বন্ধে একটি অভয়পত্রী প্রচ্ছন্ন আছে, সেই আশ্বাসের আভাস পূর্বেই দিয়েছি। নিঃসন্দেহ আমি এখানে চলে এসেছি কোনো-একটি ঋতুপরিবর্তনের মুখে। পুরাতনের সঙ্গে আমার অসংগতি থাকতে

পারে, কিন্তু নূতন বিধানের নবোদ্যম হয়তো আমাকে তার আনুচর্যে গ্রহণ করতে অপ্রসন্ন হবে না।

বিশ্ববিদ্যালয়ের কর্মক্ষেত্রে প্রথম-পদার্পণ-কালে এই কথাটির আলোচনা ক'রে অন্যের কাছে না হোক, অন্তত নিজের কাছে বিষয়টিকে স্পষ্ট ক'রে তোলার প্রয়োজন আছে। অতএব, আমাকে জড়িত করে যে ব্রতটির উপক্রম হল তার ভূমিকা এখানে স্থির করে নিই।

বিশ্ববিদ্যালয় একটি বিশেষ সাধনার ক্ষেত্র। সাধারণভাবে বলা চলে, সে সাধনা বিদ্যার সাধনা। কিন্তু তা বললে কথাটা সুনির্দিষ্ট হয় না; কেননা বিদ্যা শব্দের অর্থ ব্যাপক এবং তার সাধনা বহুবিচিত্র।

এ দেশে আমাদের বিশ্ববিদ্যালয়ের একটি বিশেষ আকার প্রকার ক্রমশ পরিণতি হয়ে উঠেছে। ভারতবর্ষের আধুনিক ইতিহাসেই তার মূল নিহিত। এই উপলক্ষে তার বিস্তারিত বিচার অসংগত হবে না। বাল্যকাল হতে যাঁরা এই বিদ্যালয়ের নিকট-সংস্রবে আছেন তাঁরা আপন অভ্যাস ও মমত্বের বেষ্টনী থেকে ছাড়িয়ে নিয়ে একে বৃহৎ কালের পরিপ্রেক্ষণিকায় দেখতে হয়তো কিছু বাধা পেতে পারেন। সামীপ্যের এবং অভ্যাসের সম্বন্ধ না থাকাতে আমার পক্ষে সেই ব্যক্তিগত বাধা নেই; অতএব আমার অসংসক্ত মনে এর স্বরূপ কিরকম প্রতিভাত হচ্ছে সেটা সকলের পক্ষে স্বীকার করবার যোগ্য না হলেও বিচার করবার যোগ্য।

বলা বাহুল্য, য়ুরোপীয় ভাষায় যাকে য়ুনিভার্সিটি বলে প্রধানত তার উদ্ভব য়ুরোপে। অর্থাৎ য়ুনিভর্সিটির যে চেহারার সঙ্গে আমাদের আধুনিক পরিচয় এবং যার সঙ্গে আধুনিক শিক্ষিতসমাজের ব্যবহার সেটা সমূলে ও শাখা-প্রশাখায় বিলিতি। আমাদের দেশের অনেক ফলের গাছকে আমরা বিলিতি বিশেষণ দিয়ে থাকি, কিন্তু দিশি গাছের সঙ্গে তাদের কুলগত প্রভেদ থাকলেও প্রকৃতিগত ভেদ নেই। আজ পর্যন্ত আমাদের

বিশ্ববিদ্যালয় সম্বন্ধে সে কথা সম্পূর্ণ বলা চলবে না। তার নামকরণ, তার রূপকরণ, এ দেশের সঙ্গে সংগত নয়; এ দেশের আবহাওয়ায় তার স্বভাবীকরণও ঘটে নি।

অথচ এই য়ুনিভর্সিটির প্রথম প্রতিরূপ একদিন ভারতবর্ষেই দেখা দিয়েছিল। নালন্দা বিক্রমশিলা তক্ষশিলার বিদ্যায়তন কবে প্রতিষ্ঠিত হয়েছিল তার নিশ্চিত কালনির্ণয় এখনো হয় নি, কিন্তু ধরে নেওয়া যেতে পারে যে, য়ুরোপীয় য়ুনিভর্সিটির পূর্বেই তাদের আবির্ভাব। তাদের উদ্ভব ভারতীয় চিত্তের আন্তরিক প্রেরণায়, স্বভাবের অনিবার্য আবেগে। তার পূর্ববর্তী কালে বিদ্যার সাধনা ও শিক্ষা বিচিত্র আকারে ও বিবিধ প্রণালীতে দেশে নানা স্থানে ব্যাপ্ত হয়েছিল, এ কথা সুনিশ্চিত। সমাজের সেই সর্বত্রপরিকীর্ণ সাধনাই পুঞ্জীভূত কেন্দ্রীভূত রূপে এক সময়ে স্থানে স্থানে দেখা দিল।

এর থেকে মনে পড়ে ভারতবর্ষে বেদব্যাসের যুগ, মহাভারতের কাল। দেশে যে বিদ্যা, যে মননধারা, যে ইতিহাসকথা দূরে দূরে বিক্ষিপ্ত ছিল, এমন-কি দিগন্তের কাছে বিলীনপ্রায় হয়ে এসেছে, এক সময়ে তাকে সংগ্রহ করা তাকে সংহত করার নিরতিশয় আগ্রহ জেগেছিল সমস্ত দেশের মনে। নিজের চিৎপ্রকর্ষের যুগব্যাপী ঐশ্বর্যকে সুস্পষ্টরূপে নিজের গোচর করতে না পারলে তা ক্রমশ অনাদরে অপরিচয়ে জীর্ণ হয়ে বিলুপ্ত হয়। কোনো-এক কালে এই আশঙ্কায় দেশ সচেতন হয়ে উঠেছিল; দেশ একান্ত ইচ্ছা করেছিল, আপন সূত্রচ্ছিন্ন রত্নগুলিকে উদ্ধার করতে, সংগ্রহ করতে, তাকে সূত্রবদ্ধ করে সমগ্র করতে এবং তাকে সর্বলোকের ও সর্বকালের ব্যবহারে উৎসর্গ করতে। দেশ আপন বিরাট চিন্ময়ী প্রকৃতিকে প্রত্যক্ষরূপে সমাজে স্থিরপ্রতিষ্ঠ করতে উৎসুক হয়ে উঠল। যা আবদ্ধ ছিল বিশেষ বিশেষ পণ্ডিতের অধিকারে তাকেই অনবচ্ছিন্নরূপে সর্বসাধারণের আয়ত্তগোচর করবার এই এক আশ্চর্য অধ্যাবসায়। এর মধ্যে একটি প্রবল চেষ্টা, অক্লান্ত সাধনা, একটি সমগ্রদৃষ্টি ছিল। এই উদ্যোগের মহিমাকে শক্তিমতী প্রতিভা

আপন লক্ষ্যীভূত করেছিল, তার স্পষ্ট প্রমাণ পাওয়া যায় মহাভারত নামটিতেই। মহাভারতের মহৎ সমুজ্জ্বল রূপ যাঁরা ধ্যানে দেখেছিল "মহাভারত' নামকরণ তাঁদেরই কৃত। সেই রূপটি একই কালে ভৌমিঙুলিক রূপ এবং মানস রূপ। ভারতবর্ষের মনকে দেখেছিলেন তাঁরা মনে। সেই বিশ্বদৃষ্টির প্রবল আনন্দে তাঁরা ভারতবর্ষে চিরকালের শিক্ষার প্রশস্ত ভূমি পত্তন করে দিলেন। সে শিক্ষা ধর্মে কর্মে রাজনীতিতে সমাজনীতিতে তত্ত্বজ্ঞানে বহুব্যাপক। তার পর থেকে ভারতবর্ষ আপন নির্ঠুর ইতিহাসের হাতে আঘাতের পর আঘাত পেয়েছে, তার মর্মগ্রন্থি বার বার বিশ্লিষ্ট হয়ে গেছে, দৈন্য এবং অপমানে সে জর্জর কিন্তু ইতিহাসবিস্মৃত সেই যুগের সেই কীর্তি এতকাল লোকশিক্ষার অবাধ জলসেকপ্রণালীকে নানা ধারায় পূর্ণ ও সচল করে রেখেছে। গ্রামে গ্রামে ঘরে ঘরে তার প্রভাব আজও বিরাজমান। সেই মূল প্রস্রবণ থেকে এই শিক্ষার ধারা যদি নিরন্তর প্রবাহিত না হত তা হল দুঃখে দারিদ্র্যে অসম্মানে দেশ বর্বরতার অন্ধকূপে মনুষ্যত্ব বিসর্জন করত। সেইদিন ভারতবর্ষে যথার্থ আপন সজীব বিশ্ববিদ্যালয়ের সৃষ্টি। তার মধ্যে জীবনীশক্তির বেগ যে কত প্রবল তা স্পষ্টই বুঝতে পারি যখন দেখতে পাই সমুদ্রপারে জাভাদ্বীপে সর্বসাধারণের সমস্ত জীবন ব্যাপ্ত ক'রে কী-একটি কল্পলোকের সৃষ্টি সে করেছে; এই আর্যেতর জাতির চরিত্রে, তার কল্পনায়, তার রূপরচনায় কিরকম সে নিরন্তর সক্রিয়।

জ্ঞানের একটা দিক আছে, তা বৈষয়িক। সে রয়েছে জ্ঞানের বিষয় সংগ্রহ করবার লোভকে অধিকার ক'রে, সে উত্তেজিত করে পাণ্ডিত্যের অভিমানকে। এই কৃপণের ভাণ্ডারের অভিমুখে কোনো মহৎ প্রেরণা উৎসাহ পায় না। ভারতে এই-যে মহাভারতীয় বিশ্ববিদ্যালয়-যুগের উল্লেখ করলেম সেই যুগের মধ্যে তপস্যা ছিল; তার কারণ ভাণ্ডার-পূরণ তার লক্ষ্য ছিল না; তার উদ্দেশ্য ছিল সর্বজনীন চিত্তের উদ্দীপন, উদ্বোধন, চারিত্রসৃষ্টি। পরিপূর্ণ মনুষ্যত্বের যে আদর্শ জ্ঞান কর্মে হৃদয়ভাবে ভারতের মনে উদ্ভাসিত হয়েছিল এই উদ্যোগ তাকেই সঞ্চারিত

করতে চেয়েছিল চিরদিনের জন্য সর্বসাধারণের জীবনের মধ্যে, তার আর্থিক ও পারমার্থিক সদগতির দিকে, কেবলমাত্র তার বুদ্ধিতে নয়।

নালন্দা বিক্রমশিলার বিদ্যায়তন সম্বন্ধেও এই কথা খাটে। সে যুগে সে বিদ্যার মহৎমূল্য দেশের লোক গভীরভাবে উপলব্ধি করেছিল; তাকে সমগ্র সম্পূর্ণতায় কেন্দ্রীভূত ক'রে সর্বজনীন জ্ঞানসত্র রচনা করবার ইচ্ছা স্বতই ভারতবর্ষের মনে সমুদ্যত হয়েছিল সন্দেহ নেই। ভগবান বুদ্ধ একদিন যে ধর্ম প্রচার করেছিলেন স ধর্ম তার নানা তত্ত্ব, নানা অনুশাসন, তার সাধনার নানা প্রণালী নিয়ে সাধারণচিত্তের আন্তর্ভৌম স্তরে প্রবেশ ক'রে ব্যাপ্ত হয়েছিল। তখন দেশ প্রবলভাবে কামনা করেছিল এই বহুশাখায়িত পরিব্যাপ্ত ধারাকে কোনো কোনো সুনির্দিষ্ট কেন্দ্রস্থলে উৎসরূপে উৎসারিত ক'রে দিতে সর্বসাধারণের স্নানের জন্য, পানের জন্য, কল্যাণের জন্য।

এই ইচ্ছাটি যে কিরকম সত্য ছিল, কিরকম উদার, কিরকম বেগবান ছিল, তার প্রমাণ পাওয়া যায় এই অনুষ্ঠানের মধ্যেই, এর অকৃপণ ঐশ্বর্যে। বিখ্যাত চৈনিক পরিব্রাজক হিউয়েন সাঙ বিস্ময়োচ্ছ্বাসিত ভাষায় এই বিদ্যানিকেতনের বর্ণনা করেছেন। তার লেখনীচিত্রে দেখতে পাই এর অলংকরণরেখায়িত শুক্তিরক্ত স্তম্ভশ্রেণী, এর অভ্রভেদী হর্ম্যশিখর, ধূপসুগন্ধি মন্দির, ছায়ানিবিড় আম্রবন, নীলপদ্মে-প্রফুল্ল গভীর সরোবর। তিনটি বড়ো বড়ো বাড়িতে এখানকার গ্রন্থাগার ছিল; তাদের নাম রত্নসাগর, রত্নোদধি, রত্নরঞ্জক। রত্নোদধি নয়তলা; সেইখানে প্রজ্ঞাপারমিতাসূত্র এবং অন্যান্য শাস্ত্রগ্রন্থ রক্ষিত ছিল। বহু রাজা পরে পরে এই সংঘের বিস্তারসাধন করেছেন; চারি দিকে উন্নত চৈত্য উঠেছে, সেই চৈত্যগুলির মধ্যে মধ্যে শিক্ষাভবন, তর্কসভাগৃহ, প্রত্যেক সরোবরের চারি দিকে বেদী ও মন্দির; স্থানে স্থানে শিক্ষক ও প্রচারকদের জন্যে চারতলা বাসস্থান। এখানকার গৃহনির্মাণে কিরকম সযত্ন সতর্কতা সেই প্রসঙ্গে ডাক্তার স্পুনার বলেন, আধুনিক কালে যে

রকমের ইঁট ও গাঁথুনি প্রচলিত এখানকার গৃহনির্মাণের উপকরণ ও যোজনাপদ্ধতি তার চেয়ে অনেক গুণে শ্রেষ্ঠ। ইৎসিঙ বললেন, এই বিদ্যায়ের প্রয়োজননির্বাহের জন্য দুই শতের অধিক গ্রাম উৎসর্গ করা হয়েছে; বহুসহস্র ছাত্র অধ্যাপকের জীবিকার উপযুক্ত ভোজ্য প্রত্যহ প্রচুর পরিমাণে গ্রামের অধিবাসীরা নিয়মিত জুগিয়ে থাকে।

এই বিদ্যায়তনগুলির মধ্যে, শুধু বিদ্যার সঞ্চয় মাত্র নয়, বিদ্যার গৌরব ছিল প্রতিষ্ঠিত। যে-সকল আচার্য অধ্যাপক ছিলেন, হিউয়েন সাঙ বললেন, তাঁদের যশ বহুদূরব্যাপী; তাঁদের চরিত্র পবিত্র, অনিন্দনীয়। তাঁরা সদ্ধর্মের অনুশাসন অকৃত্রিম শ্রদ্ধার সঙ্গে পালন করেন। অর্থাৎ যে বিদ্যা প্রচারের ভার ছিল তাঁদের 'পরে সমস্ত দেশ এবং দূরদেশের ছাত্ররা তাকে সম্মান করত; সেই সম্মানকে উজ্জ্বল ক'রে রক্ষা করার দায়িত্ব ছিল তাঁদের 'পরে— —কেবল মেধা দ্বারা নয়, বহুশ্রুতের দ্বারা নয়, চরিত্রের দ্বারা, অস্খলিত কঠোর তপস্যার দ্বারা। এটা সম্ভব হতে পেরেছিল, কেননা সমস্ত দেশের শ্রদ্ধা এই সাত্ত্বিক আদর্শ তাঁদের কাছে প্রত্যাশা করেছে। আচার্যেরা জানতেন, দূর দূর দেশকে জ্ঞানবিতরণের মহৎ ভার তাঁদের 'পরে; সমুদ্র পার হয়ে, প্রাণপণ কঠিন দুঃখ স্বীকার ক'রে, বিদেশের ছাত্ররা আসছে তাঁদের কাছে জ্ঞানপিপাসায়। এইভাবে বিদ্যার 'পরে সর্বজনীন শ্রদ্ধা থাকলে যাঁরা বিদ্যা বিতরণ করেন আপন যোগ্যতা সম্বন্ধে শৈথিল্য তাঁদের পক্ষে সহজ হয় না। সমস্ত দেশের কলাপ্রতিভাও আপন শ্রদ্ধার অর্ঘ্য এখানে পূর্ণ শক্তিতে নিবেদন করেছিল। সেই উপলক্ষ্যে দেশ আপন শিল্পরচনার উৎকর্ষ এই বিদ্যামন্দিরের ভিত্তিতে ভিত্তিতে মিলিত করেছে, ঘোষণা করেছে; ভারতের কলাবিদ্যা ভারতের বিশ্ববিদ্যাকে প্রমাণ করেছে।

একটি কথা এই প্রসঙ্গে মনে রাখা চাই, তখনকার রাজাদের প্রাসাদভবন বা ভোগের স্থান কোনো বিশেষ সমারোহে ইতিহাসের স্মৃতিকে অধিকারচেষ্টা করেছিল, তার প্রমাণ পাই নে। এই চেষ্টা

যে নিন্দনীয় তা বলি নে; কেননা সাধারণত দেশ আপন ঐশ্বর্যগৌরব প্রকাশ করবার উপলক্ষ রচনা করে আপন নৃপতিকে বেষ্টন ক'রে, সমস্ত প্রজার আত্মসম্মান সেইখানে কলানৈপুণ্যে শোভাপ্রাচুর্যে সমুজ্জ্বল হয়ে ওঠে। যে কারণেই হোক, অতীত ভারতবর্ষের সেই চেষ্টাকে আমরা আর দেখতে পাই নে। হয়তো রাজাসনের ধ্রুবত্ব ছিল না বলেই সেখানে ক্রমাগতই ধ্বংসধূমকেতুর সম্মার্জনী কাজ করেছে। কিন্তু নালন্দা বিক্রমশিলা প্রভৃতি স্থানে স্মৃতিরক্ষাচেষ্টার বিরাম ছিল না। তার প্রতি দেশের ভক্তি, দেশের বেদনা যে কত প্রবল ছিল এই তার একটি প্রমাণ।

আপন সর্বশ্রেষ্ঠ বিদ্যার প্রতি সর্বজনের যে উদার শ্রদ্ধা প্রভূতত্যাগস্বীকারে অকুণ্ঠিত সেই অকৃত্রিম শ্রদ্ধাই ছিল স্বদেশীয় বিশ্ববিদ্যালয়ের যথার্থ প্রাণ-উৎস।

এ কথা সহজেই কল্পনা করা যায় যে, জ্ঞানসাধনার এই-সকল বিরাট যজ্ঞভূমিতে মানুষের মনের সঙ্গে মনের কিরকম অতি বৃহৎ ও নিবিড় সংঘর্ষ চলেছিল, তাতে ধীশক্তি বহ্নিশিখা কিরকম নিরন্তর প্রোজ্জ্বল হয়ে থাকত। ছাপানো টেক্সট বুক থেকে নোট দেওয়া নয়, অন্তর থেকে অন্তরে অবিশ্রাম উদ্যম সঞ্চার করা। বিদ্যায় বুদ্ধিতে জ্ঞানে দেশের যাঁরা সুধীশ্রেষ্ঠ দূর দূরান্তর থেকে এখানে তাঁরা সম্মিলিত। ছাত্রেরাও তীক্ষ্নবুদ্ধি, শ্রদ্ধাবান, সুযোগ্য; দ্বারপণ্ডিতের কাছে কঠিন পরীক্ষা দিয়ে তবে তারা পেয়েছে প্রবেশের অধিকার। হিউয়েন সাঙ লিখেছেন, এই পরীক্ষায় দশ জনের মধ্যে অন্তত সাত-আট জন বর্জিত হত। অর্থাৎ তৎকালীন ম্যাট্রিকুলেশনের যে ছাঁকনি ছিল তাতে মোটা মোটা ফাঁক ছিল না। তার কারণ, সমস্ত পৃথিবীর হয়ে আদর্শকে বিশুদ্ধ ও উন্নত রাখবার দায়িত্ব ছিল জাগরুক। লোকের মনে উদ্বেগ ছিল, পাছে অযথা প্রশ্রয়ের দ্বারা বিদ্যার অধঃপতনে দেশের পক্ষে মানসিক আত্মঘাত ঘটে। নানা প্রকৃতির মন এখানে এক জায়গায় সমবেত হত; তারা একজাতীয় নয়, একদেশীয় নয়। এক লক্ষ্য দৃঢ় রেখে এক জীবিকাব্যবস্থায় তারা পরস্পরের অত্যন্ত ঘনিষ্ঠ ঐক্য লাভ

করেছিল। বিদ্যার সম্মিলনক্ষেত্রে এই ঐক্যের মূল্য যে কতকানি তাও মনে রাখা চাই। তখন পৃথিবীর আরো নানা স্থানে বড়ো বড়ো সভ্যতার উদ্ভব হয়েছিল; কিন্তু, জ্ঞানের তপস্যা-উপলক্ষে মানবমনের এমন বিশাল সমবায় আর কোথাও শোনা যায় নি। এর মূল কারণ, বিশ্বজনীন মনুষ্যত্বের প্রতি সুগভীর শ্রদ্ধা, বিদ্যার প্রতি গৌরববোধ, চিত্তসম্পদ যাঁরা নিজ পেয়েছেন বা সৃষ্টি করেছেন সেই পাওয়ার ও সৃষ্টির পরম আনন্দে সেই সম্পদ দেশবিদেশের সকলকে দান করবার একাগ্র দায়িত্বজ্ঞান। আজ নিজের প্রতি, মনুষের প্রতি, নিজের সাধনার প্রতি, আলস্যবিজড়িত অশ্রদ্ধার দিনে বিশেষ ক'রে আমাদের মনে করবার সময় এসেছে যে, মানব-ইতিহাসে সর্বাগ্রে ভারতবর্ষেই জ্ঞানের বিশ্বদানযজ্ঞ উদার দাক্ষিণ্যের সঙ্গে প্রবর্তিত হয়েছিল। বাংলাদেশের পক্ষ থেকে আরো-একটি কথা আমাদের মনে রাখবার যোগ্য নালন্দায় হিউয়েন সাঙের যিনি গুরু ছিলেন তিনি ছিলেন বাঙালি, তাঁর নাম শীলভদ্র। তিনি বাংলাদেশের কোনো-এক স্থানের রাজা ছিলেন, রাজ্য ত্যাগ করে বেরিয়ে আসেন। এই সঙ্গে যাঁরা শিক্ষাদান করতেন তাঁদের সকলের মধ্যে একলা কেবল ইনিই সমস্ত শাস্ত্র, সমস্ত সূত্র ব্যাখ্যা করতে পারতেন।

সেখানে বৌদ্ধভারতে সঙ্ঘ ছিল নানা স্থানে। সেই-সকল সঙ্ঘে সাধকেরা শাস্ত্রজ্ঞেরা তত্ত্বজ্ঞানীরা শিষ্যের সমবেত হয়ে জ্ঞানের আলোক জ্বালিয়ে রাখতেন, বিদ্যার পুষ্টিসাধন করতেন। নালন্দা বিক্রমশিলা তাদেরই বিশ্বরূপ, তাদেরই স্বাভাবিক পরিণতি।

উপনিষদের কালেও ভারতবর্ষে এরকম বিদ্যাকেন্দ্রের সৃষ্টি হয়েছিল, তার কিছু কিছু প্রমাণ পাওয়া যায়। শতপথব্রাহ্মণের অন্তর্গত বৃহদারণ্যক উপনিষদে আছে, আরুণির পুত্র শ্বেতকেতু পাঞ্চালদেশের "পরিষদ'-এ জৈবালি প্রবাহণের কাছে এসেছিলেন। এই স্থানটি আলোচনা করলে বোঝা যায়, ঐ পরিষদ ঐ দেশের বড়ো বড়ো জ্ঞনীদের সমবায়ে। এই পরিষদ জয় করতে পারলে বিশেষ প্রতিষ্ঠা লাভ হত। অনুমান করা যায় যে, সমস্ত

পাঞ্চালদেশের মধ্যে উচ্চতম শিক্ষার উদ্দেশে সম্মিলিতভাবে একটা প্রতিষ্ঠান ছিল, বিদ্যার পরীক্ষা দেবার জন্যে সেখানে অন্যত্র থেকে লোক আসত। উপনিষদ-কালের বিদ্যা যে স্বভাবতই স্থানে স্থানে শিক্ষা-আলোচনা তর্কবিতর্ক ও জ্ঞানসংগ্রহের জন্য আপন আশ্রয়রূপে পরিষদ রচনা করেছিল, তা নিশ্চিত অনুমান করা যেতে পারে।

য়ুরোপের ইতিহাসেও সেইকম ঘটেছে। সেখানে খৃস্টধর্মের আরম্ভকালে পুরাতন ধর্মের সঙ্গে নূতন ধর্মের দ্বন্দ্ব এবং নিষ্ঠুর উৎপীড়নের দ্বারা নবদীক্ষিতদের ভক্তির পরীক্ষা চলেছিল। অবশেষে ক্রমে যখন এই ধর্ম সাধারণ্যে স্বীকৃত হল তখন স্বভাবতই পূজার ধারার পাশেপাশেই তত্ত্বের ধারা প্রবাহিত হল। বাঁধ যদি বেঁধে না দেওয়া যায় তবে ব্যক্তিবিশেষের বিশেষ প্রকৃতির প্ররোচনায় ভক্তির বিষয় বিচিত্র রূপ ও বিকৃত রূপ নিতে থাকে। তখন তর্ক অবলম্বন ক'রে বিচারের প্রয়োজন হয়। বিশ্বাস তখন বুদ্ধির সাহায্যে, জ্ঞানের সাহায্যে আপন স্থায়ী ও বিশুদ্ধ ভিত্তির সন্ধান করে। তখন তার প্রশ্ন ওঠে : কস্মৈ দেবায় হবিষা বিধেম। ভক্তি তখন কেবলমাত্র পূজার বিষয় না হয়ে বিদ্যার বিষয় হয়ে ওঠে। এইরকম অবস্থায় য়ুরোপের নানা স্থানে আচার্য ও ছাত্রদের সঙ্ঘ সৃষ্টি হচ্ছিল। তার মধ্যে থেকে নির্বাচনের দরকার হল। কোথায় শিক্ষা শ্রদ্ধেয়, কোথায় তা প্রামাণিক, তা স্থির করবার ভার নিলে রোমের প্রধান ধর্মসঙ্ঘ, তারই সঙ্গে রাজার শাসন ও উৎসাহ।

সকলেই জানেন, সে সময়কার আলোচ্য বিদ্যায় প্রধান স্থান ছিল তর্কশাস্ত্রের। তখনকার পণ্ডিতেরা জানতেন, ডায়েলেকটিক সকল বিজ্ঞানের মূলবিজ্ঞান। এর কারণ স্পষ্টই বোঝা যায়। শাস্ত্রের উপদেশগুলি বাক্যের দ্বারা বদ্ধ। সেই-সকল আপ্তবাক্যের অবিসংবাদিত অর্থে পৌঁছতে গেলে শাব্দিক তর্কের প্রয়োজন হয়। য়ুরোপের মধ্যযুগে সেই তর্কের যুক্তিজাল যে কিরকম সূক্ষ্ম ও জটিল হয়ে উঠেছিল তা সকলেরই জানা আছে। শাস্ত্রজ্ঞানের

বিশুদ্ধতার জন্যে এই ন্যায়শাস্ত্র। সমাজরক্ষার জন্য আর দুটি বিদ্যার বিশেষ প্রয়োজন, আইন এবং চিকিৎসা। তখনকার য়ুরোপীয় বিশ্ববিদ্যালয় এই কয়টি বিদ্যাকেই প্রধানত গ্রহণ করেছিল। নালন্দাতে বিশেষভাবে শিক্ষার বিষয় ছিল হেতুবিদ্যা চিকিৎসাবিদ্যা, শব্দবিদ্যা। তার সঙ্গে ছিল তন্ত্র।

ইতিমধ্যে য়ুরোপের মানুষের অন্তর ও বাহিরের পরিবর্তনের সঙ্গে সঙ্গে সেখানকার য়ুনিভর্সিটিতে মস্ত দুটি মূলগত পরিবর্তন ঘটেছে। ধর্মশাস্ত্রের প্রতি সেখানকার মনুষ্যত্বের ঐকান্তিক যে নির্ভর ছিল সেটা ক্রমে ক্রমে শিথিল হয়ে এল। একদিন সেখানে মানুষের জ্ঞানের ক্ষেত্রের প্রায় সমস্তটা ধর্মশাস্ত্রের সম্পূর্ণ অন্তর্গত না হোক, অন্তত শাসনগত ছিল। লড়াই করতে করতে অবশেষে সেই অধিকারের কর্তৃত্বভার তার হাত থেকে স্খলিত হয়েছে। বিজ্ঞানের সঙ্গে যেখানে শাস্ত্রবক্যের বিরোধ সেখানে শাস্ত্র আজ পরাভূত, বিজ্ঞান আজ আপন স্বতন্ত্র বেদীতে একেশ্বররূপে প্রতিষ্ঠিত। ভূগোল ইতিহাস প্রভৃতি মানুষের অন্যান্য শিক্ষীয় বিষয় বৈজ্ঞানিক যুক্তিপদ্ধতির অনুগত হয়ে ধর্মশাস্ত্রের বন্ধন থেকে মুক্তি পেয়েছে। বিশ্বের সমস্ত জ্ঞাতব্য ও মন্তব্য বিষয় সম্বন্ধে মানুষের জিজ্ঞাসার প্রবণতা আজ বৈজ্ঞানিক। আপ্তবাক্যের মোহ তার কেটে গেছে।

এইসঙ্গে আর-একটা বড়ো পরিবর্তন ঘটেছে ভাষা নিয়ে। একদিন লাটিন ভাষাই ছিল সমস্ত য়ুরোপের শিক্ষার ভাষা, বিদ্যার আধার। তার সুবিধা এই ছিল, সকল দেশের ছাত্রই এক পরিবর্তনহীন সাধারণভাষার যোগে শিক্ষালাভ করতে পারত। কিন্তু তার প্রধান ক্ষতি ছিল এই যে, বিদ্যার আলোক পাণ্ডিত্যের ভিত্তিসীমা এড়িয়ে বাইরে অতি অল্পই পৌঁছত। যখন থেকে য়ুরোপের প্রত্যেক জাতিই আপন আপন ভাষাকে শিক্ষার বাহনরূপে স্বীকার করলে তখন শিক্ষা ব্যাপ্ত হল সর্বসাধারণের মধ্যে। তখন বিশ্ববিদ্যালয় সমস্ত দেশের চিত্তের সঙ্গে অন্তরঙ্গরূপে যুক্ত হল। শুনতে কথাটা স্বতোবিরুদ্ধ, কিন্তু সেই ভাষাস্বাতন্ত্র্যের সময় থেকেই সমস্ত য়ুরোপে

বিদ্যার যথার্থ সমবায়সাধন হয়েছে। এই স্বাতন্ত্র্য য়ুরোপের চিৎপ্রকর্ষকে খণ্ডিত না ক'রে আশ্চর্যরূপে সম্মিলিত করেছে। য়ুরোপে এই স্বদেশী ভাষার বিদ্যার মুক্তির সঙ্গে সঙ্গে তার জ্ঞানের ঐশ্বর্য বেড়ে উঠল, ব্যাপ্ত হল সমস্ত প্রজার মধ্যে, যুক্ত হল প্রতিবেশী ও দূরবাসীদের জ্ঞানসাধনার সঙ্গে, স্বতন্ত্র ক্ষেত্রের সমস্ত শস্য সংগৃহীত হল য়ুরোপের সাধারণ ভাণ্ডারে। এখন সেখানে য়ুনিভার্সিটি যেমন––উদারভাবে সকল দেশের তেমনি একান্তভাবে আপন দেশের। এইটিই হচ্ছে মানুষের প্রকৃতির অনুগত। কারণ, মানুষ যদি সত্যভাবে নিজেকে উপলব্ধি না করে তা হলে সত্যভাবে নিজেকে উৎসর্গ করতে পারে না। বিশ্বজনীনতার দাক্ষিণ্য বাস্তব হতে পারে না সেইসঙ্গে ব্যক্তিস্বাতন্ত্র্যের উৎকর্ষ যদি বাস্তব না হয়। এশিয়ার মধ্যযুগে বৌদ্ধধর্মকে তিব্বত চীন মঙ্গোলিয়া গ্রহণ করেছিল, কিন্তু গ্রহণ করেছিল নিজের ভাষাতেই। এইজন্যেই সে-সকল দেশে সে ধর্ম সর্বজনের অন্তরের সামগ্রী হতে পেরেছে, এক-একটি সমগ্রজাতিকে মানুষ করেছে, তাকে মোহান্ধকার থেকে উদ্ধার করেছে।

য়ুনিভার্সিটির উৎপত্তি সম্বন্ধে বিস্তারিত বর্ণনার প্রয়োজন নেই। আমার বলবার মোট কথাটি এই যে, বিশেষ দেশ, বিশেষ জাতি যে বিদ্যার সম্বন্ধে বিশেষ প্রীতি গৌরব ও দায়িত্ব অনুভব করেছে তাকেই রক্ষা ও প্রচারের জন্যে স্বভাবতই বিশ্ববিদ্যালয়ের প্রথম সৃষ্টি। যে ইচ্ছা সকল সৃষ্টির মূলে, সমস্ত দেশের সেই ইচ্ছাশক্তির থেকেই তার উদ্ভব। এই ইচ্ছার মূলে থাকে শক্তির ঐশ্বর্য। সেই ঐশ্বর্য দাক্ষিণ্য দ্বারা নিজেকে স্বতই প্রকাশ করতে চায়; তাকে নিবারণ করা যায় না।

সমস্ত সভ্যদেশ আপন বিশ্ববিদ্যালয়ের ক্ষেত্রে জ্ঞানের অবারিত আতিথ্য করে থাকে। যার সম্পদে উদ্‌বৃত্ত আছে সেই ডাকে অতিথিকে। গৃহস্থ আপন অতিথিশালায় বিশ্বকে স্বীকার করে। নালন্দায় ভারত আপন জ্ঞানের অন্নসত্র খুলেছিল স্বদেশ-বিদেশের সকল অভ্যাগতের জন্য। ভারত সেদিন অনুভব করেছিল, তার

এমন সম্পদ পর্যাপ্ত পরিমাণে আছে সকল মানুষকে দিতে পারলে তবেই যার চরম সার্থকতা। পাশ্চাত্য মহাদেশের অধিকাংশ দেশেই বিদ্যার এই অতিথিশালা বর্তমান। সেখানে স্বদেশী-বিদেশীর ভেদ নেই। সেখানে জ্ঞানের বিশ্বক্ষেত্রে সব মানুষই পরস্পর আপন। সমাজের আর-আর প্রায় সকল অংশেই ভেদের প্রাচীর প্রতিদিন দুর্লঙ্ঘ্য হয়ে উঠেছে : কেবল মানুষের আক্রমণ রইল জ্ঞানের এই মহাতীর্থে। কেননা এইখানে দৈন্যস্বীকার, এইখানে কৃপণতা, ভদ্রজাতির পক্ষে সকলের চেয়ে আত্মলাঘব। সৌভাগ্যবান দেশের প্রাঙ্গণ এইখানে বিশ্বের দিকে উন্মুক্ত।

আমাদের দেশে য়ুনিভার্সিটির পত্তন হল বাহিরের দানের থেকে। সে দানে দাক্ষিণ্য অধিক নেই। তার রাজানুচিত কৃপণতা থেকে আজ পর্যন্ত দুঃখ পাচ্ছি। ইংরেজের দেশে রাজদ্বারে যে অতিথিশালা খোলা আছে লন্ডন য়ুনিভর্সিটিতে, এ দেশের দরিদ্রপাড়ায় তারই একটা ছোটো শাখা স্থাপন হল। ভারতীয় বিদ্যা ব'লে কোনো-একটা পদার্থ যে কোথাও আছে এই বিদ্যালয়ে গোড়াতেই তাকে অস্বীকার করা হয়েছে। এর স্বভাবটা পৃথিবীর সকল য়ুনিভর্সিটির একেবারে বিপরীত। এর দানের বিভাগ অবরুদ্ধ, কেবল গ্রহণের বিভাগ আপন ক্ষুধিত কবল উদ্ঘাটিত করে আছে। তাতে গ্রহণের কাজও ঠিকমত ঘটে না। কেননা, যেখানে দেওয়া-নেওয়া চলাচল নেই সেখানে পাওয়াটাই থাকে অসম্পূর্ণ।

আধুনিককালে জীবনযাত্রা সকল দিকেই জটিল। নূতন নূতন নানা সমস্যার আলোড়নে মানুষের মন সর্বদাই উৎক্ষুব্ধ। নিয়ত তার নানা প্রশ্নের নানা উত্তর, তার নানা বেদনার নানা প্রকাশ সমাজে তরঙ্গিত, সাহিত্যে বিচিত্র ভঙ্গিতে আবর্তিত। বিশ্ববিদ্যালয়ে নানা যুগের ধ্রুব আদর্শগুলি যেমন মনের সামনে বিধৃত, সঞ্চিত, তেমনি প্রচলিত সাহিত্যে প্রকাশ পাচ্ছে প্রবহমান চিত্তের লীলাচাঞ্চল্য। পাশ্চাত্য বিশ্ববিদ্যালয়ে বাহিরের এই চিত্তমথনের সঙ্গে যোগ বিচ্ছিন্ন নয়। মানুষের শিক্ষার এই দুই ধারা সেখানে

গঙ্গাযমুনার মতো মেলে। কেননা সেখানে সমস্ত দেশের একই চিও তার বিদ্যাকে নিরবচ্ছিন্নভাবে সৃষ্টি করে তুলছে, পৃথিবীর সৃষ্টিকার্য যেমন জলে স্থলে উভয়তই সক্রিয়।

এ সংবাদ বোধ হয় সকলেই জানেন যে, বর্তমান কালের সঙ্গে পদক্ষেপ মিলিয়ে চলবার জন্যে ইংলণ্ডের যুনিভর্সিটিগুলিতে সম্প্রতি বিশেষভাবে আধুনিক শিক্ষাবিস্তারের চেষ্টা প্রবৃত্ত। গত য়ুরোপীয় যুদ্ধের পরে অক্‌সফোর্ডে দর্শন রাষ্ট্রতন্ত্র অর্থনীতির আধুনিক ধারার চর্চা স্বীকার করা হয়েছে। চারি দিকে কী ঘটছে, সমাজ কোন্ দিকে চলেছে, সেইটে যারা ভালো করে জানতে চায় তাদের সাহায্য করবার জন্যে য়ুনিভর্সিটির এই উদ্যোগ। ম্যাঞ্চেস্টর য়ুনিভর্সিটি আধুনিক অর্থতত্ত্ব এবং আধুনিক ইতিহাসের প্রতি বিশেষভাবে মনোযোগ করছে। বর্তমান কালের চিন্তাদ্বন্দ্ব ও কর্মসংঘাতের দিনে এইরূপ শিক্ষার ফলে ছাত্র ছাত্রীরা উপযুক্তভাবে আপন কর্তব্য ও জীবনযাত্রার জন্য প্রস্তুত হতে পারে।

আমাদের দেশে বিদেশ-থেকে-পাওয়া বিশ্ববিদ্যালয়ের সঙ্গে দেশের মনের এরকম সম্মিলন ঘটতে পারে নি। তা ছাড়া য়ুরোপীয় বিদ্যাও এখানে বদ্ধজলের মতো, তার চলৎ রূপ আমরা দেখতে পাই নে। যে-সকল প্রবীণ মত আসন্ন পরিবর্তনের মুখে, আমাদের সম্মুখে তারা স্থির থাকে ধ্রুবসিদ্ধান্তরূপে। সনাতনত্বমুগ্ধ আমাদের মত তাদের ফুলচন্দন দিয়ে পূজা করে থাকে। য়ুরোপীয় বিদ্যাকে আমরা স্থাবরভাবে পাই এবং তার থেকে বাচ্য চয়ন করে আবৃত্তি করাকেই আধুনিক রীতির বৈদগ্ধ্য ব'লে জানি, এই কারণে তার সম্বন্ধে নূতন চিন্তার সাহস আমাদের থাকে না। দেশের জনসাধরণের সমস্ত দুরূহ প্রশ্ন, গুরুতর প্রয়োজন, কঠোর বেদনা আমাদের বিশ্ববিদ্যালয় থেকে বিচ্ছিন্ন। এখানে দূরের বিদ্যাকে আমরা আয়ত্ত করি জড় পদার্থের মতো বিশ্লেষণের দ্বারা, সমগ্র উপলব্ধির দ্বারা নয়। আমরা ছিঁড়ে ছিঁড়ে বাক্য মুখস্থ করি এবং সেই টুকরো-করা মুখস্থবিদ্যার পরীক্ষা দিয়ে নিষ্কৃতি পাই।

টেক্সটবুক-সংলগ্ন আমাদের মন পরাশ্রিত প্রাণীর মতো নিজের খাদ্য নিজে সংগ্রহ করবার, নিজে উদ্ভাবন করবার শক্তি হারিয়েছে।

ইংরেজি ভাষা আমাদের প্রয়োজনের ভাষা, এইজন্যে সমস্ত শিক্ষার কেন্দ্রস্থলে এই বিদেশী ভাষার প্রতি আমাদের লোভ; সে প্রেমিকের প্রীতি নয়, কৃপণের আসক্তি। ইংরেজি সাহিত্য পড়ি, প্রধান লক্ষ্য থাকে ইংরেজি ভাষা আয়ত্ত করা। অর্থাৎ ফুলের কীটের মতো আমাদের মন, মধুকরের মতো নয়। মুষ্টিভিক্ষায় যে দান সংগ্রহ করি ফর্দ ধরে তার পরীক্ষা দিয়ে থাকি। সে পরীক্ষায় পরিমাণের হিসাব দেওয়া; সেই পরিমাণগত পরীক্ষার তাগিদ শিক্ষা করতে হয় ওজনদরে। বিদ্যাকে চিত্তের সম্পদ ব'লে গ্রহণ করা অনাবশ্যক হয় যদি তাকে বাহ্যবস্তুরূপে বহন করি। এরকম বিদ্যার দানেও গৌরব নেই, গ্রহণেও না। এমন দৈন্যের অবস্থাতেও কখনো কখনো এমন শিক্ষক মেলে শিক্ষাদান যাঁর স্বভাবসিদ্ধ। তিনি নিজগুণেই জ্ঞান দান করেন, নিজের অন্তর থেকে শিক্ষাকে অন্তরের সামগ্রী করেন, তাঁর অনুপ্রেরণায় ছাত্রদের মনে মননশক্তির সঞ্চার হয়, বিশ্ববিদ্যালয়ের বাইরে বিশ্বক্ষেত্রে আপন বিদ্যাকে ফলবান ক'রে কৃত ছাত্রেরা তার সত্যতার প্রমাণ দেয়।

যে বিশ্ববিদ্যালয় সত্য সে এইরকম শিক্ষককে আকর্ষণ করে; শিক্ষার সাহায্যে সেখান মনোলোকে সৃষ্টিকার্য চলে, এই সৃষ্টিই সকল সভ্যতার মূলে। কিন্তু আমাদের বিশ্ববিদ্যালয়ে এমনতরো যথার্থ শিক্ষক না হলেও চলে। হয়তো-বা ভালোই চলে। কেননা এখানকার পরীক্ষাপদ্ধতিতে যে ফলের প্রতি দৃষ্টি সে আহরণ– করা ফল, ফলন–করা ফল নয়। দৈন্যের নিষ্ঠুর তাগিদে এমতরো শিক্ষার প্রতি দেশের লোভ আছে, কিন্তু ভক্তি নেই। তাই শিক্ষক ও ছাত্রদের উদ্যমকে পরিপূর্ণমাত্রায় সতর্ক করে রাখবার প্রয়োজন হয় না। কেননা, দেশের প্রত্যাশা উচ্চ নয়; বাজার-দরের হিসাব করে যে পরীক্ষার মার্কা সে চায় সত্যের নিকষে তার মূল্য অতি সামান্য। এইজন্য দুর্মূল্য বিদ্যাকে সম্পূর্ণ সত্য ক'রে

তোলবার মতো শ্রদ্ধা রক্ষা করা এত কঠিন; তাই শৈথিল্য তার মজ্জায় প্রবেশ করেছে।

অভাব থেকে বিশ্ববিদ্যালয়-প্রতিষ্ঠার দৃষ্টান্ত অন্যত্র আছে। যেমন জাপানে। জাপান যখন স্পষ্ট বুঝলে যে, আধুনিক য়ুরোপ আজ যে বিদ্যার প্রভাবে বিশ্ববিজয়ী তাকে আয়ত্ত করতে না পারলে সকল দিকেই পরাভব সুনিশ্চিত তখন জাপান প্রাণপণ আকাঙ্ক্ষার বেগে আপন সদ্যপ্রতিষ্ঠিত বিশ্ববিদ্যালয়ে সেই য়ুরোপীয় বিদ্যার পীঠস্থান রচনা করলে। বিদ্যাসাধনায় আধুনিক মানব-সমাজে তার লেশমাত্র অগৌরব না ঘটে এই তার একান্ত স্পর্ধা। সুতরাং সমস্ত জাতির শিক্ষাদানকার্যে সিদ্ধির আদর্শকে খাটো ক'রে নিজেকে বঞ্চনা করার কথা তাও মনে আসতে পারে না। আমাদের দেশে বিদ্যায় সফলতার কৃত্রিম আদর্শ অনেকটা পরিমাণে পরের হাতে। বিদেশী মনিবেরা ন্যূন পরিমাণে কতটুকু হলে তাঁদের আশু প্রয়োজনের হিসাবে সন্তুষ্ট হন তার একটা ওজন বুঝে নিয়েছিলুম। প্রথম থেকেই প্রধানত এইজন্যই বিদ্যার আন্তরিক আদর্শের প্রতি নিষ্ঠা আমাদের হ্রাস হয়ে এসেছে।

জাপানে বিদ্যাকে সত্য ক'রে তোলবার ইচ্ছার প্রমাণ পাওয়া গেল যখন স্বদেশী ভাষাকে সে আপন শিক্ষার ভাষা করতে বিলম্ব করলে না। সর্বজনের ভাষার ভিতর পথ অবাধ প্রশস্ত হয়ে উঠল। তাই আজ সেখানে সমস্ত দেশে বুদ্ধির জ্যোতি অবারিতভাবে দীপ্যমান।

আমাদের দেশে মাতৃভাষায় একদা যখন শিক্ষার আসন প্রতিষ্ঠার প্রথম প্রস্তাব ওঠে তখন অধিকাংশ ইংরেজি-জানা বিদ্বান আতঙ্কিত হয়ে উঠেছিলেন। সমস্ত দেশের সামান্য যে-কয়জন লোক ইংরেজি ভাষাটাকে কোনোমতে ব্যবহার করবার সুযোগ পাচ্ছে তাদের ভাগে উক্ত ভাষার অধিকারে পাছে লেশমাত্র কমতি ঘটে এই ছিল তাঁদের ভয়। হায় রে, দরিদ্রের আকাঙ্ক্ষাও দরিদ্র!

এ কথা মানতে হবে, জাপান স্বাধীন দেশ; সেখানকার লোক বিদ্যার যে মূল্য স্থির করেছে সে মূল্য পুরো পরিমাণে মিটিয়ে দিতে কৃপণতা করে নি। আর, হতভাগা আমরা পুলিস ও ফৌজ-বিভাগের ভুরিভোজনের ভুক্তশেষ রাজস্বের উচ্ছিষ্টকণা খুঁটে তারই দামে বিদ্যার ঠাট কোনোমতে বজায় রাখছি ফাঁকা মাল-মসলায়। আমাদের কাঁথার ছিদ্র ঢাকতে হয় ছেঁড়া কাপড়ের তালি দিয়ে। তাতে গৌরব নেই; কেবল কিছু পরিমাণে লজ্জা-নিবারণ ঘটে, লোকদেখানো মান রক্ষা হয়, জীর্ণতা সত্ত্বেও আবরণটা থাকে।

এটা সত্য কথা। কিন্তু আক্ষেপ ক'রে যখন কোনোই ফল নেই তখন এর দোহাই দিয়ে নিজের চেষ্টাকে খর্ব করলে চলবে না; তুফান উঠেছে বলেই হাল আরো শক্ত করেই ধরতে হবে। যে বিদ্যাকে এতদিন আমা বিদেশের নিলামে সস্তায়-কেনা ভাঙা বেঞ্চিতে বসিয়ে রেখেছি তাকে স্বদেশর চিত্তবেদীতে সমাদরে বসাতেই হবে। বিশ্ববিদ্যালয়কে যখন যথার্থভাবে স্বদেশের সম্পদ করে তুলতে পারব তখন সমস্ত দেশের অন্তরের এই দাবি তার কাছে সার্থক হবে : শ্রদ্ধয়া দেয়ম্। দান করা চাই শ্রদ্ধার সঙ্গে। সেই শ্রদ্ধার অন্ন প্রাণের সঙ্গে মেলে, প্রাণশক্তিকে জাগিয়ে তোলে।

অনেক দিন থেকে ইংরেজি বিদ্যার খাঁচা স্থাবরভাবে আমাদের দেশে রাজবাড়ির দেউড়িতে রক্ষিত ছিল। এর দরজা খুলে দিয়ে দেশের চিত্তশক্তির জন্য যে নীড় নির্মাণ করতে হবে সব-প্রথমে আশুতোষ সে কথা বুঝেছিলেন। প্রবল বলে এই জড়ত্বকে বিচলিত করবার সাহস তাঁর ছিল। সনাতনপন্থীদের দেশে বিশ্ববিদ্যালয়ের চিরাচরিত প্রথার মধ্যে বাংলাকে স্থান দেবার প্রস্তাব প্রথমে তাঁর মনে উঠেছিল ভীরু এবং লোভীদের নানা তর্কের বিরুদ্ধে। বাংলাভাষা আজও সম্পূর্ণরূপে শিক্ষার ভাষা হবার মতো পাকা হয়ে ওঠে নি সে কথা সত্য। কিন্তু আশুতোষ জানতেন যে না হবার কারণ তার নিজের শক্তিদৈন্যের মধ্যে নেই, সে আছে তার অবস্থাদৈন্যের মধ্যে। তাকে শ্রদ্ধা ক'রে সাহস ক'রে শিক্ষার আসন দিলে তবেই সে আপন আসনের উপযুক্ত হয়ে উঠবে।

আর, তা যদি একান্তই অসম্ভব বলে গণ্য করি তবে বিশ্ববিদ্যালয় চিরদিনই বিলেতের-আমদানি টবের গাছ হয়ে থাকবে; সে টব মূল্যবান হতে পারে, অলংকৃত হতে পারে, কিন্তু গাছকে সে চিরদিন পৃথক করে রাখবে ভারতবর্ষের মাটি থেকে; বিশ্ববিদ্যালয় দেশের শখের জিনিস হবে, প্রাণের জিনিস হবে না।

তা ছাড়া বিশ্ববিদ্যালয়ের অগৌরব ঘোচাবার জন্যে পরীক্ষার শেষ দেউড়ি পার ক'রে দিয়ে আশুতোষ এখানে গবেষণাবিভাগ স্থাপন করেছিলেন--বিদ্যার ফসল শুধু জমানো নয়, বিদ্যার ফসল ফলানোর বিভাগ। লোকের অভাব, অর্থের অভাব, স্বজন-পরজনের প্রতিকূলতা, কিছুই তিনি গ্রাহ্য করেন নি। বিশ্ববিদ্যালয়ের আত্মশ্রদ্ধার প্রবর্তন হয়েছে এইখানেই। তার প্রধান কারণ, বিশ্ববিদ্যালয়কে আশুতোষ আপন করে দেখতে পেরেছিলেন, সেই অভিমানেই এই বিদ্যালয়কে তিনি সমস্ত দেশের আপন করে তোলবার ভরসা করতে পারলেন।

দেশের দিকে বিশ্ববিদ্যালয়ের যে মোটা বেড়াটা উঁচু করে তোলা ছিল তার মধ্যে অবকাশ রচনা করতে তিনি প্রবৃত্ত ছিলেন। সেই প্রবেশপথ দিয়েই আমার মতো লোকের আজ এইখানে অকুন্ঠিত মনে উপস্থিত হওয়া সম্ভবপর হয়েছে। আমার মহৎ সৌভাগ্য এই যে, বিশ্ববিদ্যালয়কে স্বদেশী ভাষায় দীক্ষিত করে নেবার পুণ্য অনুষ্ঠানে আমারও কিছু হাত রইল, অন্তত নামটা রয়ে গেল। আমি মনে করি যে, স্বদেশের সঙ্গে বিশ্ববিদ্যালয়ের মিলনসেতুরূপেই আমাকে আহ্বান করা হয়েছে। স্বদেশী ভাষায় চিরজীবন আমি যে সাধনা করে এসেছি সেই সাধনাকে সম্মান দেবার জন্যেই বিশ্ববিদ্যালয় আজ তাঁর সভায় আমাকে আসন দিলেন। দুই কালের সন্ধিস্থলে আমাকে রাখলেন একটি চিহ্নের মতো। দেখলেম যথারীতি আমাকে পদবী দেওয়া হয়েছে, অধ্যাপক। এ পদবীতে যথেষ্ট সম্মান আছে, কিন্তু আমার পক্ষে এটা অসংগত। এর দায়িত্ব আছে, সেও আমার পক্ষে গ্রহণ করা অসম্ভব। সাহিত্যের প্রকৃততত্ত্ব, তার শব্দের উৎপত্তি ও বিশ্লিষ্ট

উপাদান, অর্থাৎ সাহিত্যের নাড়ীনক্ষত্র আমার অভিজ্ঞতার বহির্ভূত। আমি অনুশীলন করেছি তার অখণ্ড রূপ, তার গতি, তার ভঙ্গি, তার ইঙ্গিত।

তখন আমার বয়স সতেরো, ইংরেজিভাষার জটিল গহনে আলো-আঁধারে কোনোমতে হাৎড়ে চলতে পারি মাত্র। সেই সময়ে লণ্ডন য়ুনিভার্সিটিতে মাস-তিনেকের জন্যে সাহিত্যের ক্লাসে ছাত্র ছিলেম। আমাদের অধ্যাপক ছিলেন শুভ্রকেশ সৌম্যমূর্তি হেন্‌রি মর্লি। সাহিত্য তিনি পড়াতেন তার অন্তরতর রসটুকু দেবার জন্যে। শেক্‌স্‌পিয়রের কোরায়োলেনস, টমাস ব্রাউনের বেরিয়ল আর্ন্‌ এবং মিল্‌টনের প্যারাডাইস রিগেন্‌ড আমাদের পাঠ্য ছিল। নোট প্রভৃতির সাহায্যে বইগুলি নিজে পড়ে আসতুম তার অর্থ গ্রহণের জন্যে। অধ্যাপক ক্লাসে বসে মূর্তিমান নোট-বইয়ের কাজ করতেন না। যে কাব্য পড়াতেন তার ছবিটি পাওয়া যেত তাঁর মুখে মুখে, আবৃত্তি করে যেতেন তিনি অতি সরসভাবে, যেটি শব্দার্থের চেয়ে অনেক বেশি, অনেক গভীর সেটি পাওয়া যেত তাঁর কন্ঠ থেকে। মাঝে মাঝে দুরূহ জায়গায় দ্রুত বুঝিয়ে যেতেন, পঠনধারার ব্যাঘাত করতেন না। রচনাশক্তির উৎকর্ষসাধন সাহিত্যশিক্ষার আর-একটি আনুষঙ্গিক লক্ষ্য। এই দায়িত্বও তাঁর ছিল। ভাষাশিক্ষা সাহিত্যশিক্ষার কাজ মুখ্যত ভাষাতত্ত্ব দিয়ে নয়, সাহিত্যের প্রস্থতত্ত্ব দিয়ে নয়, রসের পরিচয় দিয়ে ও রচনায় ভাষার ব্যবহার দিয়ে। যেমন আর্টশিক্ষার কাজ আর্কিয়লজি আইকনোগ্রাফি দিয়ে নয়, আর্টেরই আন্তরিক রসস্বরূপের ব্যাখ্যা দিয়ে। সপ্তাহে একদিন তিনি সমগ্রভাবে ছাত্রদের প্রদত্ত রচনার ব্যাখ্যা করতেন; তার পদচ্ছেদ, প্যারাগ্রাফবিভাগ, শব্দপ্রয়োগের সূক্ষ্ম ক্রটি বা শোভনতা, সমস্তই তাঁর আলোচ্য ছিল। সাহিত্য ও ভাষার স্বরূপবোধ, তার আঙ্গিকের অর্থাৎ টেকনিকের পরিচয় ও চর্চাই সাহিত্যশিক্ষার প্রধান উদ্দেশ্য, এই কথাটিই তাঁর ক্লাস থেকে জেনেছিলেম।

বয়স যদি পর্যবসিতপ্রায় না হত আর যদি আমার কর্তব্য হত ক্লাসে সাহিত্যশিক্ষকতা করা, তবে এই আদর্শ-অনুসারেই কাজ করবার চেষ্টা করতুম। সম্ভবত আমার পক্ষে তার পরিণাম শোকাবহ হত। কর্তৃপক্ষ এবং ছাত্রেরা কেউ দীর্ঘকাল আমাকে সহ্য করতেন না। সেই সম্ভবপর সংকট কাটিয়ে এসেছি।

আজ আমার শেষ বয়সে আমার কাছ থেকে কোনো রীতিমত কর্মপদ্ধতি প্রত্যাশা করা ধর্মবিরুদ্ধ, তাতে প্রত্যবায় আছে। আমার ক্লান্ত জীবনের সায়াহ্নকালে আমাকে বাংলা-অধ্যাপকের সুলভ সংস্করণরূপে আলাতে গেলে তাতে কাজেরও ক্ষতি হবে, আমার পক্ষেও সেটা স্বাস্থ্যকর হবে না। আমি এই জানি যে, আজ কলিকাতা বিশ্ববিদ্যালয়কে বঙ্গবাণী-বীণাপাণির মন্দিরদ্বারে বরণ ক'রে নেবার ভার আমার 'পরে। সেই কথা মনে রেখে আমি তাকে অভিনন্দিত করি। এই কামনা করি যে, যখন ধূমমলিন নিশীথ-প্রদীপের নির্বাপণের ক্ষণ এল তখন বঙ্গদেশের চিতাকাশে নবসূর্যোদয়ের প্রত্যুষকে যথার্থ স্বদেশীয় বিশ্ববিদ্যালয় যেন ভৈরবরাগে ঘোষণা করে, এবং বাংলার প্রতিভাকে নব নব সৃষ্টির পথ দিয়ে অক্ষয় কীর্তিলোকে উত্তীর্ণ করে দেয়।

(ORIGINAL BANGLA TEXT)

Retrieved from https://www.tagoreweb.in/Essays

শিক্ষার স্বাস্ত্রীকরণ (shikkhar swangikoron)

আমাদের দেশের আর্থিক দারিদ্র্য দুঃখের বিষয়, লজ্জার বিষয় আমাদের দেশের শিক্ষার অকিঞ্চিৎকরত্ব। এই অকিঞ্চিৎকরত্বের মূলে আছে আমাদের শিক্ষাব্যবস্থার অস্বাভাবিকতা, দেশের মাটির সঙ্গে এই ব্যবস্থার বিচ্ছেদ। চিত্তবিকাশের যে আয়োজনটা স্ববাবতই সকলের চেয়ে আপন হওয়া উচিত ছিল সেইটেই রয়েছে সব চেয়ে পর হয়ে––তার সঙ্গে আমাদের দড়ির যোগ হয়েছে, নাড়ীর যোগ হয় নি; এর ব্যর্থতা আমাদের স্বাজাতিক ইতিহাসের শিকড়কে জীর্ণ করছে, খর্ব করে দিচ্ছে সমস্ত জাতির মানসিক পরিবৃদ্ধিকে। দেশের বহুবিধ অতিপ্রয়োজনীয় বিধিব্যবস্থায় অনাত্মীয়তার দুঃসহ ভার অগত্যাই চেপে রয়েছে; আইন আদালত, সকলপ্রকার সরকারি কার্যবিধি, যা বহুকোটি ভারতবাসীর ভাগ্য চালনা করে, তা সেই বহুকোটি ভারতবাসীর পক্ষে সম্পূর্ণ দুর্বোধ, দুর্গম। আমাদের ভাষা, আমাদের আর্থিক অবস্থা, আমাদের অনিবার্য অশিক্ষার সঙ্গে রাষ্ট্রশাসনবিধির বিপুল ব্যবধান–বশত পদে পদে যে দুঃখ ও অপব্যয় ঘটে তার পরিমাণ প্রভূত। তবু বলতে পারি "এই বাহ্য'। কিন্তু শিক্ষাব্যাপার দেশের প্রাণগত আপন জিনিস না হওয়া তার চেয়ে মর্মান্তিক। ল্যাবরেটরিতে রাসায়নিক প্রক্রিয়ায় উদ্ভাবিত কৃত্রিত অন্নে দেশের পেট ভরাবার মতো সেই চেষ্টা অতি অল্পসংখ্যক পেটেই সেটা পৌঁছয়, এবং সেটাকে সম্পূর্ণ রক্তে পরিণত করবার শক্তি অতি অল্প পাকযন্ত্ররই থাকে। দেশের চিত্তের সঙ্গে দেশের শিক্ষার এই দূরত্ব এবং সেই শিক্ষার অপমানজনক স্বল্পতা দীর্ঘকাল আমাকে বেদনা দিয়েছে; কেননা নিশ্চিত জানি সকল পরাশ্রয়তার চেয়ে ভয়াবহ, শিক্ষায় পরধর্ম। এ সম্বন্ধে বরাবর আমি আলোচনা করেছি,

290

আবার তার পুনরুক্তি করতে প্রবৃত্ত হলেম; যেখানে ব্যথা সেখানে বার বার হাত পড়ে। আমার এই প্রসঙ্গে পুনরুক্তি অনেকেই হয়তা ধরতে পারবেন না; কেননা অনেকেরই কানে আমার সেই পুরোনো কথা পৌঁছয় নি। যাঁদের কাছে পুনরুক্তি ধরা পড়বে তাঁরা যেন ক্ষমা করেন। কেননা আজ আমি দুঃখের কথা বলতে এসেছি, নূতন কথা বলতে আসি নি। আমাদের দেশে ম্যালেরিয়া যেমন নিত্যই আপনার পুনরাবৃত্তি করতে থাকে, আমাদের দেশের সকল সাংঘাতিক দুঃখগুলির সেই দশা। ম্যালেরিয়া অপ্রতিহার্য নয় এ কথায় যাদের নিশ্চিত বিশ্বাস তাদেরই অজেয় ইচ্ছা ও প্রবল অধ্যবসায়ের কাছে ম্যালেরিয়া দৈববিহিত দুর্যোগের ছদ্মবেশ ঘুচিয়ে দিয়ে বিদায় গ্রহণ করে। অন্যশ্রেণীয় দুঃখও নিজের পৌরুষের দ্বারা প্রতিহত হতে পারে এই বিশ্বাসের দোহাই পাড়বার কর্তব্যতা স্মরণ করে অপটু দেহ নিয়ে আজ এসেছি।

একদা একজন অব্যবসায়ী ভদ্রসন্তান তাঁর চেয়ে আনাড়ি এক ব্যক্তির বাড়ি তৈরি করবার ভার নিয়েছিলেন। মাল-মসলার জোগাড় হয়েছিল সেরা দরের; ইমারতের গাঁথনি হয়েছিল মজবুত; কিন্তু কাজ হয়ে গেলে প্রকাশ পেল, সিঁড়ির কথাটা কেউ ভাবে নি। শনির চক্রান্তে এমনতরো পৌরব্যবস্থা যদি কোনো রাজ্যে থাকে যেখানে এক-তলার লোকের নিত্যবাস এক-তলাতেই আর দোতলার লোকের দোতলায়, তবে সেখানে সিঁড়ির কথাটা ভাবা নিতান্তই বাহুল্য। কিন্তু আলোচিত পূর্বোক্ত বাড়িটাতে সিঁড়িযোগে ঊর্ধ্বপথযাত্রায় একতলার প্রয়োজন ছিল; এইছিল তার উন্নতিলাভের একমাত্র উপায়।

এ দেশে শিক্ষা-ইমারতে সিঁড়ির সংকল্প গোড়া থেকেই আমাদের রাজমিস্ত্রির প্ল্যানে ওঠে নি। নীচের তলাটা উপরের তলাকে নিঃস্বার্থ ধৈর্যে শিরোধার্য করে নিয়েছে : তার ভার বহন করেছে, কিন্তু সুযোগ গ্রহণ করে নি; দাম জুগিয়েছে, মাল আদায় করে নি।

আমার পূর্বকার লেখায় এ দেশের সিঁড়িহারা শিক্ষাবিধানে এই মস্ত ফাঁকটার উল্লেখ করেছিলুম। তা নিয়ে কোনো পাঠকের মনে কোনো-যে উদ্বেগ ঘটেছে তার প্রমাণ পাওয়া যায় না। তার কারণ, অভ্রভেদী বাড়িটাই আমাদের অভ্যস্ত, তার গৌরবে আমরা অভিভূত, তার বুকের কাছটাতে উপর-নীচে সম্বন্ধস্থাপনের যে সিঁড়ির নিয়মটা ভদ্র নিয়ম সেটাতে আমাদের অভ্যাস হয় নি। সেইজন্যেই ইতিপূর্বে আমার আলোচ্য বিষয়টা হয়তো সেলাম পেয়ে থাকবে, কিন্তু আসন পায় নি। তবু আর-একবার চেষ্টা দেখতে দোষ নেই, কেননা ভিতরে ভিতরে কখন যে দেশের মনে হাওয়া বদল হয় পরীক্ষা না করে তা বলা যায় না।

শিক্ষা সম্বন্ধে সব চেয়ে স্বীকৃত এবং সব চেয়ে উপেক্ষিত কথাটা এই যে, শিক্ষা জিনিসটি জৈব, ওটা যান্ত্রিক নয়। এর সম্বন্ধে কার্যপ্রণালীর প্রসঙ্গ পরে আসতে পারে, কিন্তু প্রাণক্রিয়ার প্রসঙ্গ সর্বাগ্রে। ইন্‌কুবেটর যন্ত্রটা সহজ নয় ব'লেই কৌশল এবং অর্থব্যয়ের দিক থেকে তার বিবরণ শুনতে খুব মস্ত; কিন্তু মুর্গির জীবনধর্মানুগত ডিম-পাড়াটা সহজ বলেই বেশি কথা জোড়ে না, তবু সেটই অগ্রগণ্য।

বেঁচে থাকার নিয়ত ইচ্ছা ও সাধনাই হচ্ছে বেঁচে থাকার প্রকৃতিগত লক্ষণ। যে সমাজে প্রাণের জোর আছে সে সমাজ টিঁকে থাকবার স্বাভাবিক গরজেই আত্মরক্ষাঘটিত দুটি সর্বপ্রধান প্রয়োজনের দিকে অক্লান্তভাবে সজাগ থাকে, অন্ন আর শিক্ষা, জীবিকা আর বিদ্যা। সমাজের উপরের থাকের লোক খেয়ে-পরে পরিপুষ্ট থাকবে আর নীচের থাকের লোক অর্ধাশনে বা অনশনে বাঁচে কি মরে সে সম্বন্ধে সমাজ থাকবে অচেতন, এটাকে বলা যায় অর্ধাঙ্গের পক্ষাঘাত। এই অসাড়তার ব্যামোটা বর্বরতার ব্যামো।

পশ্চিম-মহাদেশে আজ সর্বব্যাপী অর্থসংকটের সঙ্গে সঙ্গে অন্নসংকট প্রবল হয়েছে। এই অভাব-নিবারণের জন্যে সেখানকার বিদ্বানের দল এবং গবর্মেন্ট যেরকম অসামান্য দাক্ষিণ্য প্রকাশ করছেন

সেরকম উদ্বেগ এবং চেষ্টা আমাদের বহুসহিষ্ণু বুভুক্ষার অভিজ্ঞতায় সম্পূর্ণ অপরিচিত। এ নিয়ে বড়ো বড়ো অঙ্কের ঋণ স্বীকার করতেও তাদের সংকোচ দেখি নে। আমাদের দেশে দু বেলা দু মুঠো খেতে পায় অতি অল্প লোক, বাকি বারো-আনা লোক আধপেটা খেয়ে ভাগ্যকে দায়ী করে এবং জীবিকার কৃপণ পথ থেকে মৃত্যুর উদার পথে সরে পড়তে বেশি দেরি করে না। এর থেকে যে নির্জীবতার সৃষ্টি হয়েছে তার পরিমাণ কেবল মৃত্যুসংখ্যার তালিকা দিয়ে নিরুপিত হতে পারে না। নিরুৎসাহ অবসাদ অকর্মণ্যতা রোগপ্রবণতা মেপে দেখবার প্রত্যক্ষ মানদণ্ড যদি থাকত তা হলে দেখতে পেতুম এ দেশের এক প্রান্ত থেকে আর-এক প্রান্ত জুড়ে প্রাণকে ব্যঙ্গ করছে মৃত্যু; সে অতি কুৎসিত দৃশ্য, অত্যন্ত শোচনীয়। কোনো স্বাধীন সভ্য দেশ মৃত্যুর এরকম সর্বনেশে নাট্যলীলা নিশ্চেষ্টভাবে স্বীকার করতেই পারে না, আজ তার প্রমাণ ভারতের বাইরে নানা দিক থেকেই পাচ্ছি।

শিক্ষা সম্বন্ধেও সেই একই কথা। শিক্ষার অভিসেচনক্রিয়া সমাজের উপরের স্তরকেই দুই-এক ইঞ্চি মাত্র ভিজিয়ে দেবে আর নীচের স্তরপরম্পরা নিত্যনীরস কাঠিন্যে সুদূর-প্রসারিত মরুময়তাকে ক্ষীণ আবরণে ঢাকা দিয়ে রাখবে, এমন চিত্তঘাতী সুগভীর মূর্খতাকে কোনো সভ্য সমাজ অলসভাবে মেনে নেয় নি। ভারতবর্ষকে মানতে বাধ্য করেছে আমাদের যে নির্মম ভাগ্য তাকে শতবার ধিক্কার দিই।

এমন কোনো কোনো গ্রহ উপগ্রহ আছে যার এক অর্ধেকের সঙ্গে অন্য অর্ধেকের চিরস্থায়ী বিচ্ছেদ; সেই বিচ্ছেদ আলোক-অন্ধকারের বিচ্ছেদ। তাদের একটা পিঠ সূর্যের অভিমুখে, অন্য পিঠ সূর্যবিমুখ। তেমনি করে যে সমাজের এক অংশে শিক্ষার আলোক পড়ে, অন্য বৃহত্তর অংশ শিক্ষাবিহীন, সে সমাজ আত্মবিচ্ছেদের অভিশাপে অভিশপ্ত। সেখানে শিক্ষিত-অশিক্ষিতের মাঝখানে অসূর্যম্পশ্য অন্ধকারের ব্যবধান। দুই ভিন্নজাতীয় মানুষের চেয়েও এদের চিত্তের ভিন্নতা আরো বেশি প্রবল। একই নদীর এক

পারের স্রোত ভিতরে ভিতরে অন্য পারের স্রোতের বিরুদ্ধ দিকে চলেছে; সেই উভয় বিরুদ্ধের পার্শ্ববর্তিতাই এদের দূরত্বকে আরো প্রবলভাবে প্রমাণিত করে।

শিক্ষার ঐক্য-যোগে চিত্তের ঐক্য-রক্ষাকে সভ্য সমাজ মাত্রই একান্ত অপরিহার্য ব'লে জানে। ভারতের বাইরে নানা স্থানে ভ্রমণ করেছি প্রাচ্য ও পাশ্চাত্য মহাদেশে। দেখে এসেছি, এশিয়ায় নবজাগরণের যুগ সর্বত্রই জনসাধারণের মধ্যে শিক্ষাপ্রচারের দায়িত্ব একান্ত আগ্রহের সঙ্গে স্বীকৃত। বর্তমান যুগের সঙ্গে যে-সব দেশ চিত্তের ও বিত্তের আদানপ্রদান বুদ্ধিবিচারের সঙ্গে চালনা করতে না পারবে তারা কেবলই হঠে যাবে, কোণ-ঠেসা হয়ে থাকবে, এই শঙ্কার কারণ দূর করতে কোনা ভদ্র দেশ অর্থাভাবের কৈফিয়ত মানে নি। আমি যখন রাশিয়ায় গিয়েছিলুম তখন সেখানে আট বছর মাত্র নূতন স্বরাজতন্ত্রের প্রবর্তন হয়েছে; তার প্রথম ভাগে অনেক কাল বিদ্রোহে বিপ্লবে দেশ ছিল শান্তিহীন, অর্থসচ্ছলতা ছিলই না। তবু এই স্বল্পকালেই রাশিয়ার বিরাট রাজ্যে প্রজাসাধারণের মধ্যে যে অদ্ভুত দ্রুতগতিতে শিক্ষাবিস্তার হয়েছে সেটা ভাগ্যবঞ্চিত ভারতবাসীর কাছে অসাধ্য ইন্দ্রজাল বলেই মনে হল।

শিক্ষার ঐক্য-সাধন, ন্যাশনল ঐক্য-সাধনের মূলে, এই সহজ কথা সুস্পষ্ট ক'রে বুঝতে আমাদের দেরি হয়েছে তারও কারণ আমাদের অভ্যাসের বিকার। একদা মহাত্মা গোখলে যখন সার্বজনিক অবশ্যশিক্ষা প্রবর্তনে উদ্যোগী হয়েছিলেন তখন সব চেয়ে বাধা পেয়েছিলেন বাংলাপ্রদেশের কোনো কোনো গণ্যমান্য লোকের কাছ থেকেই। অথচ, রাষ্ট্রীয় ঐক্যের আকাঙক্ষা এই বাংলাদেশেই সব চেয়ে মুখর ছিল। শিক্ষার অনৈক্যে বিজড়িত থেকেও রাষ্ট্রিক উন্নতির পথে এগিয়ে চলা সম্ভবপর এই কল্পনা এ প্রদেশের মনে বাধা পায় নি, এই অনৈক্যের অভ্যাস এমনিই ছিল মজ্জাগত। অভ্যাসে চিন্তার যে জড়ত্ব আনে আমাদের দেশে তার আর-একটা দৃষ্টান্ত ঘরে ঘরেই আছে। আহারে কুপথ্য

বাঙালির প্রাত্যহিক, বাঙালির মুখরোচক; সেটা আমাদের কাছে এতই সহজ হয়ে গেছে যে, যখন দেহটার আধমরা দশা বিচার করি তখন ডাক্তারে কথা ভাবি, ওষুধের কথা ভাবি, হাওয়া-বদলের কথা ভাবি, তুকতাক-মন্ত্রতন্ত্রের কথা ভাবি, এমন-কি, বিদেশী শাসনকেও সন্দেহ করি, কিন্তু পথ্যসংস্কারের কথা মনেও আসে না। নৌকোটার নোঙর থেকে মাটি আঁকড়িয়ে, সেটা চোখে পড়ে না; মনে করি পালটা ছেঁড়া ব'লেই পারঘাটে পৌঁছনো হচ্ছে না।

আমার কথার জবাবে এমন তর্ক হয়তো উঠবে, আমাদের দেশে সমাজ পূর্বেও তো সজীব ছিল, আজও একেবারে মরে নি-- তখনো কি আমাদের দেশ শিক্ষায় অশিক্ষায় যেন জলে স্থলে বিভক্ত ছিল না? তখনকার টোলে চতুষ্পাঠীতে তর্কশাস্ত্র ব্যাকরণশাস্ত্রের যে প্যাঁচ-কষাকষি চলত সে তো ছিল পণ্ডিত পালোয়ানদের ওস্তাদি-আখড়াতেই বদ্ধ : তার বাইরে যে বৃহৎ দেশটা ছিল সেও কি সর্বত্র ঐরকম পালোয়ানি কায়দায় তাল ঠুকে পাঁয়তারা করে বেড়াত? যা ছিল বিদ্যানামধারী পরিণত গজের বপ্রক্রীড়া সেই দিগ্গজ পণ্ডিতি তো তার শুঁড় আস্ফালন করে নি দেশের ঘরে ঘরে। কথাটা মেনে নিলুম। বিদ্যার যে আড়ম্বর, নিরবচ্ছিন্ন পাণ্ডিত্য, সকল দেশেই সেটা প্রাণের ক্ষেত্র থেকে দূরবর্তী। পাশ্চাত্য দেশেও স্থূলপদবিক্ষেপে তার চলন আছে, তাকে বলে পেডেন্ট্রি। আমার বক্তব্য এই যে, এ দেশে একদা বিদ্যার যে ধারা সাধনার দুর্গম তুঙ্গ শৃঙ্গ থেকে নির্ঝরিত হত সেই একই ধারা সংস্কৃতিরূপে দেশকে সকল স্তরেই অভিষিক্ত করেছে। এজন্যে যান্ত্রিক নিয়মে এডুকেশন ডিপার্টমেন্টের কারকানা-ঘর বানাতে হয় নি; দেহে যেমন প্রাণশক্তির প্রেরণায় মোটা ধমনীর রক্তধারা নানা আয়তনের বহুসংখ্যক শিরা-উপশিরা-যোগে সমস্ত দেহে অঙ্গপ্রত্যঙ্গে প্রবাহিত হতে থাকে তেমনি ক'রেই আমাদের দেশের সমস্ত সমাজদেহে একই শিক্ষা স্বাভাবিক প্রাণপ্রক্রিয়ায় নিরন্তর সঞ্চারিত হয়েছে--নাড়ীর বাহনগুলি কোনোটা-বা স্থূল কোনোটা-বা অতি সূক্ষ্ম, কিন্তু তবু

তারা এক কলেবর-ভুক্ত নাড়ী, এবং রক্তও একই প্রাণ-ভরা রক্ত।

অরণ্য যে মাটি থেকে প্রাণরস শোষণ করে বেঁচে আছে সেই মাটিকে আপনিই প্রতিনিয়ত প্রাণের উপাদান অজস্র জুগিয়ে থাকে। তাকে কেবলই প্রাণময় করে তোলে। উপরের ডালে যে ফল সে ফলায় নীচের মাটিতে তার আয়োজন তার নিজকৃত। অরণ্যের মাটি তাই হয়ে ওঠে আরণ্যিক, নইলে সে হত বিজাতীয় মরু। যেখানে মাটিতে সেই উদ্ভিদসার পরিব্যাপ্ত নয় সেখানে গাছপালা বিরল হয়ে জন্মায়, উপবাসে বেঁকেচুরে শীর্ণ হয়ে থাকে। আমাদের সমাজের বনভূমিতে একদিন উচ্চশীর্ষ বনস্পতির দান নীচের ভূমিতে নিত্যই বর্ষিত হত। আজ দেশে যে পাশ্চাত্য শিক্ষা প্রবর্তিত হয়েছে মাটিকে সে দান করেছে অতি সামান্য; ভূমিকে সে আপন উপাদানে উর্বরা করে তুলছে না। জাপান প্রভৃতি দেশের সঙ্গে আমাদের এই প্রভেদটাই লজ্জাজনক এবং শোকাবহ। আমাদের দেশ আপন শিক্ষার ভূমিকা সৃষ্টি সম্বন্ধে উদাসীন। এখানে দেশের শিক্ষা এবং দেশের বৃহৎ মন পরস্পরবিচ্ছিন্ন। সেকালে আমাদের দেশের মস্ত মস্ত শাস্ত্রজ্ঞ পণ্ডিতের সঙ্গে নিরক্ষর গ্রামবাসীরা মনঃপ্রকৃতির বৈপরীত্য ছিল না। সেই শাস্ত্রজ্ঞানের প্রতি তাদের মনের অভিমুখিতা তৈরি হয়ে গিয়েছিল। সেই ভোজে অর্ধভোজন তাদের ছিল নিত্য, কেবল ঘ্রাণে নয়, উদ্‌বৃত্ত-উপভোগে।

কিন্তু সায়ান্সে-গড়া পাশ্চাত্যবিদ্যার সঙ্গে আমাদের দেশের মনের যোগ হয় নি; জাপানে সেটা হয়েছে পঞ্চাশ বছরের মধ্যে, তাই পাশ্চাত্যশিক্ষার ক্ষেত্রে জাপান স্বরাজের অধিকারী। এটা তার পাস-করা বিদ্যা নয়, আপন-করা বিদ্যা। সাধারণের কথা ছেড়ে দেওয়া যাক, সায়ান্সে ডিগ্রি-ধারী পণ্ডিত এ দেশে বিস্তর আছে যাদের মনের মধ্যে সায়ান্সের জমিনটা তলতলে, তাড়াতাড়ি যা-তা বিশ্বাস করতে তাদের অসাধারণ আগ্রহ, মেকি সায়ান্সের মন্ত্র পড়িয়ে অন্ধ সংস্কারকে তারা সায়ান্সের জাতে তুলতে কুন্ঠিত

হয় না। অর্থাৎ, শিক্ষার নৌকোতে বিলিতি দাঁড় বসিয়েছি, হাল লাগিয়েছি, দেখতে হয়েছে ভালো, কিন্তু সমস্ত নদীটার স্রোত উলটো দিকে--নৌকো পিছিয়ে পড়ে আপনিই। আধুনিক কালে বর্বর দেশের সীমানার বইরে ভারতবর্ষই একমাত্র দেশ যেখানে শতকরা আট-দশ জনের মাত্র অক্ষর-পরিচয় আছে। এমন দেশে ঘটা ক'রে বিদ্যাশিক্ষার আলোচনা করতে লজ্জা বোধ করি। দশ জন মাত্র যার প্রজা তার রাজত্বের কথাটা চাপা দেওয়াই ভালো। বিশ্ববিদ্যলয় অক্সফোর্ডে আছে, কেম্ব্রিজে আছে, লণ্ডনে আছে। আমাদের দেশেও স্থানে স্থানে আছে, পূর্বোক্তের সঙ্গে এদের ভাবভঙ্গি ও বিশেষণের মিল দেখে আমরা মনে ক'রে বসি এরা পরস্পরের সবর্ণ : যেন ওটিন ক্রিম ও পাউডার মাখলেই মেমসাহেবের সঙ্গে সত্যসত্যই বর্ণভেদ ঘুচে যায়। বিশ্ববিদ্যালয় যেন তার ইমারতের দেওয়াল এবং নিয়মাবলীর পাকা প্রাচীরে মধ্যেই পর্যাপ্ত। অক্সফোর্ড কেম্ব্রিজ বলতে শুধু এটুকুই বোঝায় না, তার সঙ্গে সঙ্গে সমস্ত শিক্ষিত ইংলণ্ডকেই বোঝায়। সেইখানেই তারা সত্য, তারা মরীচিকা নয়। আর আমাদের বিশ্ববিদ্যালয় হঠাৎ থেমে গেছে তার আপন পাকা প্রাচীরের তলাটাতেই। থেমে যে গেছে সে কেবল বর্তমানের অসমাপ্তিবশত নয়। এখনো বয়স হয় নি ব'লে যে মানুষটি মাথায় খাটো তার জন্যে আক্ষেপ করবার দরকার নেই, কিন্তু যার ধাতের মধ্যেই সম্পূ বাড়বার জৈবধর্ম নেই তাকে যেন গ্রেনেডিয়ারের স্বজাতীয় বলে কল্পনা না করি।

গোড়ায় যাঁরা এ দেশে তাঁদের রাজতন্ত্রের সঙ্গে সঙ্গে শিক্ষাব্যবস্থার পত্তন করেছিলেন, দেখতে পাই, তাঁদেরও উত্তরাধিকারীরা বাইরের আসবাব এবং ইঁট-কাঠ-চুন -সুরকির প্যাটার্ন দেখিয়ে আমাদের এবং নিজেদেরকে ভোলাতে আনন্দ বোধ করেন। কিছুকাল পূর্বে একদিন কাগজে পড়েছিলুম, অন্য-এক প্রদেশের রাজ্যসচিব বিশ্ববিদ্যালয়ের ভিত-পত্তনের সময়ে বলেছিলেন যে, যারা বলে উমারতের বাহুল্যে আমরা শিক্ষার সম্বল খর্ব করি তারা অবুঝ, কেননা শিক্ষা তো কেবল জ্ঞানলাভ

নয়, ভালো দালানে বসে পড়াশুনো করা সেও একটা শিক্ষা। অর্থাৎ ক্লাসে বড়ো অধ্যাপকের চেয়ে বড়ো দেওয়ালটা বেশি বৈ কম নয়। আমাদের নালিশ এই যে, তলোয়ারটা যেখানে তালপাতার চেয়ে বেশি দামি করা অর্থাভাববশত অসম্ভব ব'লে সংবাদ পাই সেখানে তার থাপটাকে ইস্পাত দিয়ে বাঁধিয়ে দিলে আসল কাজ এগোয় না। তার চেয়ে ঐ ইস্পাতকে গলিয়ে একটা চলনসই গোছের ছুরি বানিয়ে দিলেও কতকটা সান্ত্বনার আশা থাকে।

আসল কথা, প্রাচ্য দেশে মূল্যবিচারের যে আদর্শ তাতে আমরা উপকরণকে অমৃতের সঙ্গে পাল্লা দেওয়ার দরকার বোধ করি নে। বিদ্যা জিনিসটি অমৃত, ইঁটকাঠের দ্বারা তার পরিমাপের কথা আমাদের মনেই হয় না। আন্তরিক সত্যের দিকে যা বড়ো বাহ্য রূপের দিকে তার আয়োজন আমাদের বিচারে না হলেও চলে। অন্তত, এতকাল সেইরকমই আমাদের মনের ভাব ছিল। বস্তুত, আমাদের দেশের প্রাচীন বিশ্ববিদ্যালয় আজও আছে বারাণসীতে। অত্যন্ত সত্য, নিতান্ত স্বভাবিক, অথচ মস্ত ক'রে চোখে পড়ে না। এ দেশের সনাতন সংস্কৃতির মূল উৎস সেইখানেই, কিন্তু তার সঙ্গে না আছে ইমারত, না আছে অতিজটিল ব্যায়সাধ্য ব্যবস্থাপ্রণালী। সেখানে বিদ্যাদানের চিরন্তন ব্রত দেশের অন্তরের মধ্যে অলিখিত অনুশাসনে লেখা। বিদ্যাদানের পদ্ধতি, তার নিঃস্বার্থ নিষ্ঠা, তার সৌজন্য, তার সরলতা, গুরুশিষ্যের মধ্যে অকৃত্রিম হৃদ্যতার সম্বন্ধ, সর্বপ্রকার আড়ম্বরকে উপেক্ষা করে এসেছে--কেননা, সত্যেই তার পরিচয়। প্রাচ্য দেশের কারিগররা যেরকম অতি সামান্য হাতিয়ার দিয়ে অতি অসামান্য শিল্পদ্রব্য তৈরি ক'রে থাকে পাশ্চাত্য বুদ্ধি তা কল্পনা করতে পারে না। যে নৈপুণ্যটি ভিতরের জিনিস তার বাহন প্রাণে এবং মনে। বাইরের স্থূল উপাদানটি অত্যন্ত হয়ে উঠলে আসল জিনিসটি চাপা পড়ে।

দুর্ভাগ্যক্রমে এই সহজ কথাটা আমরাই আজকাল পাশ্চাত্যের চেয়েও কম বুঝি। গরিব যখন ধনীকে মনে মনে ঈর্ষা করে তখন এইরকমই বুদ্ধিবিকার ঘটে। কোনো অনুষ্ঠানে যখন আমরা পাশ্চাত্যের অনুকরণ করি তখন ইঁট-কাঠের বাহুল্যে এবং যন্ত্রের চক্রে উপচক্রে নিজেকে ও অন্যকে ভুলিয়ে গৌরব করা সহজ। আসল জিনিসের কার্পণ্যে এইটেরই দরকার হয় বেশি। আসলের চেয়ে নকলের সাজসজ্জা স্বভাবতই যায় বাহুল্যের দিকে। প্রত্যহই দেখতে পাই, পূর্বদেশে জীবনসমস্যার আমরা যে সহজ সমাধান করেছিলুম তার থেকে কেবলই আমরা স্খলিত হচ্ছি। তার ফলে হল এই যে, আমাদের অবস্থাটা রয়ে গেল পূর্ববৎ, এমন-কি, তার চেয়ে কয়েক ডিগ্রি নীচের দিকে, অথচ আমাদের মেজাজটা ধার করে এনেছি অন্য দেশ থেকে যেখানে সমারোহের সঙ্গে তহবিলের বিশেষ আড়াআড়ি নেই।

মনে করে দেখো-না--এ দেশে বহুরোগজর্জর জনসাধারণের আরোগ্যবিধানের জন্যে রিক্ত রাজকোষের দোহাই দিয়ে ব্যয়সংকোচ করতে হয়, দেশজোড়া অতিবিরাট মূর্খতার কালিমা যথোচিত পরিমার্জন করতে অর্থে কুলোয় না, অর্থাৎ যে-সব অভাবে দেশ অন্তরে-বাহিরে মৃত্যুর তলায় তলাচ্ছে তার প্রতিকারের অতি ক্ষীণ উপায় দেউলে দেশের মতোই; অথচ এ দেশে শাসনব্যবস্থায় ব্যয়ের অজস্র প্রাচুর্য একেবারেই দরিদ্র দেশের মতো নয়। তার ব্যয়ের পরিমাণ স্বয়ং পাশ্চাত্য ধনী দেশকেও অনেক দূর এগিয়ে গেছে। এমন-কি, বিদ্যাবিভাগের সমস্ত বাহ্য ঠাট বজায় রাখবার ব্যয় বিদ্যা-পরিবেশনের চেয়ে বেশি। অর্থাৎ গাছের পাতাকে দর্শনধারী আকারে ঝাঁকড়া ক'রে তোলবার খাতিরে ফল ফলাবার রস-জোগানে টানাটানি চলছে। তা হোক, এর এই বাইরে দিকের অভাবের চেয়ে এর মর্মগত গুরুতর অভাবটাই সব চেয়ে দুশ্চিন্তার বিষয়। সেই কথাটাই বলতে চাই। সেই অভাবটা শিক্ষার যথাযোগ্য আধারের অভাব।

আজকালকার অস্ত্রচিকিৎসায় অঙ্গপ্রত্যঙ্গে বাইরে থেকে জোড়া লাগাবার কৌশল ক্রমশই উৎকর্ষ লাভ করছে। কিন্তু বাইরে-থেকে-জোড়া-লাগা জিনিসটা সমস্ত কলেবরের সঙ্গে প্রাণের মিলে মিলিত না হলে সেটাকে সুচিকিৎসা বলে না। তার ব্যাণ্ডেজ-বন্ধনের উত্তরোত্তর প্রভূত পরিস্ফীতি দেখে স্বয়ং রোগীর মনেও গর্ব এবং তৃপ্তি হতে পারে, কিন্তু মুমূর্ষু প্রাণপুরুষের এতে সান্ত্বনা নেই। শিক্ষা সম্বন্ধে এই কথাটা পূর্বেই বলেছি। বলেছি, বাইরের থেকে আহরিত শিক্ষাকে সমস্ত দেশ যতক্ষণ আপন করতে না পারবে ততক্ষণ তার বাহ্য উপকরণের দৈর্ঘ্যপ্রস্থের পরিমাপটাকে হিসাবের খাতায় লাভের কোঠায় ফেললে হন্ডি-কাটা ধারের টাকাটাকে মূলধনহারা ব্যবসায়ে মুনাফা ব'লে আনন্দ করার মতো হয়। সেই আপন করবার সর্বপ্রধান সহায় আপন ভাষা। শিক্ষার সকল খাদ্য ঐ ভাষার রসায়নে আমাদের আপন খাদ্য হয়। পক্ষীশাবক গোড়া থেকেই পোকা খেয়ে মানুষ; কোনো মানবসমাজে হঠাৎ যদি কোনো পক্ষীমহারাজের একাধিপত্য ঘটে তা হলেই কি এমন কথা বলা চলবে যে, সেই রাজখাদ্যটা খেলেই মানুষ প্রজাদেরও পাখা গজিয়ে উঠবে।

শিক্ষায় মাতৃভাষাই মাতৃদুগ্ধ, জগতে এই সর্বজনস্বীকৃত নিরতিশয় সহজ কথাটা বহুকাল পূর্বে একদিন বলেছিলেম; আজও তার পুনরাবৃত্তি করব। সেদিন যা ইংরেজি-শিক্ষার মন্ত্র-মুগ্ধ কর্ণকুহরে অশ্রাব্য হয়েছিল আজও যদি তা লক্ষ্যভ্রষ্ট হয় তবে আশা করি, পুনরাবৃত্তি করবার মানুষ বারে বারে পাওয়া যাবে।

আপন ভাষায় ব্যাপকভাবে শিক্ষার গোড়াপত্তন করবার আগ্রহ স্বভাবতই সমাজের মনে কাজ করে, এটা তার সুস্থ চিত্তের লক্ষণ। রামমোহন রায়ের বন্ধু পাদ্রি এডাম সাহেব বাংলাদেশের প্রাথমিক শিক্ষার যে রিপোর্ট প্রকাশ করেন তাতে দেখা যায় বাংলা-বিহারে এক লক্ষের উপর পাঠশালা ছিল, দেখা যায় প্রায় প্রত্যেক গ্রামেই ছিল জনসাধারণকে অন্তত ন্যূনতম শিক্ষাদানের ব্যবস্থা। এ ছাড়া প্রায় তখনকার ধনী মাত্রেই আপন চণ্ডীমণ্ডপে সামাজিক

কর্তব্যের অঙ্গরূপে পাঠশালা রাখতেন, গুরুমশায় বৃত্তি ও বাসা পেতেন তাঁরই কাছ থেকে। আমার প্রথম অক্ষরপরিচয় আমাদেরই বাড়ির দালানে, প্রতিবেশী পোড়োদের সঙ্গে। মনে আছে এই দালানের নিভৃত খ্যাতিহীনতা ছেড়ে আমার সতীর্থ আত্মীয় দুজন যখন অশ্বরথযোগে সরকারি বিদ্যালয়ে প্রবেশাধিকার পেলেন তখন মানহানির দুঃসহ দুঃখে অশ্রুপাত করেছি এবং গুরুমশায় আশ্চর্য ভবিষ্যৎদৃষ্টির প্রভাবে বলেছিলেন, ঐখান থেকে ফিরে আসবার ব্যর্থ প্রয়াসে আরো অনেক বেশি অশ্রু আমাকে ফেলতে হবে। তখনকার প্রথম শিক্ষার জন্য শিশুশিক্ষা প্রভৃতি যে-সকল পাঠ্যপুস্তক ছিল, মনে আছে, আবকাশকালেও বার বার তার পাতা উল্টিয়েছি। এখনকার ছেলেদের কাছে তার প্রত্যক্ষ পরিচয় দিতে কুণ্ঠিত হব, কিন্তু সমস্ত দেশের শিক্ষা-পরিবেশনের স্বাভাবিক ইচ্ছা ঐ অত্যন্ত গরিব-ভাবে-ছাপানো বইগুলির পত্রপুটে রক্ষিত ছিল––এই মহৎ গৌরব এখনকার কোনো শিশুপাঠ্য বইয়ে পাওয়া যাবে না। দেশের খাল-বিল-নদী-নালায় আজ জল শুকিয়ে এল, তেমনি রাজার অনাদরে আধমরা হয়ে এল সর্বসাধারণের নিরক্ষরতা দূর করবার স্বাদেশিক ব্যবস্থা।

দেশে বিদ্যাশিক্ষার যে সরকারি কারখানা আছে তার চাকায় সামান্য কিছু বদল করতে হলে অনেক হাতুড়ি-পেটাপিটির দরকার হয়। সে খুব শক্ত হাতের কর্ম। সেই শক্ত হাতই ছিল আশু মুখুজ্জে মশায়ের। বাঙালির ছেলে ইংরেজিবিদ্যায় যতই পাকা হোক, তবু শিক্ষা পুরো করবার জন্যে তাকে বাংলা শিখতেই হবে, ঠেলা দিয়ে মুখুজ্জেমশায় বাংলার বিশ্ববিদ্যালয়কে এতটা দূর পর্যন্ত বিচলিত করেছিলেন। হয়তো ঐ পথটায় তার চলৎশক্তির সূত্রপাত করে দিয়েছেন, হয়তো তিনি বেঁচে থাকলে চাকা আরো এগোত। হয়তো সেই চালনার সংকেত মন্ত্রণাসভার দফতরে এখনো পরিণতির দিকে উন্মুখ আছে।

তবু আমি যে আজ উদ্‌বেগ প্রকাশ করছি তার কারণ, বিশ্ববিদ্যালয়ের যানবাহনটা অত্যন্ত ভারী এবং বাংলাভাষার পথ

এথনো কাঁচা পথ। এই সমস্যা-সমাধান দুরূহ ব'লে পাছে হতে-করতে এমন একটা অতি অস্পষ্ট ভাবী কালে তাকে ঠেলে দেওয়া হয় যা অসম্ভাবিতের নামান্তর, এই আমাদের ভয়। আমাদের গতি মন্দাক্রান্তা, কিন্তু আমাদের অবস্থাটা সবুর করবার মতো নয়। তাই আমি বলি পরিপূর্ণ সুযোগের জন্যে সুদীর্ঘ কাল অপেক্ষা না করে অল্প বহরে কাজটা আরম্ভ করে দেওয়া ভালো, যেমন ক'রে চারাগাছ রোপণ করে সেই সহজ ভাবে। অর্থাৎ তার মধ্যে সমগ্র গাছেরই আদর্শ আছে; বাড়তে বাড়তে দিনে দিনে সেই আদর্শ সম্পূর্ণ হয়। বয়স্ক ব্যক্তির পাশে শিশু যখন দাঁড়ায় সে আপন সমগ্রতার সম্পূর্ণ ইঙ্গিত নিয়েই দাঁড়ায়। এমন নয়, একটা ঘরে বছর-দুয়েক ধ'রে ছেলেটার কেবল পা'খানা তয়ের হচ্ছে, আর-একটা ঘরে এগিয়েছে হাতের কনুইটা পর্যন্ত। এতদূর অত্যন্ত সতর্কতা সৃষ্টিকর্তার নেই। সৃষ্টির ভূমিকাতেও অপরিণতি সত্ত্বেও সমগ্রতা থাকে।

তেমনি বাংলা-বিশ্ববিদ্যালয়ের একটি সজীব সমগ্র শিশুমূর্তি দেখতে চাই, সে মূর্তি কারখানাঘরে-তৈরি থণ্ড থণ্ড বিভাগের ক্রমশ যোজনা নয়। বয়স্ক বিদ্যালয়ের পাশে এসেই সে দাঁড়াক বালকবিদ্যালয় হয়ে। তার বালকমূর্তির মধ্যেই দেখি তার বিজয়ী মূর্তি, দেখি ললাটে তার রাজাসন-অধিকারের প্রথম টিকা।

বিদ্যালয়ের কাজে যাঁরা অভিজ্ঞ তাঁরা জানেন, এক দল ছাত্র স্বভাবতই ভাষাশিক্ষা অপটু। ইংরেজি ভাষায় অনধিকার সত্ত্বেও যদি তারা কোনোমতে ম্যাট্রিকের দেউড়িটা পেরিয়ে যায় উপরের সিঁড়ি ভাঙবার বেলায় বসে পড়ে, আর ঠেলে তোলা যায় না।

এই দুর্গতির অনেকগুলো কারণ আছে। একে তো যে ছেলের মাতৃভাষা বাংলা, ইংরেজি ভাষার মতো বালাই তার আর নেই। ও যেন বিলিতি তলোয়ারের খাপে দিশি খাঁড়া ভরবার কসরত। তার পরে, গোড়ার দিকে ভালো শিক্ষকের কাছে ভালো নিয়মে ইংরেজি শেখার সুযোগ অল্প ছেলেরই হয়, গরিবের ছেলের তো হয়ই না। তাই অনেক স্থলেই বিশল্যকরণীর পরিচয় ঘটে না

বলেই গোটা ইংরেজি বই মুখস্থ করা ছাড়া উপায় থাকে না। সেরকম ত্রেতাযুগীয় বীরত্ব ক'জন ছেলের কাছে আশা করা যায়?

শুধু এই কারণেই কি তারা বিদ্যামন্দির থেকে আণ্ডামানে চালান যাবার উপযুক্ত? ইংলণ্ডে একদিন চুরির দণ্ড ছিল ফাঁসি, এ যে তার চেয়েও কড়া আইন, এ যে চুরি করতে পারে না ব'লেই ফাঁসি। না বুঝে বই মুখস্থ ক'সে পাস করা কি চুরি করে পাস করা নয়? পরীক্ষাগারে বইখানা চাদরের মধ্যে নিয়ে গেলেই চুরি, আর মগজের মধ্যে করে গিয়ে গেলে তাকে কী বলব? আস্ত-বই-ভাঙা উত্তর বসিয়ে যারা পাস করে তারাই তো চোরাই কড়ি দিয়ে পারানি জোগায়।

তা হোক, যে উপায়েই তারা পার হোক, নালিশ করতে চাই নে। তবু এ প্রশ্নটা থেকে যায় যে, বহুসংখ্যক যে-সব হতভাগা পার হতে পারল না তাদের পক্ষে হাওড়ার পুলটাই নাহয় দু-ফাঁক হয়েছে, কিন্তু কোনো রকমেরই সরকারি খেয়াও কি তাদের কপালে জুটবে না—একটা লাইসেন্স-দেওয়া পান্সি, মোটর-চালিত নাই-বা হল, নাহয় হল দিশি হাতে-দাঁড়-টানা?

অন্য স্বাধীন দেশের সঙ্গে আমাদের একটা মস্ত প্রভেদ আছে। সেখানে শিক্ষার পূর্ণতার জন্যে যারা দরকার বোঝে তারা বিদেশী ভাষা শেখে। কিন্তু, বিদ্যার জন্যে যেটুকু আবশ্যক তার বেশি তাদের না শিখলেও চলে। কেননা, তাদের দেশের সমস্ত কাজই নিজের ভাষায়। আমাদের দেশের অধিকাংশ কাজই ইংরেজি ভাষায়। যাঁরা শাসন করেন তাঁরা আমাদের ভাষা শিখতে, অন্তত যথেষ্ট পরিমাণে শিখতে, বাধ্য নন। পর্বত নড়েন না, কাজেই সচল মানুষকেই প্রয়োজনের গরজে পর্বতের দিকে নড়তে হয়। ইংরেজি ভাষা কেবল যে আমাদের জানতে হবে তা নয়, তাকে ব্যবহার করতে হবে। সেই ব্যবহার বিদেশী আদর্শে যতই নিখুঁত হবে সেই পরিমাণেই স্বদেশীদের এবং কর্তাদের কাছে আমাদের সমাদর। আমি একজন ইংরেজ ম্যাজিস্ট্রেটকে জানতুম; তিনি

বাংলা সহজেই পড়তে পারতেন। বাংলাসাহিত্যে তাঁর রুচির আমি প্রশংসা করবই; কারণ, রবীন্দ্রনাথের রচনা তিনি পড়তেন এবং পড়ে আনন্দ পেতেন। একবার গ্রামবাসীদের এক সভায় তিনি উপস্থিত ছিলেন। গ্রামহিতৈষী বাঙালী বক্তাদের মধ্যে যা যা বক্তব্য ছিল বলা হলে পর ম্যাজিস্ট্রেটের মনে হল, গ্রামের লোককে বাংলায় কিছু বলা তাঁরও কর্তব্য। কোনো প্রকারে দশ মিনিট কর্তব্য পালন করেছিলেন। গ্রামের লোকেরা বাড়ি ফিরে গিয়ে আত্মীয়দের জানালো যে, সাহেবের ইংরেজি বক্তৃতা এইমাত্র তারা শুনে এসেছে। পরভাষা ব্যবহার সম্বন্ধে বিদেশীর কাছে খুব বেশি আশা না করলেও তাকে অসম্মান করা হয় না। ম্যাজিস্ট্রেট নিজেই জানতেন, তাঁর বাংলা-কথনের ভাষা এমন নয় যে, গৌড়জন আনন্দে যার অর্থবোধ করতে পারে সম্যক্। তাই নিয়ে তিনি হেসেও ছিলেন। আমরা হলে কিছুতেই হাসতে পারতুম না, ধরণীকে অনুনয় করতুম দ্বিধা হতে। ইংরেজি সম্বন্ধে আমাদের বিদেশিত্বের কৈফিয়ত আত্মীয় বা অনাত্মীয়-সমাজে গ্রাহ্য হয় না। একদা বিশ্ববিখ্যাত জর্মান তত্ত্বজ্ঞানী অয়কেনের ইংরেজি বক্তৃতা শুনেছিলেম। আশা করি এ কথাটা অত্যুক্তি ব'লে মনে করবেন না যে, ইংরেজি শুনলে আমি বুঝতে পারি সেটা ইংরেজি। কিন্তু অয়কেনের ইংরেজি শুনে আমার ধাঁধা লেগেছিল। এ নিয়ে অয়কেনকে অবজ্ঞা করতে কেউ পারে নি। কিন্তু এ দশা আমার হলে কী হত সে কথা কল্পনা করলেও কর্ণমূল রক্তবর্ণ হয়ে ওঠে। বাবু-ইংলিশ নামে নিরতিশয় অবজ্ঞা-সূচক একটা শব্দ ইংরেজিতে আছে; কিন্তু ইংরেজি-বাংলা তার চেয়ে বহুগুণে বিকৃত হলেও ওটাকে অনিবার্য ব'লে মেনে নিই, অবজ্ঞা করতে পারি নে। আমাদের কারো ইংরেজিতে ত্রুটি হলে দেশের লোকের কাছে সেটা যেমন হসনীয় হয় এমন কোনো প্রহসন হয় না। সেই হাসির মধ্য থেকে পরাধীনতারই কলঙ্ক দেখা দেয় কালো হয়ে। যতদিন আমাদের এই দশা বহাল থাকবে ততদিন আমাদের শিক্ষাভিমানীকে কেবল যথেষ্ট ইংরেজি নয়, অতিরিক্ত ইংরেজি শিখতে হবে। তাতে যে অতিরিক্ত সময় লাগে সেই

সময়টা যথোচিত শিক্ষার হিসাব থেকে কাটা যায়। তা হোক, অত্যাবশ্যকের চেয়ে অতিরিক্তকে যতদিন আমাদের মেনে চলতেই হবে ততদিন ইংরেজি -ভাষায়-পেটাই-করা বিশ্ববিদ্যালয়ের বিজাতীয় ভার আমাদের আগাগোড়াই বহন করা অনিবার্য। কেননা, ভালো ক'রে বাংলা শেখার দ্বারাতেই ভালো ক'রে ইংরেজি শেখার সহায়তা হতে পারে, এ কথা মনে করতে সাহস হবে না। গরজটা অতিশয় জরুরি, তাই মন বলতে থাকে, কী জানি! আমার সেই শিক্ষানেতা গুরুজনের মতো অভিভাবক বাংলাদেশে বেশি পাওয়া যাবে না, তাই বেশি দাবি ক'রে লাভ নেই। বাংলা-বিশ্ববিদ্যালয়ের একেশ্বরত্বের অধিকার আজ সহ্য হবে না। নূতন স্বাধীনতার দাবিকে পুরাতন অধীনতার সেফ্‌গার্ড্‌স্‌এর দ্বারা বেড়া তুলে দেবার আশ্বাস না দিতে পারলে সবটাই ফেঁসে যেতে পারে, এই আমার ভয় তাই বলছি, আমাদের বিশ্ববিদ্যালয়ের ভিতরের দালানে বিদ্যার ভোজের যে আয়োজন চলছে তার রান্নাটা বিলিতি মসলায় বিলিতি ডেকচিতে, তার আহারটা বিলিতি আসনে বিলিতি পাত্রেই চলুক; তার জন্যে প্রাণপণে আমরা যে মূল্য দিতে পারি তাতে ভূরিভোজের আশা করা চলবে না। যারা কার্ড পেয়েছে তারা ভিতর-মহলেই বসুক, আর যারা রবাহূত বাইরের আঙিনায় তাদের জন্যে পাত পেড়ে দেওয়া যাক-না। টেবিল পাতা নাই হল, কলাপাত পড়ুক।

বাংলাদেশে উচ্চশিক্ষাকে চিরকাল অথবা অতি দীর্ঘকাল পরান্নভোজী পরাবসথশায়ী হয়ে থাকতেই হবে, কেননা এ ভাষায় পাঠ্যপুস্তক নেই, এই কঠিন তর্ক তুললে একদা সেটা কথা-কাটাকাটির ঘূর্ণি হাওয়াতেই আবর্তিত হতে পারত; দূর দেশ ছাড়া কাছের পাড়া থেকে দৃষ্টান্ত আহরণ ক'রে ঐ উৎপাতটাকে শান্ত করা যেতে পারত না। আজ হাতের কাছেই সুযোগ মিলেছে।

ভারতের অন্যান্য বিশ্ববিদ্যালয়ের তুলনায় দক্ষিণ হায়দ্রাবাদ বয়সে অল্প; সেইজন্যই বোধ করি তার সাহস বেশি, তা ছাড়া এ কথা বোধ করি সেখানে স্বীকৃত হওয়া সহজ হয়েছে যে,

শিক্ষাবিধানে কৃপণতা করার মতো নিজেকে ফাঁকি দেওয়া আর-কিছুই হতে পারে না। ঐ বিশ্ববিদ্যালয়ে অবিচলিত নিষ্ঠার সহায়তায় আদ্যন্তমধ্যে উর্দু ভাষার প্রবর্তন হয়েছে। তারই প্রবল তাড়নায় ঐ ভাষায় পাঠ্যপুস্তক-রচনা প্রায় পরিপূর্ণ হয়ে উঠল। ইমারতও হল, সিঁড়িও হল, নীচে থেকে উপরে লোক-যাতায়াত চলছে। হতে পারে, সেখান যথেষ্ট সুযোগ ও স্বাধীনতা ছিল। কিন্তু তবুও চারি দিকের প্রচলিত মত ও অভ্যাসের দুস্তর বাধা অতিক্রম ক'রে যিনি এমন মহৎ সংকল্পকে মনে এবং কাজের ক্ষেত্রে স্থান দিতে পেরেছেন সেই স্যর আকবর হয়দরির সাহসকে ধন্য বলি। বিনা দ্বিধায় জ্ঞানসাধনার দুর্গমতাকে তাঁদের মাতৃভাষা ক্ষেত্রে সমভূম করে দিয়ে উর্দুভাষীদের তিনি যে মহৎ উপকার করেছেন তার দৃষ্টান্ত যদি আমাদের মন থেকে সংশয় দূর এবং শিক্ষাসংস্কৃতির বিলম্বিত গতিকে ত্বরান্বিত করতে পারে তবে একদা আমাদের বিশ্ববিদ্যালয় অন্য সকল সভ্য দেশের বিশ্ববিদ্যালয়ের সমপর্যায়ে দাঁড়িয়ে গৌরব করতে পারবে। নইলে প্রতিধ্বনি ধ্বনির সঙ্গে একই মূল্য দাবি করবে কোন্ স্পর্ধায়? বনস্পতির শাখায় যে পরগাছা ঝুলছে সে বনস্পতির সমতুল্য নয়।

বিদেশ থেকে যেখানে আমরা যন্ত্র কিনে এনে ব্যবহার করি সেখানে তার ব্যবহারে ভয়ে ভয়ে অক্ষরে পুঁথি মিলিয়ে চলতে হয়, কিন্তু সজীব গাছের চারার মধ্যে তার আত্মচালনা-আত্মপরিবর্ধনার তত্ত্ব অনেক পরিমাণে ভিতরে ভিতরে কাজ করতে থাকে। যন্ত্র আমাদের স্বায়ত্ত হতে পারে, কিন্তু তাতে আমাদের স্বানুবর্তিতা থাকে না। স্বাধীন পরিচালনার ক্ষেত্রে সেখানে ন্যাশনল কলেজ গড়া হয়েছে, হিন্দু-বিশ্ববিদ্যালয়-স্থাপনায় যেখানে দেখা গেল অর্থব্যয় অজস্র হয়েছে, সেখানেও ছাঁচ-উপাসক আমরা ছাঁচের মুঠো থেকে আমাদের স্বাতন্ত্র্যকে কিছুতে ছাড়িয়ে নিতে পারছি নে। সেখানেও শুধু যে ইংরেজি য়ুনিভর্সিটির গায়ের মাপে ছেঁটেছুঁটে কুর্তি বানাচ্ছি তা নয়, ইংরেজের জমি থেকে তার ভাষাসুদ্ধ উপড়ে এনে দেশের চিত্তক্ষেত্রকে কোদালে কুড়ুলে ক্ষত

বিক্ষত ক'রে বিরুদ্ধ ভূমিতে তাকে রোপণের গলদ্‌ঘর্ম চেষ্টা করছি; তাতে শিকড় না ছড়াচ্ছে চারি দিকে, না পৌঁচছে গভীরে।

বাংলাভাষার দোহাই দিয়ে যে শিক্ষার আলোচনা বারংবার দেশের সামনে এনেছি তার মূলে আছে আমার ব্যক্তিগত অভিজ্ঞতা। যখন বালক ছিলেম, আশ্চর্য এই যে, তখন অবিমিশ্র বাংলাভাষায় শিক্ষা দেবার একটা সরকারি ব্যবস্থা ছিল। তখনো যে-সবস্কুলের রাস্তা ছিল কলকাতা য়ুনিভর্সিটির প্রবেশদ্বারের দিকে সৃষ্টিত, যারা ছাত্রদের আবৃত্তি করাচ্ছিল "he is up তিনি হন উপরে', যারা ইংরেজি ঐ সর্বনাম শব্দের ব্যাখ্যা মুখস্থ করাচ্ছিল "I, by myself I, তাদের আহ্বানে সাড়া দিচ্ছিল সেই-সব পরিবারের ছাত্র যারা ভদ্রসমাজে উচ্চ পদবীর অভিমান করতে পারত। এদের দূর পার্শ্বে সংকুচিতভাবে ছিল প্রথমোক্ত শিক্ষাবিভাগ, ছাত্রবৃত্তির পোড়োদের জন্য। তারা কনিষ্ঠ অধিকারী, তাদের শেষ সদ্‌গতি ছিল "নর্মাল স্কুল'-নামধারী মাথা-হেঁট করা বিদ্যালয়ে। তাদের জীবিকার শেষ লক্ষ্য ছিল বাংলা-বিদ্যালয়ে স্বল্পসন্তুষ্ট বাংলা-পণ্ডিতি ব্যবসায়ে। আমার অভিভাবক সই নর্মাল স্কুলের দেউড়ি-বিভাগে আমাকে ভর্তি করেছিলেন। আমি সম্পূর্ণ বাংলাভাষার পথ দিয়েই শিখেছিলেম ভূগোল, ইতিহাস, গণিত, কিছু-পরিমাণ প্রাকৃত বিজ্ঞান, আর সেই ব্যাকরণ যার অনুশাসনে বাংলাভাষা সংস্কৃতভাষার আভিজাত্যের অনুকরণে আপন সাধু ভাষার কৌলীন্য ঘোষণা করত। এই শিক্ষার আদর্শ ও পরিমাণ বিদ্যা হিসাবে তখনকার ম্যাট্রিকের চেয়ে কম দরের ছিল না। আমার বারো বৎসর বয়স পর্যন্ত ইংরেজি-বর্জিত এই শিক্ষাই চলেছিল। তার পরে ইংরেজি বিদ্যালয় প্রবেশের অনতিকাল পরেই আমি ইস্কুল-মাস্টারের শাসন হতে ঊর্ধ্বশ্বাসে পলাতক।

এর ফলে শিশুকালেই বাংলাভাষার ভাণ্ডারে আমার প্রবেশ ছিল অবারিত। সে ভাণ্ডারে উপকরণ যতই সামান্য থাক, শিশুমনের পোষণ ও তোষণের পক্ষে যথেষ্ট ছিল। উপবাসী মনকে দীর্ঘকাল বিদেশী ভাষার চড়াই পথে খুঁড়িয়ে খুঁড়িয়ে দম হারিয়ে চলতে

হয় নি, শেখর সঙ্গে বোঝার প্রত্যহ সাংঘাতিক মাথা-ঠোকাঠুকি না হওয়াতে আমাকে বিদ্যালয়ের হাসপাতালে মানুষ হতে হয় নি। এমন-কি, সেই কাঁচা বয়সে যখন আমাকে মেঘনাদবধ পড়তে হয়েছে তখন একদিন মাত্র আমার বাঁ গালে একটা বড়ো চড় খেয়েছিলুম, এইটেই একমাত্র অবিস্মরণীয় অপঘাত; যতদূর মনে পড়ে মহাকাব্যের শেষ সর্গ পর্যন্তই আমার কানের উপরেও শিক্ষকের হস্তক্ষেপ ঘটে নি, অথবা, সেটা অত্যন্তই বিরল ছিল।

কৃতজ্ঞতার কারণ আরো আছে। মনে চিন্তা এবং ভাব কথায় প্রকাশ করবার সাধনা শিক্ষার একটি প্রধান অঙ্গ। অন্তরে বাহিরে দেওয়া-নেওয়া এই প্রক্রিয়ার সামঞ্জস্যসাধনাই সুস্থ প্রাণের লক্ষণ। বিদেশী ভাষাই প্রকাশচর্চার প্রধান অবলম্বন হলে সেটাতে যেন মুখোশের ভিতর দিয়ে ভাবপ্রকাশের অভ্যাস দাঁড়ায়। মুখোশ-পরা অভিনয় দেখেছি; তাতে ছাঁচে-গড়া ভাবকে অবিচল করে দেখানো যায় একটা বাঁধা সীমানার মধ্যে, তার বাইরে স্বাধীনতা পাওয়া যায় না। বিদেশী ভাষার আবরণের আড়ালে প্রকাশের চর্চা সেই জাতের। একদা মধুসূদনের মতো ইংরেজি-বিদ্যায় অসামান্য পণ্ডিত এবং বঙ্কিমচন্দ্রের মতো বিজাতীয় বিদ্যালয়ের কৃতী ছাত্র এই মুখোশের ভিতর দিয়ে ভাব বাংলাতে চেষ্টা করেছিলেন; শেষকালে হতাশ হয়ে সেটা টেনে ফেলে দিতে হল।

রচনার সাধনা অমনিতেই সহজ নয়। সেই সাধনাকে পরভাষার দ্বারা ভারাক্রান্ত করলে চিরকালের মতো তাকে পঙ্গু করার আশঙ্কা থাকে। বিদেশী ভাষার চাপে বামন হওয়া মন আমাদের দেশে নিশ্চয়ই বিস্তর আছে। প্রথম থেকেই মাতৃভাষার স্বাভাবিক সুযোগে মানুষ হলে সেই মন কী হতে পারত আন্দাজ করতে পারি নে ব'লে, তুলনা করতে পারি নে।

যাই হোক, ভাগ্যবলে অখ্যাত নর্মাল স্কুলে ভর্তি হয়েছিলুম, তাই কচি বয়সে রচনা করা ও কুস্তি করাকে এক ক'রে তুলতে হয় নি; চলা এবং রাস্তা খোঁড়া ছিল না একসঙ্গে। নিজের ভাষায়

চিন্তাকে ফুটিয়ে তোলা, সাজিয়ে তোলার আনন্দ গোড়া থেকেই পেয়েছি। তাই বুঝেছি মাতৃভাষায় রচনার অভ্যাস সহজ হয়ে গেলে তার পরে যথাসময়ে অন্য ভাষা আয়ত্ত ক'রে সেটাকে সাহসপূর্বক ব্যবহার করতে কলমে বাধে না; ইংরেজির অতিপ্রচলিত জীর্ণ বাক্যাবলী সাবধানে সেলাই ক'রে ক'রে কাঁথা বুনতে হয় না। ইস্কুল-পালানো অবকাশে যেটুকু ইংরেজি আমি পথে-পথে সংগ্রহ করেছি সেটুকু নিজের খুশিতে ব্যবহার করে থাকি; তার প্রধান কারণ, শিশুকাল থেকে বাংলাভাষায় রচনা করতে আমি অভ্যস্ত। অন্তত, আমার এগারো বছর বয়স পর্যন্ত আমার কাছে বাংলাভাষার কোনো প্রতিদ্বন্দ্বী ছিল না। রাজসম্মানগর্বিত কোনো সুয়োরানী তাকে গোয়ালঘরের কোণে মুখ চাপা দিয়ে রাখে নি। আমার ইংরেজি-শিক্ষায় সেই আদিম দৈন্য সত্ত্বেও পরিমিত উপকরণ নিয়ে আমার চিত্তবৃত্তি কেবল গৃহিণীপনার জোরে ইংরেজিজানা ভদ্র সমাজে আমার মান বাঁচিয়ে আসছে; যা-কিছু ছেঁড়া-ফাটা, যা-কিছু মাপে খাটো, তাকে কোনোরকমে ঢেকে বেড়াতে পেরেছে। নিশ্চিত জানি তার কারণ, শিশুকাল থেকে আমার মনের পরিণতি ঘটেছে কোনো-ভেজাল-না-দেওয়া মাতৃভাষায়; সেই খাদ্যে খাদ্যবস্তুর সঙ্গে যথেষ্ট খাদ্যপ্রাণ ছিল, যে খাদ্যপ্রাণে সৃষ্টিকর্তা তাঁর জাদুমন্ত্র দিয়েছেন।

অবশেষে আমার নিবেদন এই যে, আজ কোনো ভগীরথ বাংলাভাষায় শিক্ষাস্রোতকে বিশ্ববিদ্যার সমুদ্র পর্যন্ত নিয়ে চলুন, দেশের সহস্র সহস্র মন মূর্খতার অভিশাপে প্রাণহীন হয়ে পড়ে আছে, এই সঞ্জীবনী ধারার স্পর্শে বেঁচে উঠুক, পৃথিবীর কাছে আমাদের উপেক্ষিত মাতৃভাষার লজ্জা দূর হোক, বিদ্যাবিতরণের অন্নসত্র স্বদেশের নিত্যসম্পদ হয়ে আমাদের আতিথ্যের গৌরব রক্ষা করুক।জানি নে হয়তো অভিজ্ঞ ব্যক্তি বলবেন, এ কথাটা কাজের কথা নয়, এ কবিকল্পনা। তা হোক, আমি বলব, আজ পর্যন্ত কেজো কথায় কেবল জোড়াতাড়ার কাজ চলেছে, সৃষ্টি হয়েছে কল্পনার বলে।

স্বাধীন শিক্ষা (swadhin shikkha)

দেশের শিক্ষাকে বিদেশী রাজার অধীনতা হইতে মুক্তি দিবার জন্য কী উপায় করা যাইতে পারে, এই প্রশ্ন ভাঙারেউঠিয়াছে।

যতদিন বিদ্যালয়ের উপাধিলাভের উপরে অন্নলাভ নির্ভর করিবে, ততদিন মুক্তির আশা করা যায় না এই কথাই সকলে বলিতেছেন। কিন্তু কথাটা কেবল উচ্চশিক্ষা সম্বন্ধেই খাটে, তাহা আমাদিগকে মনে রাখিতে হইবে। পাড়াগাঁয়ে প্রাকৃতগণ যে শিক্ষালাভের জন্য ছেলেকে পাঠশালায় পাঠায়, সে শিক্ষার দ্বারা গবর্মেন্টের চাকরি কেহ প্রত্যাশা করে না। আমাদের দেশে এই পাঠশালা চিরকাল স্বাধীন ছিল। আজও এই-সকল পাঠশালার অধিকাংশ ব্যয় দেশের লোক বহন করে; কেবল তাহার উপর আর সামান্য দুই-চার-আনার লোভে এই আমাদের নিতান্তই দেশীয় ব্যবস্থা পরের হাতে আপনাকে বিকাইয়াছে।

এই প্রাথমিক পাঠশালার চেয়ে উপর পর্যন্ত উঠে অথচ কলেজ পর্যন্ত পৌঁছে না এমন একদল ছাত্র আছে, সাধারণত ইহারাও সরকারি চাকরির দাবি করিতে পারে না। ইহারা অনেকেই সদাগরের আপিসে, জমিদারের সেরেস্তায়, ধনিগৃহের দপ্তরখানায়, গৃহস্থঘরের বাজার-সরকার প্রভৃতি কাজে নিযুক্ত হইবার জন্য চেষ্টা করে। কিন্তু দেশে ইহাদের শিক্ষার তেমন ভালো ব্যবস্থা নাই। পূর্বে ছাত্রবৃত্তি স্কুল ইহাদের কতকটা উপযোগী ছিল। কিন্তু মাইনর স্কুল এখন ছাত্রবৃত্তিকে প্রায় চাপিয়া মারিল। ইংরেজি শিক্ষাই যে-সব স্কুলের প্রধান লক্ষ্য এবং কলেজই যাহার গম্য স্থান, সে-সকল স্কুলে কিছুদূর পর্যন্ত পড়িয়া পড়াশুনা ছাড়িয়া দিলে না বাংলা না ইংরেজি না কিছুই শেখা হয়। অতএব যাহারা

পাঠশালা পর্যন্ত পড়ে এবং যাহারা নানাপ্রকার অভাব ও অসুবিধা বশত তাহার চেয়ে আর-কিছুদূর মাত্র পড়িবার আশা করিতে পারে, দেশ তাহাদের শিক্ষার ভার নিজের হাতে লইলে বাধার কারণ তো কিছুই দেখা যায় না। গুনতি করিয়া দেখিলে কলেজে পাস-করা ছাত্রদের চেয়ে ইহাদের সংখ্যা অনেক বেশি হইবে। এই বহুবিস্তৃত নিম্নতন শ্রেণীর শিক্ষা আমরা যদি উপযুক্তভাবে দিতে পারি, তবে দেশের শ্রী ফিরিয়া যায় সন্দেহ নাই। ইহাদের শিক্ষা গোড়া হইতে এমনভাবে দিতে হইবে যাহাতে লোকহিত কাহাকে বলে তাহা ইহারা ভালো করিয়া জানিতে এবং জীবিকা উপার্জনের জন্য হাতে-কলমে সকল রকমে তৈরি হইয়া উঠিতে পারে। পাঠশালায় শিশুবয়সে যে-সকল ভাব, জ্ঞান ও অভ্যাস সঞ্চার করিয়া দেওয়া যায়, বড়োবয়সে বক্তৃতার দ্বারা তাহা কখনোই সম্ভবপর হয় না।

যাই হোক, উচ্চশিক্ষায় দেশের লোকের পক্ষে গবর্মেন্টের প্রতিযোগিতা করিবার যে-সকল বাধা আছে নিম্নশিক্ষায় তাহা নাই। কিন্তু এতবড়ো দেশব্যাপী কাজের ভার আমাদিগকে নিজের হাতে গ্রহণ করিতে হইবে, এ কথা বলিলেই বিজ্ঞ ব্যক্তিরা হতাশ হইয়া পড়েন। অথচ তাঁহারা ইহাও জানেন, এ কাজ সরকারের হাতে দিলে কিণ্ডারগার্টেনের ধুয়া ধরিয়া নিতান্ত ছেলেখেলা হইতে থাকিবে এবং লাভের মধ্যে ম্যাকমিলন কোম্পানির উদরপূরণ হইবে। কিছু না-হউক, এ শিক্ষা আমরা যেমন চাই তেমন হইবে না, বরঞ্চ কতক অংশে বিপরীত হইবে।

অন্যত্র ইহা তো দেখিয়াছি দয়ানন্দের দল আপন সম্প্রদায়ের জন্য স্বচেষ্টায় বিদ্যালয় স্থাপন করিতেছে। আমাদের দেশেও এইরূপ চেষ্টা কী করিলে সাধ্য হইতে পারে এবং এই-সকল নিম্নতন বিদ্যালয়গুলিতে কী কী বিষয় কী নিয়মে শিক্ষা দিতে হইবে, সুধীগণ ভাণ্ডারপত্রে তাহার আলোচনা করিলে সম্পাদক কৃতার্থ হইবেন।

(ORIGINAL BANGLA TEXT)

স্ত্রীশিক্ষা (strishikkha)

আমরা শ্রীমতী লীলা মিত্রের কাছ হইতে স্ত্রীশিক্ষা সম্বন্ধে একখানি চিঠি পাইয়াছি, তাহা আলোচনা করিয়া দেখিবার যোগ্য। চিঠিখানি এই--

এক দল লোক বলেন, স্ত্রীশিক্ষার প্রয়োজন নাই, কারণ স্ত্রীলোক শিক্ষিতা হইলে পুরুষের নানা বিষয়ে নানা অসুবিধা। শিক্ষিতা স্ত্রী স্বামীকে দেবতা বলিয়া মনে করে না, স্বামীসেবায় তার তেমন মন থাকে না, পড়াশুনা লইয়াই সে ব্যস্ত ইত্যাদি।

আবার আর-এক দল বলেন, স্ত্রীশিক্ষার প্রয়োজন খুবই আছে, কেননা আমরা পুরুষরা শিক্ষিত, আমরা যাহাদের লইয়া ঘরসংসার করিব তাহারা যদি আমাদের ভাব চিন্তা আশা আকাঙ্ক্ষা বুঝিতেই না পারে তবে আমাদের পারিবারিক সুখের ব্যাঘাত হইবে ইত্যাদি।

দুই দলই নিজেদের দিক হইতে স্ত্রীশিক্ষার বিচার করিতেছেন। নারীর যে পুরুষের মতো ব্যক্তিত্ব আছে, সে যে অন্যের জন্য সৃষ্ট নয়, তাহার নিজের জীবনের যে সার্থকতা আছে, তাহা স্ত্রীশিক্ষার স্বপক্ষের বা বিপক্ষের কোনো উকিল স্বীকার করেন না। উকিলরা যে পক্ষ লইয়াছেন বস্তুত তাহা তাঁহাদের নিজেরই পক্ষ। মামলার নিষ্পত্তিতে যাঁহাদের প্রকৃত স্বার্থ তাঁহাদের কথা কাহারও মনে উদয় হয় না, এইটেই আশ্চর্য।

বিদ্যা যদি মনুষ্যত্বলাভের উপায় হয় এবং বিদ্যালাভে যদি মানবমাত্রেরই সহজাত অধিকার থাকে তবে নারীকে কোন্ নীতির

দোহাই দিয়া সে অধিকার হইতে বঞ্চিত করা যাইতে পারে বুঝিতে পারি না।

আবার, যাঁরা স্ত্রীলোককে তাঁহাদের নিজের জন্যই সৃষ্ট বলিয়া স্থির করিয়া বসিয়াছেন, তাঁরা যেটুকু বিদ্যা স্ত্রীর জন্য উচ্ছিষ্ট রাখিতে চান তাহা হইতে স্ত্রীলোকের মনুষ্যত্বের যথোচিত পুষ্টি আশা করা বাতুলতা।

যাঁহারা শিক্ষাদানে স্ত্রী-পুরুষ উভয়কেই সমভাবে সাহায্য করিতে প্রস্তুত তাঁহারা সাধারণ পুরুষের পঙ্‌ক্তিতে পড়েন না; তাঁহাদের আসন অনেক উচ্চে, সুতরাং তাঁহাদের কথা ছাড়িয়া দেওয়ই উচিত।

অতএব, গরজ যাঁহাদের তাঁহাদিগকেই কার্যক্ষেত্রে নামিতে হইবে। নিজের উদ্যমে ও শক্তিতে নিজেকে মুক্ত না করিলে অন্যে মুক্তি দিতে পারে না। অন্যে যেটাকে মুক্তি বলিয়া উপস্থিত করে সেটা বন্ধনেরই অন্য মূর্তি। পুরুষ যে স্ত্রীশার ছাঁচ গড়িয়াছে সেটা পুরুষের খেলার যোগ্য পুতুল গড়িবার ছাঁচ।

কিন্তু যিনি এ কার্যে অবতীর্ণা হইবেন তাঁহাকে সাধারণ স্ত্রীলোকের মতো গতানুগতিক হইলে চলিবে না। সংসারে লোকে যাহাকে সুখ বলে সেটাকে তিনি আদর্শ করিবেন না। এ কথা তাঁহাকে মনে রাখিতে হইবে, সন্তান গর্ভে ধারণ করাই তাঁহার চরম সার্থকতা নয়। তিনি পুরুষের আশ্রিতা, লজ্জাভয়ে লীনাঙ্গিনী, সামান্য ললনা নহেন; তিনি তাহার সংকটে সহায়, দুরূহ চিন্তায় অংশী এবং সুখে দুঃখে সহচরী হইয়া সংসারপথে তাহার প্রকৃত সহযাত্রী হইবেন। --

এই চিঠির মূল কথাটা আমি মানি। যাহা-কিছু জানিবার যোগ্য তাহাই বিদ্যা, তাহা পুরুষকেও জানিতে হইবে, মেয়েকেও জানিতে হইবে--শুধু কাজে খাটাইবার জন্য যে তাহা নয়, জানিবার জন্যই।

মানুষ জানিতে চায়, সেটা তার ধর্ম; এইজন্য জগতের আবশ্যক অনাবশ্যক সকল তত্ত্বই তার কাছে বিদ্যা হইয়া উঠিয়াছে। সেই তার জানিতে চাওয়াকে যদি থোরাক না জোগাই কিংবা তাকে কুপথ্য দিয়া ভুলাইয়া রাখি তবে তার মানবপ্রকৃতিকেই দুর্বল করি, এ কথা বলাই বাহুল্য।

কিন্তু, মানুষকে পুরা পরিমাণে মানুষ করিব এ কথা আমাদের সকলের অন্তরের কথা নয়। যখন সর্বসাধারণকে শিক্ষা দেওয়ার প্রস্তাব হয় তখন এক দল শিক্ষিত লোক বলিয়া থাকেন, তাহা হইলে আমরা চাকর পাইব কোথা হইতে? বোধ হয় শীঘ্রই এ সম্বন্ধে রসিক লোকে প্রহসন লিখিবেন যাহাতে দেখা যাইবে-- বাবুর চাকর কবিতা লিখিতেছে কিংবা নক্ষত্রলোকের নাড়িনক্ষত্র গণনা করিবার জন্য বড়ো বড়ো অঙ্ক ফাঁদিয়া বসিয়াছে, বাবু তাহাকে ধুতি কোঁচাইবার জন্য ডাকিতে সাহস করিতেছেন না পাছে তার ধ্যানের ব্যাঘাত হয়। মেয়েদের সম্বন্ধেও সেই এক কথা যে, তারা যদি লেখাপড়া শেখে তবে যে ঝাঁটা বঁটি ও শিলনোড়া বাবুদের ভাগে পড়ে।

অথচ ইঁহাদের তর্কের যুক্তিটা এই যে, মেয়েদের প্রকৃতিই স্বতন্ত্র। কিন্তু তাই যদি হয় তবে তাঁহাদের ভয়টা কিসের? পৃথিবীকে আমরা চ্যাপ্টা ভাবি কিন্তু তাহা গোল, এ কথা জানিলে পুরুষের পৌরুষ কমে না। তেমনি, বাসুকির মাথার উপর পৃথিবী নাই এ খবরটা পাইলে মেয়েদের মেয়েলিভাব নষ্ট হইবে এ কথা যদি বলি তবে বুঝিতে হইবে, মেয়েরা মেয়েই নয়, আমরা তাহাদিগকে অজ্ঞানের ছাঁচে ঢালিয়া মেয়ে করিয়া গড়িয়া তুলিয়াছি।

বিধাতা একদিন পুরুষকে পুরুষ এবং মেয়েকে মেয়ে করিয়া সৃষ্টি করিলেন, এটা তাঁর একটা আশ্চর্য উদ্ভাবন, সে কথা কবি হইতে আরম্ভ করিয়া জীবতত্ত্ববিৎ সকলেই স্বীকার করেন। জীবলোকে এই যে একটা ভেদ ঘটিয়াছে এই ভেদের মুখ দিয়া একটা প্রবল শক্তি এবং পরম আনন্দের উৎস উৎসারিত হইয়া উঠিয়াছে। ইস্কুল-মাস্টার কিংবা টেক্সবুক-কমিটি তাঁহাদের

এক্সেসাইজের খাতা কিংবা পাঠ্য ও অপাঠ্য বইয়ের বোঝা দিয়া এই শক্তি এবং সৌন্দর্যপ্রবাহের মুখে বাঁধ বাঁধিয়া দিতে পারেন, এমন কথা আমি মানি না। মোটের উপর, বিধাতা এবং ইস্কুল-মাস্টার এই দুইয়ের মধ্যে আমি বিধাতাকে বেশি বিশ্বাস করি। সেইজন্য আমার ধারণা এই যে, মেয়েরা যদি বা কান্ট-হেগেল‌ও পড়ে তবু শিশুদের স্নেহ করিবে এবং পুরুষদের নিতান্ত দূর-ছাই করিবে না।

কিন্তু তাই বলিয়া শিক্ষাপ্রণালীতে মেয়ে পুরুষ কোথাও কোনো ভেদ থাকিবে না, এ কথা বলিলে বিধাতাকে অমান্য করা হয়। বিদ্যার দুটো বিভাগ আছে। একটা বিশুদ্ধ জ্ঞানের, একটা ব্যবহারের। যেখানে বিশুদ্ধ জ্ঞান সেখানে মেয়ে-পুরুষের পার্থক্য নাই, কিন্তু যেখানে ব্যবহার সেখানে পার্থক্য আছেই। মেয়েদের মানুষ হইতে শিখাইবার জন্য বিশুদ্ধ জ্ঞানের শিক্ষা চাই, কিন্তু তার উপরে মেয়েদের মেয়ে হইতে শিখাইবার জন্য যে ব্যবহারিক শিক্ষা তার একটা বিশেষত্ব আছে, এ কথা মানিতে দোষ কী?

মেয়েদের শরীরের এবং মনের প্রকৃতি পুরুষের হইতে স্বতন্ত্র বলিয়াই তাহাদের ব্যবহারের ক্ষেত্র স্বভাবতই স্বতন্ত্র হইয়াছে। আজকাল বিদ্রোহের ঝোঁকে এক দল মেয়ে এই গোড়াকার কথাটাকেই অস্বীকার করিতেছেন। তাঁরা বলেন, মেয়েদের ব্যবহারের ক্ষেত্র পুরুষের সঙ্গে একেবারে সমান।

এটা তাঁদের নিতান্তই ক্ষোভের কথা। ক্ষোভের কারণ এই যে, পুরুষ আপন কর্মের পথ ধরিয়া জগতে নানা বিচিত্র ক্ষেত্রে কর্তৃত্ব লাভ করিয়াছে, কিন্তু মেয়েদের কর্ম যেখানে সেখানে অধিকাংশ বিষয়েই তাহাদিগকে দায়ে পড়িয়া পুরুষের অনুগত হইতে হইয়াছে। এই আনুগত্যকে তাঁরা অনিবার্য বলিয়া মনে করেন না।

তাঁরা বলেন, পুরুষ এতদিন কেবলমাত্র গায়ের জোরেই মেয়েদের কাঁধের উপর এই আনুগত্যটা চাপাইয়া দিয়াছে। জগতের সর্বত্রই

এই কথাটা যদি এতদিন ধরিয়া সত্য হইয়া থাকে, যদি মেয়েদের প্রকৃতির বিরুদ্ধে পুরুষের শক্তি তাহাদিগকে সংসারের তলায় ফেলিয়া রাখিয়া থাকে তবে বলিতেই হইবে, দাসত্বই মেয়েদের পক্ষে স্বাভাবিক। দাসত্ব বলিতে এই বোঝায়, দায়ে পড়িয়া অনিচ্ছাসত্ত্বে পরের দায় বহন করা। যাদের পক্ষে এটা প্রকৃতিসিদ্ধ নয়, তারা বরঞ্চ মরে তবু এমন উৎপাত সহ্য করে না।

এতদিনের মানবের ইতিহাসে যদি এই কথাটাই সর্বদেশে সপ্রমাণ হইয়া থাকে যে দাসীত্ব মেয়েদের স্বাভাবিক, তবে পৃথিবীর সেই অর্ধেক মানুষের লজ্জায় সমস্ত পৃথিবী আজ মুখ তুলিতে পারিত না। কিন্তু আমি বলি, বিদ্রোহী মেয়েরা স্বজাতির বিরুদ্ধে এই যে অপবাদ ঘোষণা করিয়া বেড়াইতেছেন এটা সম্পূর্ণ মিথ্যা।

আসল কথা এই, স্ত্রী হওয়া, মা হওয়া, মেয়েদের স্বভাব; দাসী হওয়া নয়। ভালোবাসার অংশ মেয়েদের স্বভাবে বেশি আছে-- এ নহিলে সন্তান মানুষ হইত না, সংসার টিঁকিত না। স্নেহ আছে বলিয়াই মা সন্তানের সেবা করে, তার মধ্যে দায় নাই; প্রেম আছে বলিয়াই স্ত্রী স্বামীর সেবা করে, তার মধ্যে দায় নাই।

কিন্তু দায় আসিয়া পড়ে যখন স্নেহপ্রেমের সম্বন্ধ স্বাভাবিক সম্বন্ধ না হয়। সকল স্বামীকেই সকল স্ত্রী যদি স্ববাবতই ভালোবাসিতে পারিত তাহা হইলে কথাই ছিল না, তাহা সম্ভবপর নহে। অথচ যতদিন সমাজ বলিয়া একটা পদার্থ আছে ততদিন মানুষকে অনেক বিষয়ে এবং অনেক পরিমাণে একটা নিয়ম মানিয়া চলিতেই হইবে।

কিন্তু, সেই নিয়ম সৃষ্টি করিবার সময় সমাজ ভিতরে ভিতরে স্বভাবেরই অনুসরণ করিতে থাকে। মেয়েদের সম্বন্ধে সমাজ আপনিই এটা ধরিয়া লইয়াছে যে, মেয়েদের পক্ষে ভালোবাসাটাই সহজ। তাই মেয়েদের সম্বন্ধে নিয়ম ভালোবাসার নিয়ম। সমাজ তাই মেয়েদের কাছে এই দাবি করে যে, তারা এমন করিয়া কাজ করিবে যেন তারা সংসারকে ভালেবাসিতেছে। বাপ মা

ভাই বোন স্বামী ও ছেলেমেয়ের সেবা তারা করিবে। তাদের কাজ ভালোবাসার কাজ, এইটেই তাদের আদর্শ।

এইজন্য মেয়েদের সংসারে কোনো কারণে যেখানে তাদের ভালোবাসা নাই সেখানেও তাহাদিগকে সমাজ ভালোবাসার আদর্শেই বিচার করিয়া থাকে। যে স্বামীকে স্ত্রী ভালোবাসিতে পারে নাই তার সম্বন্ধেও তার ব্যবহারকে ভালোবাসার মাপকাঠিতেই মাপিতে হয়। সংসারকে সে ভালো বাসুক আর না বাসুক তার আচরণকে কষিয়া দেখিবার ঐ একটিমাত্র কষ্টিপাথর আছে, সেটা ভালোবাসার কষ্টিপাথর।

ভালোবাসার ধর্মই আত্মসমর্পণে, সুতরাং তার গৌরবও তাহাতেই। যেটাকে আনুগত্য বলিয়া লজ্জা করা হইতেছে সেটা লজ্জার বিষয় হয় যদি তাহাতে প্রীতি না থাকে, কেবলমাত্র দায় থাকে। মেয়েরা আপনার স্বভাবের দ্বারাই সমাজে এমন একটা জায়গা পাইয়াছে যেখানে সংসারের কাছে তারা আত্মসমর্পণ করিতেছে। যদি কোনো কারণে সমাজের এমন অবস্থা ঘটে যাতে এই আত্মসমর্পণ ভালোবাসার আদর্শ হইতে বহুল পরিমাণে ভ্রষ্ট হইয়া থাকে, তবে তাহা মেয়েদের পক্ষে পীড়া ও অবমাননা।

মেয়েরা স্বভাবতই ভালোবাসে এবং একনিষ্ঠ আত্মসমর্পণের আদর্শকেই সামাজিক শিক্ষায় তাদের মনে বদ্ধমূল করিয়া দিয়াছে, এই সুবিধাটুকু ধরিয়া অনেক স্বার্থপর পুরুষ তাদের প্রতি অত্যাচার করে। যেখানে পুরুষ যথার্থ পৌরুষের আদর্শ হইতে ভ্রষ্ট সেখানে মেয়েরা আপন উচ্চ আদর্শের দ্বারাই পীড়িত ও বঞ্চিত হইতে থাকে, ইহার দৃষ্টান্ত আমাদের দেশে যত বেশি এমন আর-কোনো দেশে আছে কিনা আমি সন্দেহ করি। কিন্তু তাই বলিয়া এ কথাটাকে উড়াইয়া দেওয়া যায় না যে, সমাজে মেয়েরা যে ব্যবহারের ক্ষেত্রটি অধিকার করিয়াছে সেখানে স্বভাববশতই তারা আপনিই আসিয়া পৌঁছিয়াছে, বাহিরের কোনো অত্যাচার তাহাদিগকে বাধ্য করে নাই।

এ কথা মনে রাখিতে হইবে, সমাজে পুরুষের দাসত্ব মেয়েদের চেয়ে অল্প নহে, বরঞ্চ বেশি। এতকালের সভ্যতার সাধনার পরেও মানুষের সমাজ আজও দাসের হাতের থাটুনিতে চলিতেছে। এ সমাজে যথার্থ স্বাধীনতা অতি অল্প লোকেই ভোগ করে। রাজ্যতন্ত্রে বাণিজ্যতন্ত্রে এবং সমাজের সর্ববিভাগেই দাসের দল প্রাণপাত করিয়া সমাজ-জগন্নাথের প্রকাণ্ড রথ টানিয়া চলিতেছে। কোথায় লইয়া চলিতেছে তাহাও জানে না, কাহার রথ টানিতেছে তাহাও দেখিতে পায় না। সমস্ত জীবন দিনের পর দিন এ মন দায় বহন করিতেছে যাহারা মধ্যে প্রীতি নাই, সৌন্দর্য নাই। এই দাসত্বের বারো-আনা ভাগ পুরুষের কাঁধে চাপিয়াছে। মেয়েদের ভালোবাসার উপরই সমাজ ঝোঁক দিয়াছে এইজন্য মেয়েদের দায় ভালোবাসার দায়। পুরুষের শক্তির উপরই সমাজ ঝোঁক দিয়াছে, এইজন্য পুরুষের দায় শক্তির দায়। অবস্থাগতিকে সেই দায় এত অতিরিক্ত হইতে পারে যহাতে ভালোবাসা উৎপীড়িত হয় ও শক্তি দুর্বল হইয়া পড়ে। তখন সমাজের সংস্কার আবশ্যক হয়। সেই সংস্কারের জন্য আজ সমস্ত মানবসমাজে বেদনা জাগিয়াছে। কিন্তু সংস্কার যতদূর পর্যন্তই যাক সৃষ্টির গোড়া পর্যন্ত গিয়া পৌঁছিবে না এবং শেষ পর্যন্ত কবির দল এই বলিয়া আনন্দ করিতে পারিবেন যে, পুরুষ পুরুষই থাকিবে, মেয়েরা মেয়ে থাকিয়া যাইবে বলিয়াই তার "সংকটে সহায়, দুরূহ চিন্তায় অংশী এবং সুখে দুঃখে সহচরী হইয়া সংসারে তাহার প্রকৃত সহযাত্রী হইবেন'।

শিক্ষা ও সংস্কৃতি (shikkha o songskriti)

শিক্ষাবিধি সম্বন্ধে আলোচনা করব স্থির করেছিলুম, ইতিমধ্যে কোনো-একটি আমেরিকান কাগজে এ বিষয়ে একটি প্রবন্ধ পড়লুম; পড়ে খুশি হয়েছি। আমার মতটি এই লেখায় ঠিকমত ব্যক্ত হয়েছে। হবার প্রধান কারণ এই, আমেরিকা দীর্ঘকাল থেকে বৈষয়িক সিদ্ধির নেশায় মেতে ছিল। সেই সিদ্ধির আয়তন ছিল অতি স্থূল, তার লোভ ছিল প্রকাণ্ড মাপের। এর ব্যাপ্তি ক্রমশ বেড়েই চলেছিল। তার ফলে সামাজিক মানুষের যে পূর্ণতা সেটা চাপা পড়ে গিয়ে বৈষয়িক মানুষের কৃতিত্ব সব ছাড়িয়ে উঠেছিল। আজ হঠাৎ সেই অতিকায় বৈষয়িক মানুষটি আপন সিদ্ধিপথের মাঝখানে অনেক দামের জটিল যানবাহনের চাকা ভেঙে, কল বিগড়িয়ে, ধুলায় কাত হয়ে পড়েছে। এখন তার ভবনার কথা এই যে, সব ভাঙাচোরা বাদ দিয়ে মানুষটার বাকি রইল কী? এত কাল ধরে যা-কিছুকে সে সর্বোর্ধ্ব মূল্য দিয়েছিল, তার প্রায় সমস্তই বাইরের। বাইরে যখন ভাঙন ধরে তখন ভিতরটাতে যদি দেখে সমস্ত ফাঁক তা হলে সান্ত্বনা পাবে কী নিয়ে? আসবাবগুলো গেল, কিন্তু মানুষটা কোথায়? সে এই বলে শোক করছে যে, সে আজ ভিক্ষুক; বলতে পারছে না "আমার অন্তরে সম্পদ আছে'। আজ তার মূল্য নেই; কেননা সে আপনাকে হাটের মানুষ ক'রে তুলেছিল, সেই হাট গেছে ভেঙে।

একদিন ভারতবর্ষে যখন তার নিজের সংস্কৃতি ছিল পরিপূর্ণ তখন ধনলাঘবকে সে ভয় করত না, লজ্জা করত না; কেননা তার প্রধান লক্ষ্য ছিল অন্তরের দিকে। সেই লক্ষ্য নির্ণয় করা,

অভ্যাস করা, তার শ্রেষ্ঠতা স্বীকার করা শিক্ষার সর্বপ্রধান অঙ্গ। অবশ্য, তারই এক সীমানায় বৈষয়িক শিক্ষাকে স্থান দেওয়া চাই, কেননা মানুষের সত্তা ব্যবহারিক-পারমার্থিককে মিলিয়ে। সংস্কৃতির অভাব আছে অথচ দক্ষতা পুরোমাত্রায়, এমন খোঁড়া মানুষ চলেছিল বাইসিক্‌ল্‌ চড়ে। ভাবে নি কোনো চিন্তার কারণ আছে, এমন সময় বাইসিক্‌ল্‌ পড়ল ভেঙে। তখন বুঝল, বহুমূল্য যন্ত্রটার চেয়ে বিনা মূল্যের পায়ের দাম বশি। যে মানুষ উপকরণ নিয়ে বড়াই করে সে জানে না আসলে সে কতই গরিব। বাইসিক্‌লের আদর কমাতে চাই নে, কিন্তু দুটো সজীব পায়ের আদর তার চেয়ে বেশি। যে শিক্ষায় এই সজীব পায়ের জীবনীশক্তিকে বাড়িয়ে তোলে তাকেই ধন্য বলি, যে শিক্ষায় প্রধানত আসবাবের প্রতিই মানুষকে নির্ভরশীল ক'রে তোলে তাকে মূঢ়তার বাহন বলব। যখন শান্তিনিকেতনে প্রথম বিদ্যালয় স্থাপন করি তখন এই লক্ষ্যটাই আমার মনে প্রবল ছিল। আসবাব জুটে গেলে তাকে ব্যবহার করার জন্যে সাধনার দরকার নেই, কিন্তু আসবাব-নিরপেক্ষ হয়ে কী ক'রে বাহিরে কর্মকুশলতা ও অন্তরে আপন সম্মানবোধ রক্ষা করা যায় এইটেই শিক্ষাসাধ্য। তখন আশ্রমে গরিবের মতোই ছিল জীবনযাত্রা, সেই গরিবিয়ানাকে লজ্জা করাই লজ্জাকর এ কথাটা তখন মনে ছিল। উপকরণবানের জীবনকে ঈর্ষা করা বা বিশেষভাবে সম্মান করাই যে কুশিক্ষা, এ কথাটা আমি তখনকার শিক্ষকদের স্মরণ করিয়ে রেখেছিলুম। বলা বাহুল্য, যে দারিদ্র্য শক্তিহীনতা থেকে উদ্ভূত সে কুৎসিত। কথা আছে : শক্তস্য ভূষণং ক্ষমা। তেমনি বলা যায়, সামর্থ্যবানেরই ভূষণ অকিঞ্চনতা। অতএব সামর্থ্য শিক্ষা করাই চাই ভোগের অভ্যাস বর্জন ক'রে। সামর্থ্যহীন দারিদ্র্যেই ভারতবর্ষের মাথা হেঁট হয়ে গেছে, অকিঞ্চনতায় নয়। অক্ষমকে দেবতা ক্ষমা করেন না।

"আমি সব পারি, সব পারব' এই আত্মবিশ্বাসের বাণী আমাদের শরীর মন যেন তৎপরতার সঙ্গে বলতে পারে। "আমি সব জানি' এই কথা বলবার জন্যে আমাদের ইন্দ্রিয় মন উৎসুক হয়

তো হোক, কিন্তু তার পরেও চরমের কথা "আমি সব পারি'। আজ এই বাণী সমস্ত য়ুরোপের। সে বলে, "আমি সব পারি, সব পারব।' তার আপন ক্ষমতাকে শ্রদ্ধা করার অন্ত নেই। এই শ্রদ্ধার দ্বারা সে নির্ভীক হয়েছে, জলে স্থলে আকাশে সে জয়ী হয়েছে। আমরা দেবের দিকে তাকিয়ে আছি, সেইজন্যে বহু শতাব্দী ধরে আমরা দৈবকর্তৃক প্রবঞ্চিত। সুইডেনের বিখ্যাত ভূপর্যটক স্বেন হেডিনের ভ্রমণবৃত্তান্ত অনেক দিন পরে আবার আমি পড়েছিলুম। এশিয়ার দুর্গম মরুপ্রদেশে আবহতত্ত্ব পর্যবেক্ষণের উপায় করবার জন্যে তিনি দুঃসাধ্য অধ্যবসায়ে প্রবৃত্ত হয়েছিলেন। এই অধ্যবসায়ের মূলমন্ত্র হচ্ছে, "আমি সব জানব, সব পারব।' এই পারবার শক্তি বলতে কি বোঝায় সে তাঁর বই পড়লে বোঝা যায়। আমরা কথায় কথায় ওদের বলে থাকি বস্তুতান্ত্রিক। আত্মার শক্তি যার এত প্রবল, যে জ্ঞান-অর্জনের জন্যে সে প্রাণকে তুচ্ছ করে, যার কিছুতে ভয় নেই, সাংঘাতিক বাধাকে সে স্বীকার করে না, দুঃসহ কৃচ্ছ্রসাধনে যাকে পরাহত করতে পারে না--প্রাণপণ সাধনা এমন-কিছুর জন্যে যা আর্থিক নয়, জীবিকার পক্ষে যা অত্যাবশ্যক নয়, বরঞ্চ বিপরীত--তাকে বলব বস্তুতান্ত্রিক! আর, সে কথা বলবে আমাদের মতো দুর্বল আত্মা!"আমরা সব-কিছু পারব' এই কথা সত্য ক'রে বলবার শিক্ষাই আত্মাবমাননা থেকে আমাদের দেশকে পরিত্রাণ করতে পারে, এ কথা ভুললে চলবে না। আমাদের বিদ্যালয়ে সকল কর্মে সকল ইন্দ্রিয়মনের তৎপরতা প্রথম হতেই অনুশীলিত হোক, এইটেই শিক্ষাসাধনার গুরুতর কর্তব্য বলে মনে করতে হবে। জানি এর প্রধান অন্তরায় অভিভাবক; পড়া মুখস্থ করতে করতে জীবনীশক্তি মননশক্তি কর্মশক্তি সমস্ত যতই কৃশ হতে থাকে তাতে বাধা দিতে গেলে তাঁরা উদ্বিগ্ন হয়ে ওঠেন। কিন্তু মুখস্থ বিদ্যার চাপে এই-সব চির-পঙ্গু মানুষের অকর্মণ্যতার বোঝা দেশ বহন করবে কী করে? উদ্যোগিনং পুরুষসিংহমুপৈতি লক্ষ্মীঃ। আমাদের শিক্ষালয়ে নবীন প্রাণের মধ্যে অক্লান্ত উদ্যোগিতার হাওয়া বয়েছে যদি দেখতে পাই তা হলেই বুঝব, দেশে লক্ষ্মীর আমন্ত্রণ সফল

হতে চলল। এই আমন্ত্রণ ইকনমিক্সে ডিগ্রি নেওয়ায় নয় : চরিত্রকে বলিষ্ঠ কর্মিষ্ঠ করায়, সকল অবস্থার জন্যে নিজেকে নিপুণভাবে প্রস্তুত করায়, নিরলস আত্মশক্তির উপর নির্ভর ক'রে কর্মানুষ্ঠানের দায়িত্ব সাধনা করায়। অর্থাৎ কেবল পাণ্ডিত্যচর্চায় নয়, পৌরুষচর্চায়। সাধারণ ইস্কুলে এই সাধনার সুযোগ নেই, আমাদের আশ্রমে আছে। এখানে নানা বিভাগে নানা কর্ম চলছে, তার মধ্যে শক্তি প্রয়োগ করাতে পারে এমন অবস্থা থাকা চাই। এই কৃতিত্বশিক্ষা অত্যাবশ্যক হলেও এই-যে যথেষ্ট নয় সে কথা মানতে হবে। আমেরিকান লেখক এই কথাটারই আলোচনা করেছেন। তিনি বলেন, আধুনিক শিক্ষা থেকে একটা জিনিস কেমন করে স্খলিত হয়ে পড়েছে, সে হচ্ছে সংস্কৃতি। চিত্তের ঐশ্বর্যকে অবজ্ঞা ক'রে আমরা জীবনযাত্রার সিদ্ধিলাভকেই একমাত্র প্রাধান্য দিয়েছি। কিন্তু সংস্কৃতিকে বাদ দিয়ে এই সিদ্ধিলাভ কি কখনো যথার্থভাবে সম্পূর্ণ হতে পারে?

সংস্কৃতি সমগ্র মানুষের চিত্তবৃত্তিকে গভীরতর স্তর থেকে সফল করতে থাকে। তার প্রভাবে মানুষ অন্তর থেকে স্বতই সর্বাঙ্গীণ সার্থকতা লাভ করে। তার প্রভাবে নিষ্কাম জ্ঞানার্জনের অনুরাগ এবং নিঃস্বার্থ কর্মানুষ্ঠানের উৎসাহ স্বাভাবিক হয়ে ওঠে। যথার্থ সংস্কৃতি জড়ভাবে প্রথাপালনের চেয়ে অকৃত্রিম সৌজন্যকে বড়ো মূল্য দিয়ে থাকে। মানুষের সঙ্গে ব্যবহার কাজ উদ্ধার করবার উপযোগী বিনয়কৌশল তার অনুশাসন নয়; সংস্কৃতিবান্ মানুষ নিজের ক্ষতি করতে পারে, কিন্তু নিজেকে হেয় করতে পারে না। সে আড়ম্বরপূর্বক নিজেকে প্রচার করতে বা স্বার্থপরভাবে সবাইকে ঠেলে নিজেকে অগ্রসর করতে লজ্জা বোধ করে। যা-কিছু ইতর বা কপট তার গ্লানি তাকে বেদনা দেয়। শিল্পে সাহিত্যে মানুষের ইতিহাসে যা-কিছু শ্রেষ্ঠ তার সঙ্গে আন্তরিক পরিচয় থাকাতে সকলপ্রকার শ্রেষ্ঠতাকে সম্মান করতে সে আনন্দ পায়। সে বিচার করতে পারে, ক্ষমা করতে পারে, মতবিরোধের বাধা ভেদ ক'রেও যেখানে যেটুকু ভালো আছে সে তা দেখতে পায়, অন্যের সফলতাকে ঈর্ষা করাকে সে নিজের লাঘব বলেই জানে।

সমগ্র মনুষ্যত্বের স্বকীয় আদর্শ প্রত্যেক বড়ো সমাজেই আছে। সেই আদর্শ কেবল পাঠাগারে নয়, পরিবারের মধ্যেও। আমাদের দেশের বর্তমান দুর্গতির দিনে সেই আদর্শ দুর্বল হয়ে গেছে, তার শোচনীয় দৃষ্টান্ত প্রতিদিন দেখতে পাই। তাই বীভৎস কুৎসা আমাদের দেশে আয়জনক পণ্যদ্রব্য হয়ে উঠেছে। তারস্বরে নিন্দা বিস্তার করে বাতাসকে বিষাক্ত করার অপরাধকে আমরা গ্রাহ্যই করি নে; একটু উপলক্ষ ঘটবা-মাত্র এই বীভৎসতাকে উদ্ভাবিত করার ও প্রশ্রয় দেবার লোক দলে দলে ভিড় করে আসে, ইতর হিংস্রতায় সমস্ত দেশ মারীগ্রস্ত হয়ে ওঠে। তীক্ষ্ণ মেধার গুণে আমার পড়া মুখস্থ করি। বি. এ., এম. এ. পাস করি; কিন্তু আত্মলাঘবকারী পরস্পরের সৌভাগ্যবিদ্বেষী নিন্দালোলুপ যে চরিত্রদৈন্য শুভকর্মে পরস্পর মিলিত হবার পথে পথে সচেষ্টভাবে কাঁটার বীজ বপন করে চলেছে, সকল প্রকার সদনুষ্ঠানকে জীর্ণ বিদীর্ণ করে দেবার জন্যে মহোল্লাসে উঠে পড়ে লেগেছে, সে কেবল সংস্কৃতির অভাবে মনুষ্যত্বের আদর্শ ক্ষুন্ন হয়েছে বলেই সম্ভব হল। সকল কর্মানুষ্ঠানে উৎসাহপূর্বক নিজেদেরকে অকৃতার্থ করে আজ বাঙালি সমস্ত পৃথিবীর কাছে অশ্রদ্ধেয় হয়ে উঠল। শিশুকাল থেকে এই ইতরতার বিষবীজ শিক্ষার ভিতর দিয়ে উন্মূলিত করা আমাদের বিদ্যালয়ের সর্বপ্রধান লক্ষ হোক, এই আমি একান্ত মনে কামনা করি। এর একমাত্র উপায় হচ্ছে পরীক্ষা-পাসের জন্যে পড়া মুখস্থ করা নয়, মানুষের ইতিহাসে যা-কিছু ভালো তার সঙ্গে আনন্দময় পরিচয়সাধন করিয়ে তার প্রতি শ্রদ্ধা অনুভব করবার সুযোগ সর্বদা ঘটিয়ে দেওয়া। একদা আশ্রমে আমার কবিসহযোগী সতীশ রায় এই কাজ করতেন এবং আর একজন সহযোগী ছিলেন অজিত চক্রবর্তী। তেমন শিক্ষক নিঃসন্দেহ এখনো আমাদের মধ্যে আছেন, কিন্তু রক্তপিপাসু পরীক্ষাদানবের কাছে শিশুদের মন বলি দিতে তাঁদের এত অত্যন্ত ব্যস্ত থাকতে হয় যে শিক্ষার উপরের তলায় ওঠবার সময় থাকে না। আমেরিকান লেখক সংস্কৃতির এই ফলশ্রুতি বর্ণনা করেছেন; তিনি বলেন সংস্কৃতির প্রভাবে চিত্তের সেই ঔদার্য ঘটে যাতে

ক'রে অন্তঃকরণে শান্তি আসে, আপনার প্রতি শ্রদ্ধা আসে, আত্মসংযম আসে এবং মনে মৈত্রীভাবের সঞ্চার হয়ে জীবনের প্রত্যেক অবস্থাকেই কল্যাণময় করে। একদিন দেখেছিলাম শান্তিনিকেতনের পথে গোরুর গাড়ির চাকা কাদায় বসে গিয়েছিল; আমার ছাত্ররা সকলে মিলে ঠেলে গাড়ি উদ্ধার করে দিলে। সেদিন কোনো অভ্যাগত আশ্রমে যখন উপস্থিত হলেন তাঁর মোট বয়ে আনবার কুলি ছিল না; আমাদের কোনো তরুণ ছাত্র অসংকোচে তাঁর বোঝা পিঠে করে নিয়ে যথাস্থানে এনে পৌঁছিয়ে দিয়েছিল। অপরিচিত অতিথিমাত্রের সেবা আনুকূল্য তারা কর্তব্য বলে জ্ঞান করত। সেদিন তারা আশ্রমের পথ নির্মাণ করেছে, গর্ত বুজিয়ে দিয়েছে। এ-সমস্তই তাদের সতর্ক ও বলিষ্ঠ সৌজন্যের অঙ্গ ছিল, বইয়ের পাতা অতিক্রম করে তাদের শিক্ষার মধ্যে সংস্কৃতি প্রবেশ করেছিল। সেই-সব ছেলেদের প্রত্যেককে তখন আমি জানতাম; তার পরে অনেক দিন তাদের অনেককে দেখি নি। আশা করি তারা নিন্দাবিলাসী নয়, পরশ্রীকাতর নয়, অক্ষমকে সাহায্য করতে তারা তৎপর এবং ভালোকে তারা ঠিকমত যাচাই করতে জানে। ১৫ জুলাই ১৯৩৫